The Life and Work of
Henry Parry Liddon
(1829–1890)

To Janet
with gratitude and love

The Life and Work of Henry Parry Liddon (1829–1890)

Michael Chandler

First published in 2000

Gracewing
2 Southern Avenue
Leominster
Herefordshire HR6 0QF

ISBN 0 85244 494 X

Typesetting by
Action Publishing Technology Ltd, Gloucester, GL1 1SP

Printed in England by MPG Books Ltd.,
Bodmin PL31 1EG

Contents

By the same author:

The Life and Work of John Mason Neale (1818–1866)

Chapter One

'A man of modesty and sense'[1]

There are two unrelated facts about the early life of Henry Parry Liddon that may be seen as symbolic of what was to follow. Born on 20 August 1829 he was baptised at the end of the following month by Frederick Beadon, who with his father before him, served as vicar of the parish of North Stoneham (in the Diocese of Winchester) for the remarkable total of one hundred and thirty-nine years.[2] Beadon senior served the parish from 1740 to 1810, and his son, who died at the age of 101, was vicar from 1810–1879. The two clergy thus providing examples of perseverance and loyalty that would have appealed to the adult Liddon. The second fact is to do with Liddon's middle name. He got it from his godfather, Lieutenant Edward Parry, who was later knighted and under whom his father had served with distinction in the Royal Navy in a demanding expedition in search of the North West Passage. Parry was a notable naval officer who was both courageous and tenacious, qualities not lacking in the later, very different, career of his godson. Liddon's career remained unchronicled for nearly fifteen years after his death, until early in the twentieth century when three biographies appeared. The most significant came out in 1904 and is *The Life and Letters of Henry Parry Liddon* by John Octavius Johnston, Principal of Cuddesdon Theological College. The second is *Henry Parry Liddon* by a former Canon of Truro, A. B. Donaldson, which appeared in 1905. Finally, published later in the same year, in the series *Leaders of the Church 1800–1900*, edited by G. W. E. Russell, came a book which is simply called *Dr Liddon*. It was written by Russell himself who, as a schoolboy and young man, had known Liddon. Despite their publication, however, Liddon is a Victorian Anglican divine whose reputation has remained consistently under-appreciated, largely because his devotion to Dr E. B. Pusey the Regius Professor of Hebrew and Canon of Christ Church, Oxford, appeared to be over-whelming. A younger contemporary, Francis Paget later Bishop of Oxford, described Liddon's devotion to Pusey as casting him in the role of 'always a henchman,' and this has been the verdict of history. This assessment is incorrect, but unfortunately, it strengthened the erroneous view that Liddon had nothing of his own to offer the Church of England which he served with unswerving loyalty. In fact he was a theologian of considerable intellectual power. He was blessed with spiritual resources and pastoral acumen which he made readily available. In his own day he was famous for his preaching ministry which enabled him to exercise his remarkable gift for communication.

His father, Captain Matthew Liddon, retired from the Royal Navy because of poor health in 1820 at the age of twenty-nine. He married Ann Bilke in 1828. They moved from North Stoneham in Hampshire to Colyton in Devon in 1832 when Henry Parry Liddon was still an infant. He was their first son, although their second-born, and was their first surviving child out of an eventual ten. He began his education there in a local school, but at the age of ten became a boarder at a school in Lyme Regis run by a Mr Roberts. Liddon seems to have been an ordinary little boy. He began to collect coins, which remained a lifelong hobby; a fondness for cats was another lifelong trait. He played and fought at school and found Greek difficult. He wrote several plays and acted in at least one of his own compositions. The Lyme Regis years were uneventful, and in the autumn of 1844 he was sent to London to be a pupil at King's College School in the Strand. This removed him from the influence of the Vicar of Lyme Regis, a clergyman named Frederick Hodges whose anti-Roman Catholic polemics influenced the young Liddon who, as was by no means unusual at the time, had already tried his hand at writing sermons. The religious atmosphere at King's was different from that at Lyme Regis. The motto of the school was *Sancte et Sapienter*, but in later years Liddon remarked that the second half was given much greater emphasis than the first.

A contemporary of Liddon's at King's College School recalled him as a serious-minded young man, and spoke of him as 'sweet, somewhat fatherly, somewhat melancholy.' He was already pious, and did not engage in sport, horse-play or the common practical jokes of his school fellows. Someone called him a 'priest among boys' and remarked that his attitudes were already fixed. If this is correct, it seems that as an adolescent Liddon was priggish and rather different from his earlier school days. However, it is not entirely accurate. Liddon did enjoy some conventional pastimes. He is known to have been a good swimmer, and in his last long vacation at University, saved from drowning the historian William Stubbs, a Fellow of

Trinity College who later became a colleague at St Paul's and eventually Bishop of Oxford. He noted in his diary, but without any comment, that he was confirmed as a schoolboy, on 29 May 1846. A nephew of Liddon's recalled that his uncle asked the Vicar of Colyton, Dr Frederick Barnes, to prepare him for confirmation. He was invited to breakfast and over the meal was asked if he knew the Catechism. 'Oh! Yes! I know it by heart.' Barnes said that this was satisfactory and made the necessary arrangements. Liddon's nephew located this conversation in Liddon's undergraduate days, but his own diary indicates that he was confirmed during his last term at school. It is, nevertheless, quite possible that Barnes saw Liddon at Colyton because, although he was an absentee incumbent, he took care of the parish for a month in each year to enable his curate to have a holiday. About this time Liddon came into contact with the Oxford Movement[3] and its 'Church Principles.' How this came about is, regrettably, lost but there had been a great change in his views since the Lyme Regis days when he had echoed Hodges' opinions. He wanted to go to Oxford but, at first, fear of 'popery' seemed likely to prevent it. Despite the fact that the Vicar of Colyton, Dr Barnes, was sub-Dean and a Canon of Christ Church, the curate thought that Liddon's soul might be in danger from the Puseyites. He persuaded Liddon's mother of the spiritual danger, but not Captain Liddon. The young man was allowed to sit the matriculation examination at Christ Church which he did 'in a great fright.' He was successful and went up in the autumn of 1846 with an admonition from the headmaster of King's College School that he should not undermine his health by overworking. He started his university career on the same day as Richard Meux Benson, who became a personal friend. Benson became Vicar of Cowley and founded the Society of St John the Evangelist, the first Religious Order for men in the post Reformation Church of England. Senior members of the university whom he got to know included Richard William Church, later Dean of St Paul's, and Charles Marriott who became the first principal of Chichester Theological College and later Vicar of St Mary the Virgin, the University church of Oxford.

The ethos of Oxford University in the mid-1840s was exclusively Church of England, although that ethos was soon to be challenged. In addition it was still suffering from the aftermath of John Henry Newman's secession to Rome just twelve months before, and the followers of the Tractarians were not popular. Newman's former friends and colleagues were distrusted by many, and the fear of 'popery' was strong. Chief among Newman's former associates was Dr Pusey. After Newman's departure, he became the most learned protagonist for the Oxford Movement, along with John Keble, from 1831 Professor of Poetry at Oxford, a man whom Liddon liked and admired intensely. How Liddon came to meet Pusey is not recorded, but it is unlikely to have been through Barnes. Liddon soon became a frequent visitor at Pusey's home in Tom Quad, but he received a 'very kindly' note of admonition after being seen on Pusey's doorstep by the son of one of the other Canons. The friendship of Pusey was considered by many to be detrimental to the career prospects of a young man, but Liddon was already interested in Church principles and willingly placed himself under Pusey's learning and profound spirituality. Liddon's devotion to Pusey did not prevent him from following his own mind in many things, although subsequent history has not given Liddon the credit that he deserved for his independence. Unfortunately, after Pusey died, Liddon revered his memory to the extent that he spoke and acted as though he had always accepted the old man's views and followed his lead. In reality, Pusey was not the sort of man to accept sycophancy as the basis of a friendship and Liddon's character was too strong for him to have offered uncritical devotion. Pusey was, however, important to Liddon for the rest of his life.

Liddon's mother died in February 1849, and as late as 1866 he still remembered her fear that he might become a great scholar whilst failing to becoming a good Christian. He graduated in the summer of 1850, with a second class degree in the Final Classical School. He was too young to be ordained, but had already decided to seek ordination, and was beginning to think that he ought to remain unmarried because he thought that the Church of England needed 'men of decided and earnest cast to serve her, quite disentangled from the work of this world . . .' Regrettably there is no record of his intellectual and spiritual progress to these decisions, but there can be no doubt that Pusey encouraged him. In the summer of 1851 he entered for, and won, the Johnson Theological Scholarship but was not successful the following year when he tried to win the Ellerton Essay Prize. He kept a diary at this time but, apart from the odd notebook, it has not survived, although there are many volumes for later years.

There were two significant controversies which affected the Church of England at this time and Liddon, as an ordinand with an enquiring mind, was aware of both. The first was a famous legal dispute. The Bishop of Exeter was a high churchman of the old school, a fiercely opinionated man named Henry Phillpotts. In his diocese an equally intransigent clergyman, but of protestant views, was seeking to move to another parish. He was Charles Cornelius Gorham, and the Bishop examined his theology and concluded that

Gorham's views were inconsistent with the doctrine of the Church of England with regard to baptismal regeneration. Gorham was secure in the freehold of his existing parish, but the Bishop felt that he could not conscientiously institute him to the new living of Brampford Speke. The matter was only resolved after recourse to the Privy Council which overturned the Bishop's decision. The point of contention then moved away from the doctrine of baptism and became, for High Churchmen, the equally important matter that a secular court, the Privy Council, was defining the doctrines of the Church and was thereby seriously exceeding what they could accept. A number of prominent Anglicans, particularly Archdeacon Henry Manning and Robert Wilberforce, also an Archdeacon and a brother of Samuel Wilberforce, the Bishop of Oxford, seceded to Rome.

It was Roman Catholicism which provided the second source of distress to catholic-minded members of the Church of England in 1850. In an act which its opponents called the 'papal aggression,' Rome decided that the time was ripe to re-establish a proper hierarchy for Roman Catholics in England. Astonishingly the new Cardinal Archbishop of Westminster, Nicholas Wiseman, said later that he did not expect the move to be controversial. But it was, and he fanned the flames of the dispute with an unwise pastoral letter in the autumn of 1850 at the time when the new dioceses were established. These events occurred during a period when those who sought to emphasise the protestant nature of the Church of England were convinced that the followers of Doctor Pusey and Mr Keble were really traitors to the Church to which they professed allegiance. Liddon, as an ardent disciple, was acutely aware of all this and was eager to associate his own reputation with that of his mentors. He was eager also to assert their loyalty, and his own, at a time when some of his acquaintances converted to Roman Catholicism.

In July 1851 he visited Scotland and took a dislike to presbyterianism. St Giles' Cathedral in Edinburgh earned his particular criticism. At that time it was divided into three separate 'meeting houses' and the place was dismissed by him as 'the Kebla of Presbyterian devotion.' At Stirling he dared to criticise John Knox and was surprised not to earn a rebuke. Later he paid a visit to the continent and reacted in much the same way to the Calvinism which he encountered in Geneva. He went back to Scotland in 1852, but in the same year his travels took him as far as Rome, via Milan and Pisa, and there occurred one of the most remarkable events of Liddon's life. His diary is crowded with descriptions of buildings and people. He had with him a letter of introduction to Monsignor George Talbot, the Chamberlain to Pope Pius IX. Talbot had himself converted to

Roman Catholicism in 1847 and was eager to promote the Church he had espoused. He arranged for Liddon to have a good view of a Mass attended by the Pope on St Michael's day, 29 September. Liddon observed that the Pope 'wears an expression truly beautiful ... I think that the most ferocious Protestant could not but appreciate it.' Talbot continued his campaign by engaging Liddon in discussion and controversy and by making further use of the attractions of the Vatican, but Liddon felt that the appeal was addressed to his imagination and feelings rather than to his convictions. This perception is indicative of his rather intellectual and detached character which, in later years, led some people to think of him as unemotional. Talbot persevered, and Liddon was shown the sights. On 30 September, the visit to Rome culminated in an audience with the Pope which Liddon recorded in his diary. Talbot took him through

> a great number of antechambers, well stocked with guards and attendants ... At length I reached the apartment in which the Pope was sitting. He was at a desk, writing, surrounded with books and papers. I knelt first on entering the room, and a second time to kiss his feet. He was anxious to talk, and spoke for some minutes. He spoke in French; said that he hoped I had enjoyed Rome – of course I had – and then went on to express his hope that I should pursue my studies with constant recourse to prayer to God, without Whose aid nothing would be obtained, and Who would ultimately lead me to the Truth ... He spoke for about five minutes. I proffered some *objets* to be blessed, and then knelt and left the apartment. The apartment in which the Pope was sitting was very plain and unadorned, with a brick floor, and it contrasted strangely with the magnificent antechambers through which I had to pass to reach it.
>
> What a wonderful day in my life! The first time I ever found myself in the presence of Royalty; strange that this should have been in the court of the successor of Peter!

Liddon did not succumb to the blandishments of Roman Catholicism, although Talbot still persevered. Eventually he sent a note to the Monsignor in which he terminated the discussion. He returned to England, and arrived at his uncle's house on 5 November, having been away just on two months. He was sure that he should not become a Roman Catholic, but was uneasy about the position of the Church of England. A week after his return from the continent he went to see Bishop Wilberforce, and was reassured that the Church had not been fatally compromised by the Gorham case.

The Bishop was impressed by the young Liddon; they established an enduring friendship, and he often dined with the Bishop. With his mind at rest on the Gorham case and one or two other matters, which unfortunately he did not list but which he also discussed with Dr Barnes, Liddon was ordained deacon by Wilberforce on 19 December 1852, and priest on 18 December 1853. He recorded in his diary that he had spent 'three days delightfully at Cuddesdon.' Wilberforce was among the pioneers of the practice of expecting ordinands to go into retreat. Liddon's intention seems to have been that he would work as a parochial clergyman with academic interests. This was very much in keeping with the ideals of the Tractarians. Examples of this type of High Church parish priest may be seen in John Keble who combined his Oxford activities with a parish ministry at Hursley, and Keble's brother, Thomas, the Vicar of Bisley; R. W. Church in his days as Rector of Whatley, and Liddon's own Vicar, W. J. Butler at Wantage. However his experience of parish life was to be short lived, so much so that his biographers were subsequently confused as to the precise extent of this aspect of his work, and the following has been reconstructed from his diaries and papers. He did not take up his duties as Butler's curate at Wantage until he was able to move into lodgings, which he shared with his fellow curate, A. H. Mackonochie who later achieved notoriety as the ritualist first vicar of the newly-built St Alban's, Holborn, a post which Liddon declined and for which he recommended his former colleague. He commenced his duties on 29 January 1853, and the following day, in a letter to his Aunt Louisa to whom he often wrote, he described Mackonochie as 'a little stiff, but a genuine Christian . . . [and] . . . a most excellent fellow.' That day was a Sunday, and Liddon was not impressed with the arrangements for worship. By Easter it had become clear that Liddon was not strong enough for the rigours of parish ministry if his work was also to include serious study. He had lost his voice after preaching an extemporary sermon on Maundy Thursday. On Wednesday 30 March 1853, exactly two months after beginning there, and three days after Easter, Liddon left Wantage. He remained on good terms with W. J. Butler and later arranged, as he told his aunt, to bring Cuddesdon students 'over one by one to study parish work . . . so that any how they will get a fine ideal of what a Christian ministry is into their heads.' By the end of May he felt sufficiently recovered to look after the small parish of Finedon in Northamptonshire for a few weeks. The following assessment was written in his diary on 1st July 1853 and applies to that parish, although it is not specifically identified. A letter to his aunt, however, confirms that he was in Finedon at that date:

this parish is indeed in a deplorable state. About two thirds of the people are dissenters. Of the fourteen farmers, twelve go to meetings. The dissenters are Quakers, Independents, Wesleyans, original and Reformed. The Wesleyan Sunday School alone is larger than that belonging to the Church. Immorality is exactly proportionate to schism. Within the church: huge doctrinal error, eg., the other day in widow Wallis' cottage Mary Freeman 'withstood me' on the subject of Baptism. Many, she observed, approved of my ministry, except in that one particular. And I find the tone, even of our religious people, thoroughly Wesleyan. Their 'feelings' and 'experiences' and 'apprehensions' and 'interest' are the staple of their religious life. Conscience is left out of the question.

Nothing would do but a staff of three clergy: earnest extempore preaching and the sacramental system in its fullness.

These two brief experiences are the sum total of Liddon's parochial work and their brevity cannot have had much impact upon the formation of his pastoral attitudes or his priestly ideals and work. The view of Henry Scott Holland, who wrote the original article on Liddon for the *Dictionary of National Biography,* that at Wantage he 'came into touch with that development of parish work in town and country into which the Oxford Movement was then passing,' makes too great an implicit claim. A similar verdict must be given against George Russell's comment that 'the poor people loved Liddon as they knew him in the fields, in their cottages, and at their sick beds,'[4] and against the Donaldson biography which went even further and claimed that 'this pastoral experience was a valuable element in the formation of his character.'[5]

It was Butler who recommended Liddon to Bishop Wilberforce as a suitable person to be Vice-Principal of the newly built theological college at Cuddesdon, a few miles outside Oxford, although J.O. Johnston claimed that the Bishop had Liddon in mind from the time of his ordination retreat. Both men were impressed by the twenty-four year old Liddon's learning and spirituality, and Wilberforce personally liked him. Wilberforce's relationship with his new college, which opened in the Michaelmas term 1854, was close, and some of its worship was offered in the private chapel of his palace which was close by, the grounds only separated by a narrow country road. However, when Liddon accepted the post, Wilberforce had second thoughts and hesitated, largely because he was anxious that Liddon's reputation as Pusey's leading disciple might harm the fledgling institution, so it was a few days before the appointment was confirmed. The Bishop was anxious about Liddon's churchmanship, but he was reassured when Liddon said that he would not try to impose the practice of sacramental confession on the students, although he wished to continue with his own adherence to the practice. The Bishop compelled him to change his spiritual director from Pusey, whose teaching Wilberforce distrusted, to Keble. Liddon felt awkward at having to tell Pusey, but it was made easier for him when Pusey observed that he was 'changing brass for gold.'

Liddon's new work brought him back closer to his University. He frequently walked the five or six miles to the city but he was far enough away to be safe when the town suffered its second outbreak of cholera in five years. The Oxford association, having been renewed, was later strengthened and lasted until the end of his life. For the five years that he was at the College, Liddon was, in theory, under the direction and leadership of Alfred Pott who had been the Bishop's curate in the days when the bishop was incumbent of Cuddesdon. The parochial arrangement had changed in 1852 and Pott became the Vicar of Cuddesdon in his own right. Such was the Bishop's confidence in Pott that he readily appointed him Principal of the College, but he was to prove not strong enough to provide the necessary checks that Liddon's personality needed. Pott himself commented on his younger colleague's unwillingness to compromise. Liddon's strength of character was apparent to those who met him. Physically he was slight and not tall, he had a swarthy complexion and dark hair which went very grey towards the end of his life. At Cuddesdon he dressed in a cassock, which was remarkable at that time. A Cambridge graduate who went to Cuddesdon described, in terms reminiscent of a novel, the impact which the Vice-Principal made on him:

> I was 'in amazement lost' on being received at the College by an Italian-looking ecclesiastic, glittering-eyed, clean-shaven, and closely-cropped, wearing a white band for a collar . . . who, offering me his hand, welcomed me to the College . . .[6]

Pott and Liddon were the only academic members of the College staff, until they were joined later by Alfred Barff as Chaplain, with whom Liddon established a friendship which lasted until his death. Occasionally they received help from Edward King, at that time curate at nearby Wheatley, and also destined to be a friend for the whole of Liddon's life. In 1855, Liddon was offered a Christ Church living, Drayton, three and a half miles from Cuddesdon, with the suggestion that he should, as he told his aunt, 'keep a pony and a curate' and 'work it from this place.' He declined on the grounds that there were 'anxieties enough' connected with the college where he undertook the customary teaching work and was remembered as a stimulating lecturer. The curriculum was very traditional, including the eighteenth century Bishop Joseph Butler's famous *Analogy of Religion* and also Pearson's *Exposition of the Creed*.[7] He combined his teaching with an intense concern for the spiritual formation of the students. There was much personal contact with the students which he often recorded in his diary. A typical entry is that of 24 April 1858, 'a capital talk with A. Cave who is much improving,' although only two days earlier he had written of the same man, 'I fear I felt very impatient with him.' He also followed the conventional academic habit of walking with the men in the afternoons, but did not often record details of their conservation, although some of the students remembered for the rest of their lives the advice they had received. It may have been during one of these walks that an incident occurred which illustrated Liddon's seriousness of mind and, regretfully, a limitation of his pastoral ability with ordinary people. In a footnote to *The Founding of Cuddesdon*, Owen Chadwick recorded that, 'a Cuddesdon legend described how Liddon found a little girl crying in the village. He knelt down beside her and pleaded with her to "reconsider the situation" because he was sure she would discover "alleviating circumstances." Chadwick used this incident to illustrate his observation that 'in the young Liddon you feel, sometimes, that the burden of responsibility has weighed down youth's simplicity.'[8]

In addition to his pastoral concern he did hear confessions and gave advice frequently to students troubled by what he called 'Roman questions,' sometimes speaking with considerable frankness and severity. He exercised considerable influence over the students, and this was indirectly part of his contribution towards the spread of 'Church principles' through the Church of England. He was a more powerful force in the College than its Principal, as Pott also acknowledged later, and it is interesting to note that history repeated itself in this respect when Charles Gore was Vice-Principal between 1880 to 1883 when C. W. Furse was the Principal. This gave rise to the pun that the College was more renowned for its 'Vices' than its 'Principals'. Despite his comparative youth, Liddon had clear ideas about priesthood, and he was forthright in setting them before the students training for ordination at Cuddesdon. His views were remarkably consistent throughout his life in this as in most other theological matters, so an analysis of them can range across his whole ministry. He had, by this time, definitely arrived at the conviction that, personally, he should remain unmarried. He advocated celibacy, although he did not discourage his friends or students from marrying. He taught his students the truth of the Tractarian insight that an important aspect of priesthood is an emphasis on personal holiness. It was 'the sense that all life must be consecrated to God and offered for his glory [which] we soon come to recognise as the guiding force in the lives of Newman, Keble, Pusey and many of their companions and followers.'[9] Liddon was a chief among those companions and followers, and in his teaching, preaching and pastoral work, as well as in his own private life, he did his utmost to recommend and promote sanctity and obedience to the perceived will of God. This was particularly important for ordinands at a time when there began to occur fundamental changes in the role of the clergy brought about by the gradual development of a perception of their work as professional men. This was as a result of the clergy being forced to re-assess their role in society as their former activities as civil administrators, local educators and parochial philanthropists were gradually taken over by others. Liddon was not directly involved in this process because he was not a parish priest, but as one of the intel-ligentsia among the clergy he helped to form attitudes and to interpret theologically the developments that were taking place in English society. His whole understanding of the Christian ministry was rooted in the Catholic tradition as rediscovered by the Tractarians. Consequently, he was convinced, in accordance with the Anglican Ordinal, that admission to any of the orders of ministry can only be conferred upon men who have received a call from God.[10] It should never arise as a form of social convenience. Preaching on 'The secret of Clerical Power' at a Salisbury Cathedral ordination in 1865, he said:

> No clerical duty would be tolerable to a man of modesty and sense who supposed himself to be acting in his own strength, and putting forth his own ideas; no clerical duty can give any anxiety to those who know that they are sent by Jesus Christ Himself, and who are sure that He will make good His word for all who in simple sincer-ity place themselves at His disposal.[11]

At Oxford in 1867, he expressed the same conviction more forcibly, 'a true inward call to the priesthood and the commission which descends from the Apostles, are alike the gifts of Jesus Christ alone.'[12] Speaking in more general terms in a lecture, Liddon claimed that failure 'to confess Him before men is to break with Him for ever,' and this assertion lies at the heart of his claims about the nature and function of the ordained ministry. He was convinced that a genuine call from God brought unavoidable consequences in terms of work and witness, especially sanctification of life. Liddon was sure that no one is left to meet these demands alone, for recognition of such a call endows each person with the grace of God and with a 'moral power' which enables them to meet their responsibilities and not be overwhelmed by the disappointments that even what Liddon called the most 'successful' ministerial 'career' encounters.[13] The work of a Christian minister, Liddon presumed, will in many respects be its own reward, especially when the prospect of heaven is included in the assessment. However, he observed that there are occasions when 'a great deal of honest clerical work, of necessary, inevitable clerical work' brings no reward but 'exposes the worker to much obloquy and distress.' He taught that a complete conviction of the reality and validity of his calling would help a priest endure such times, and he was to demonstrate this in his own ministry, and chronicle it in that of Pusey which he so faithfully observed.

But a man does not seek ordination simply because he has an inward calling, nor because the grace of ordination would sustain him when his work is difficult. The reason for anyone to seek ordination, is, according to Liddon, fundamentally more significant. He explained the underlying motive in the following passage in the sermon 'Clerical Motives:'

> For, after all, why is it that we do take Orders? Is it not because we believe and are sure that eighteen centuries ago an event occurred, compared with which all that has happened since, all that can happen in this eventful day, happen what may – is utterly insignificant? Is it not because, like St Paul at Ephesus, we believe that the Everlasting Son of God really entered into conditions of space and time, and died upon the cross for the sins of all men, and rose from the grave, and ascended, and has been pleading for us all ever since, and is doing so at this moment, and has sent His Spirit, and given us His Sacraments? Is it not because we are convinced that if He has done so much for us – for each of us, – the least we can do is to yield Him a free and cheerful service, in such circumstances as He wills, in storm or sunshine, in battle or repose, in hopeful times or days of despondency, it matters little? Surely this is so, brethren, and, when we think of it, the present scene, the nearer horizon, the tangled web of ecclesiastical and political change, dwarfs down into its true proportions, and we see only Jesus Christ Crucified, and souls perishing all around for lack of knowledge or lack of grace, and our own one duty – the duty of our predecessors, the duty of the great Apostle to bring each within our reach, by whatever moral or intellectual instruments, close to the Atoning Cross, to have a share in the sprinkling of the

Cleansing Blood, to know something of that Power and Wisdom of God which is still a stumbling-block to the self-righteous, and foolishness to the self-opinionated. And for this blessed work – blessed in its results to others, blessed in its reflex effect upon all who earnestly undertake it in dependence on God's grace – we have at this day great opportunities.[14]

This was not an original perception by Liddon but it was fresh sounding in an age which still saw 'the Church' as an acceptable career for a gentleman. This Tractarian rejection of worldliness in favour of a sense of vocation and seriousness of purpose had received early expression in the form of a rhetorical question posed in 1833 by Benjamin Harrison in *Tracts For the Times, no. 17,* 'I would . . . ask, **for whose benefit** this high and sacred office has been instituted? For the Clergy, or for the people?' The motive for seeking ordination must be a disinterested response to the love of God: 'alas for those who press to the steps of the sanctuary only that they may keep a fellowship or please a friend or parent,' said Liddon in one of his University sermons criticising a common attitude that the Tractarians helped to eradicate.[15] He believed that such behaviour would invite disaster and judgement. Liddon constantly reiterated that the only source from which ministerial authority is ultimately derived is Christ and the priest must always recall that he does not retain his ministerial authority by right; he would, however, be zealous in his efforts to protect and maintain the spiritual privileges which God has given to the Church and in which the ordained man shares. The certainty of these privileges although theologically defensible, could drive a man of a certain cast of mind into advocating his own understanding of ministry in the guise of uncompromising principles. This seems to have been a fault of Liddon as a young man; at least, Edward King thought so. In 'the great explosion', as it was called, at Cuddesdon, King was appointed chaplain in succession to Alfred Barff and was asked by Bishop Wilberforce to report on how he interpreted the situation at the College. Chadwick quoted from an unidentified source that King thought 'there is something wrong' and 'I think the cause of the wrong will be found in the dear Vice-Principal', whose strong will and personality made him determined 'to fit the Cuddesdon shoe on every foot,' even in inessentials where it is 'most productive of division – this pertinacity in doubtful things appears to me most hurtful to a strong and healthy judgement.'[16] Later the Bishop himself complained that from Cuddesdon the men 'come out too much cut out by a machine.'

Edward King's fear that Liddon was imposing his opinions too rigidly on the students at Cuddesdon was correct, and proved to be his undoing at the College. Bishop Wilberforce sometimes referred to the College as a 'diocesan seminary.' This was unwise in that it generated suspicions in the Oxford Diocese and beyond at a time when many loyal members of the Church of England were bemused by events within the Church in the preceding twenty years, and were anxious about the influence of 'popery'. The Reverend Charles Pourtales Golightly was a former curate of Newman and had become a vigorous opponent of all for which Tractarianism stood. He was a fiercely loyal Church of England clergyman who was utterly opposed to Roman Catholicism. He was also a willing controversialist who believed that the Oxford Movement had introduced an incipient Romanism into the Church of England. Golightly had written to the Bishop from Oriel College, Oxford, in the late summer of 1857 expressing exactly that fear about Cuddesdon. Wilberforce had dealt with him in a friendly and courteous manner, referring to him privately as 'my gossiping friend.' He pointed out that some of the matters about which Golightly complained had been dealt with at once when they arose soon after the College had opened three years before. He also stated that Liddon, as Vice-Principal, was 'eminently endued with the power of leading men to earnest and devoted piety [and] with such a man I do not think I ought to interfere except as to anything substantially important'.[17] Events were to reveal that serious minded and devout men could have very different interpretations of what was substantially important. Liddon's methods were motivated by his own Anglo-Catholicism and Pott did little or nothing to restrain him. Rumours gradually spread about the churchmanship of the place, and these were fuelled when visitors reported that the altar had a frontal and that an enthusiastic ordinand had been permitted to decorate the chapel walls with murals, although it was later conceded that the figures were small. Wilberforce kept in close touch with Liddon who was a frequent visitor to the palace, and he attached the highest priority to supporting the College and its staff. He acted to reduce the provocation but he acted too late, because in September 1857 the College was inspected by Golightly. He had also been there in 1855 and liked it no more on his second visit, although on neither occasion did he have any official right to look around. It was after the second visit, that he wrote to Wilberforce in terms critical of the College and its Vice-Principal. Golightly, who was gradually gaining a hearing among the public, was too incensed to be persuaded by episcopal reassurances which conceded nothing. Gradually the situation deteriorated as Golightly persisted in his criticisms and Wilberforce tried to protect the College and Liddon, whose piety and devotion the Bishop continued to admire. In addition to his other traits, Golightly was an enthusiastic and able author. The Bishop and his circle were anxious that Golightly should not issue circulars or pamphlets. The attack eventually came from a different quarter. A clergyman named Whitwell Elwin[18] anonymously wrote an article in the *Quarterly Review* of January 1858. The article was about 'Church Extension' but it contained criticisms of Cuddesdon College, which he had visited briefly. These were expressed, as Wilberforce's biographer put it, in 'somewhat severe strictures.' In general he believed that men should be prepared for the ordained ministry alongside others who intended to remain laymen, as had hitherto been the case at Oxford and Cambridge. Certainly, the writer urged, the theological colleges should not become the chief means by which men were prepared for ordination. In particular, he argued that theological colleges were not only wrong in principle, they also failed to provide the technical training that they claimed as their speciality. Further, they were to be criticised for the way in which they invariably inculcated what he called a 'party spirit' in their students. It was at this point that the author criticised Cuddesdon Theological College, which he claimed to have visited. Predictably he cited the chapel and its ornaments and was also critical of an Office Book of services and prayers which Liddon had compiled. The article inevitably increased the temperature of the debate and served to encourage Golightly. He renewed his attack on 28 January 1858 by sending a circular letter to clergy and lay people in the Diocese of Oxford. He said that the activities of the College and the demeanour of its staff tended to 'unprotestantise' the Church of England,[19] he also asserted that his protests to Bishop Wilberforce had not been answered satisfactorily.

The Bishop knew that something had to be done and had to be seen to be done, not least because he sensed that what he called his 'usefulness' in the Diocese of Oxford was being damaged by the controversy. He acceded to a suggestion from Pott, the Principal, that he should commission his archdeacons to make a proper enquiry. They met at the College, with Golightly in attendance, on 6 February 1858 and interviewed Pott and Liddon who returned especially from a visit to his mortally sick Aunt Louisa, who was his godmother, in order to be present. In his diary Liddon was pleased to record that Golightly was somewhat wrong-footed by what went on. He reached the conclusion that Golightly's reputation was beginning to rebound on him and that opinion in favour of the College would begin to strengthen as a result. It is possible, however, that Liddon was deceiving himself. Golightly was happy with what he perceived to be the attitude of the archdeacons. Their report, which W. E. Gladstone, the adherent to Tractarian doctrine and future Prime Minister, later said was in 'clumsy dress',[20] was not long in coming and Wilberforce wrote to Pott, enclosing a copy, on 15 February. It was not a document which gave much comfort to either Wilberforce or to Liddon. The archdeacons upheld the criticism that the chapel was decorated too ornately, the word 'gaudy' had been used by one visitor, and alleged that that fact 'has a tendency on the one hand to strengthen a prejudice which already exists in some minds against Theological Colleges, and on the other hand to encourage in the students a disproportionate regard for the mere accessories of Public Worship, and to invest them with an over-prominent importance'.[21] Some detailed criticisms followed, but it was when the report considered Liddon's Office Book that more discomfort was generated. To start with there was a genuinely helpful declaration that it contained nothing contrary to the doctrine of the Church of England and a rejection of some of Golightly's criticisms as factually incorrect. However the assessors did object to some of the terminology in the book, particularly the use of the term 'antiphon,' and to the design of the Book according to the pattern of 'hours', or services for use at particular times of the day, which gave it a quasi-monastic feel. The whole thing, they said, had 'been cast in a form which bears an unfortunate resemblance to the Breviary of the Church of Rome'.[22] As part of the process of repudiating the charge of 'Romanism,' it was necessary for Liddon to re-cast the Book, and he set about the task with a heavy heart. Pott, for his part, sent a letter to incumbents of parishes which had former Cuddesdon students as curates. He asked about Roman tendencies and was reassured when he learned that virtually all of them were entirely satisfied with the denominational loyalty of their assistant curates. The curates themselves combined to issue their own statement in support of Pott and Liddon, 'We can truly say that the lectures of both the Principal and the Vice-Principal have furnished us with the soundest and most conclusive arguments against Roman errors.'[23] However, the simplicity of this endorsement by ordained former students was partially undermined in September 1858 when a man named Mande, who had left the College without being ordained, did become a Roman Catholic. On his conversion, Mande received two unequivocal, but carefully friendly, letters from Liddon. In December of the same year the reputation of Cuddesdon suffered another blow when a student called Burnard, who was still a member of the College, left in order to convert to Roman Catholicism. Liddon had counselled Mande against leaving the College, and he also tried to persuade Burnard not to secede. After the events he tried to minimise the publicity, but the situation was such that the outcome was what mattered, rather than the efforts of those involved. Liddon was not perceived to have moderated his churchmanship, and the Bishop eventually came to share Edward King's conclusion that he was part of the problem and could not become part of the solution.

Wilberforce continued to protect his foundation by expressing his confidence in it and its loyalty to the Church of England. At the same time he ensured that the necessary changes were made to the liturgy and to the chapel ceremonies and ornaments. He also began to deal with the problem of the staff. Barff, the chaplain, was replaced by King for the Michaelmas term of 1858. As has been noticed, he was compelled by Wilberforce to report what he discovered. What he said inevitably weakened Liddon's position. Throughout 1858, following the report of the archdeacons, Liddon had declared himself willing to resign if the Bishop concluded that his departure would benefit the College. Wilberforce did not want to lose him, but was beginning to see that it was inevitable. King's reluctant report strengthened the case against him. During those difficult months, Pott had been unwell and he had made up his own mind that he should leave the College. Liddon wrote a sensitive prayer which he distributed 'to the men on November 3, 1858 – the day after the resignation of the Principal was formally announced in chapel.' In the process of looking for a new Principal, it became clear to Wilberforce that the new man would find Liddon a difficult lieutenant. After a considerable amount of effort, Wilberforce eventually found a man who he felt would adequately replace Pott. He was the devout and unworldly Reverend Henry Hutchinson Swinny. The arrangement was made that Pott would leave at Easter 1859 and it was agreed that Liddon would go at the same time, thereby preserving a sense of order but also allowing Swinny and the new Vice-Principal to begin the new phase of the College's life together. King declined to be promoted to Vice-Principal and a priest named William Harrison Davy was appointed in Liddon's place. It is noteworthy that Liddon retained the trust and affection of Wilberforce and also King. He described leaving Cuddesdon as 'the only great disappointment of my life' and felt that his 'first great attempt at work in life' had failed. However, he did his best to help the students, some of whom were devoted to him personally, to come to terms with the new arrangements. Several of them asked for copies of the old Office Book, Liddon's original compilation, and they made a collection which raised enough to buy him seventy-three theological books.

As the storm at Cuddesdon was beginning to gather, Liddon involved himself in a controversial pastoral problem which Johnston incorrectly dated as having taken place in 1858-9, although the internal evidence of Liddon's diary is clear. He spent part of the 1857 Christmas vacation at Taunton where he ministered to a man named Beale who had been sentenced to death for the murder of a woman called Charlotte Pugsley. Liddon had met Beale before the crime; he had been the butler at a friend's house. Liddon's compassion was engaged because Beale refused the ministrations of the prison chaplain at Bristol where he was awaiting execution. Liddon, in the company of his uncle Henry, visited the prisoner on 1 January 1858 and spent some time with him. Not unnaturally, the man was preoccupied with what he called 'his situation.' However, Liddon was rather more successful than the unfortunate chaplain, and helped the man turn his thoughts to 'the impending eternity.' Two days later he returned in the evening, '. . . saw Beale for an hour and a half. He seemed to join with me earnestly in prayer. He said that he was "sold" by his attorney.' Liddon persevered and returned to the prison twice during the next three days. The diary entries are brief, but he worked with Beale through the passion of Christ in the gospels of St Matthew, St Mark and St John. However, on 6 January, Beale's attitude was different. He had received a visit from someone who had greatly disturbed him. Liddon's diary entry is incomplete. It fails to record the visitor's name and what was said, but the visit had 'sadly checked the spiritual tone of the conversation.' Liddon continued to visit Beale frequently and evidently won the man's confidence. His diary reveals that Beale talked about his past and was helped to appreciate the saving nature of Christianity. Liddon hoped that Beale would make 'an act of contrition,' but it was not to be. Liddon preached at the gaol on Sunday 7 January and returned in the evening. The next significant diary entry came on 11 January, 'Beale would not confess, "God knows all, and no good would come of it, and it is such a task."' Despite this reluctance, Liddon noted that Beale prayed 'most earnestly.' The situation had begun to affect Liddon's imagination, for he continued, 'unable to do any thing for thinking of poor B[eale]. It is terrible to think that tomorrow those eyes will be closed and that hand cold and stiff. Deus misereatur.' Nevertheless, he returned once again to the gaol that night at ten, and worked through the account of the Passion in the Fourth Gospel and also the Burial Service in the Book of Common Prayer. Beale was deeply appreciative of Liddon's efforts, in contrast to his earlier attitude to the prison chaplain. He told Liddon that he had prevented him from attempting suicide.

The execution took place on 12 January 1858 and Liddon was among those present. He recorded his involvement in his diary:

At 6 a.m. I was again at the gaol, engaged in prayer with B. until 7.15. The service in chapel and Holy Communion was at 8. B. communicated with much devotion. He thanked me very warmly, and said that I had saved him. O my Saviour, grant that he may be right. At 9 I went with Uncle Henry to the scaffold, when B. gave me the manual [of prayers] and his wife's last letter ... He seemed to die without any severe struggle.

He concluded by recording that he was advised by a prison official not to preach to the people gathered outside the gaol. Among Liddon's biographers, Johnston devotes most space to this matter, but he failed to record that on the day following the execution, Liddon recorded in his diary that he visited the man's widow and 'sat an hour with her. She entertains no doubt of her husband's guilt.' As a result of his sustained concern Liddon found his concept of a priest's pastoral duty calumnied in the press under the heading 'Flagrant Tractarian Scandal'. Beale was described as a 'hardened and miserable man' who

had the Sacrament administered to him before his execution, either by the Principal or Chaplain of Cuddesdon – it is not ascertained which. There is something truly awful in so flagrant a prostitution of the most sacred and solemn of all the ordinances of religion ... [The journalist claimed to have evidence that Beale was unrepentant] ... The circumstance has caused a most painful sensation in Bristol and Clifton, and it is to give utterance to the prevailing feeling in these places on the subject, that we have called attention to it. Both the Rev. Gentlemen are Puseyites. We need say no more as to the character and tendency of Tractarianism ...[24]

Liddon was wounded by the allegations that he had been either a fool or had been deceived by a hardened criminal, and wrote in his diary on 13 January 1858, 'in *The Times* of today's date a full account of Beale's execution with a series of unfortunate references to myself ... Give me grace, O my Saviour utterly to reject what is said of me by men.' However, he replied rather disingenuously, in a letter to *The Morning Advertiser,* by stating that neither the Principal nor the Chaplain of Cuddesdon had administered the Holy Communion to Beale and he stressed that he alone of the College staff had visited the man; he did not state that he was present when Beale received the sacrament from another priest. The newspaper printed his letter but added a note from the editor which stated that, although 'bound to believe the statement of our Rev. Correspondent', he was far from convinced of the veracity of Liddon's assertions. The prison visiting and care for Beale seems to have been unique in Liddon's career. There is a contrast at this point with the ministry of Edward King, who as Bishop of Lincoln ministered similarly to a condemned man in 1887: 'from that time on it became the Bishop's practice to visit prisoners lying under sentence of death at Lincoln, and to spend long periods with them in private devotion'.[25] Most of Liddon's pastoral work was less sombre in its associations, and there are occasionally more light-hearted incidents. In the diary for 11 July 1867 he described himself, while in Edinburgh, as having 'interfered between a man and his wife: the latter got drunk and was carrying off some shawls to pawn for whisky. She was a RC, he a Presbyterian. He promised to be patient with her, but was much distressed.' On an earlier occasion he had also concerned himself with an aspect of family life which he felt to be unsatisfactory. While calling on someone he encountered a governess who seemed to be a suitable person, except 'as to religious matters dry and unattractive for a child-guide. I tried to get her to interest herself in *Hymns Ancient and Modern*'.[26]

Chapter Two

To 'The centre of the world's concourse'[1]

Although Liddon's departure from Cuddesdon Theological College had been an entirely gentlemanly business, he felt bruised by what had happened. Certainly this is suggested by his investigation of the possibility of serving as a missionary in India. However, the idea did not survive for long. He was already convinced that he was not strong enough for the hurly-burly of English parish life, and his medical adviser told him that he would not survive more than a year in the climate of the colony. He always retained an affection for the idea, and in his will left the Oxford Mission to Calcutta a legacy which was sufficient to pay for a lecture hall. But his friends wanted to keep him in England. Curacies were suggested, St Paul's, Knightsbridge was one; the chaplaincy of Lancing College was another possibility which was not fully explored. His theological mentors wanted to keep him in Oxford, if possible, although he claimed that he was not enamoured at the prospect of college life and was keen to continue in work similar to that from which he was reluctantly resigning. It seems that Pusey's views were not sought at an early stage for he only learned that Liddon had left Cuddesdon when he read about it in a newspaper about three weeks after the event, although he had visited Liddon at the College on at least one occasion. However Pusey did, once again, become a central factor in his life and the friendship dominated the rest of Liddon's life even in the remaining years after Pusey died in 1882.

Just at the point when Liddon was most concerned about his future, the post of Vice-Principal of St Edmund Hall was vacant. His friend William Bright, a Fellow of University College and later Regius Professor of Ecclesiastical History and a Canon of Christ Church cathedral, Oxford, had turned it down and the Principal offered it to Liddon who began work in May 1859. He had not sought the post and it was not quite what he was after. He was teased by some of his friends for accepting it, but nevertheless it gave him a position in

Oxford and the opportunity to work pastorally among undergraduates and to pursue his own academic interests. He planned to contribute to the Bible commentary on which Pusey had been engaged for some years, and began work on the Pastoral Epistles. He did not get very far and the only published outcome was a rather sparse analysis which appeared after his death. One reason for his failure with the commentary was that he abandoned work on the Pastoral Epistles in favour of the Book of Leviticus, but in reality his Biblical work soon took a different direction. Pusey was not pleased with him, as he noted on 2 June 1864: 'Called on Dr P., who was very sharp about my having done nothing with the Commentary ... "When I was your age, I had finished my Tract on Baptism, and my Arabic Catalogue."' The change of direction followed a lunch-time discussion at Cowley Vicarage with R. M. Benson. Liddon decided to give lectures in his College rooms on Sunday evenings to anyone who cared to attend. He began on 6 November 1859 and noted in his diary, 'my first lecture; Prolegomena on the Epistle to the Hebrews; seven men present.' He added a wistful note that none were from St Edmund Hall. He persevered with the idea and numbers grew to about forty within two years, which meant that he had to move them into the dining hall. In 1865 another move was necessary and the venue was switched to the hall of The Queen's College at the invitation of the Provost. Even this was not the final location of his lectures. They were moved eventually to the hall at Christ Church, where sometimes as many as four hundred men attended. Concerning the latter change of venue, Bright wrote, 'Is not this grand? Liddon calls it the Feast of the Translation. His face was quite radiant ...' Liddon kept the lectures going until 1869 and started them again in 1883, so they formed a significant part of his ministry in Oxford.

It was during his time at St Edmund Hall that Liddon's reputation as a preacher began to develop. Bishop Wilberforce, despite the developing difficulties at Cuddesdon, had sufficient confidence to ask him to contribute to a series of Lenten sermons in St Giles' church in Oxford in 1858, and the arrangement was continued in subsequent years. Liddon, as earlier biographers noted, was the youngest priest to contribute to the series. It was the address he gave in the 1858 series which became the first of Liddon's published sermons. Its text was 1 Kings 21.29 and it had the simple title, 'The Repentance of Ahab.' Liddon became the recipient of an increasing number of invitations to preach outside Oxford and found himself travelling a good deal. Even in term time the demands were made, and he had to learn gradually to limit the number of acceptances. However, in 1860 he accepted invitations to preach in no fewer than forty-two different locations. In the time of the Cuddesdon troubles he had complained that preaching was difficult for him, but it is clear that he overcame his problems.

In the spring of 1861, Liddon committed what can only be described as an error of judgement. During the previous year a volume called *Essays and Reviews* was published by a group of liberal theologians. Benjamin Jowett, the Master of Balliol College, was one contributor. Jowett was Professor of Greek, but his post was one of a number which was poorly endowed and the annual salary small, forty pounds, having been fixed during the reign of King Henry VIII. Dr A. P. Stanley proposed that Jowett's stipend should be increased. Stanley was Professor of Ecclesiastical History at Oxford and later a Canon of Canterbury and then Dean of Westminster, and generally acknowledged as the leader of the country's theological liberals although not a contributor to the book. High Churchmen were fearful that support for such an obviously just proposal would, however, be construed as some sort of approval of Jowett's theology. Liddon, who read *Essays and Reviews* within ten days of its publication, was among those utterly opposed to the views it expressed, and was probably the first to attack the volume.[2] It was because of his antipathy towards the theological liberals that he made his mistake when Pusey, ever judicious, sought a compromise. Pusey made a counter proposal in May 1861 when the *Essays and Reviews* controversy was at its height, that the emoluments of a number of poorly endowed professorships should be increased, Jowett's among them. In this way, he thought, justice would be served without theology being compromised. Liddon opposed the move along with a number of others, including William Bright and C. L. Dodgson, a Christ Church colleague and personal friend who achieved lasting fame under the pen-name Lewis Carroll, and who wrote an anonymous pamphlet on the matter. The proposal was defeated, and Liddon incurred Pusey's wrath, and also that of John Keble. They both realised that the action of the opponents of the proposal showed them in an uncharitable and partisan light, and Liddon found himself in the unhappy position of someone who had earned rebukes from two of the men whom he most admired. He never forgot the experience. In 1865 the matter was raised again, and Jowett's stipend was raised from its sixteenth century level to five hundred pounds. At that time, Dodgson, a mathematics don, parodied the attitude of Liddon, who had changed his view, and Pusey in an article, 'The New method of Evaluation as Applied to π.' In a spoof formula he represented Jowett's stipend and said that 'the locus of HPL will be found almost entirely to coincide with ... the locus of EBP.' It was, Dodgson said, 'hopeless to obtain any real value for π by this method'.[3] This was not the only time when Dodgson used his skill as a humorous writer at the expense of his friend.

Liddon's involvement in University politics and his preaching were in addition to his ordinary work among undergraduates at St Edmund Hall. His pastoral earnestness was apparent in his expressed conviction that Oxford dons 'are really answerable for the souls of undergraduates.' He was frequently pained at what he believed to be his pastoral ineffectiveness, even though he recorded many occasions when he walked or talked with his students and gave them pamphlets and other printed religious material. An example of Liddon's pastoral care of new university students is to be found in the biography of Francis Paget although the incident occurred several years later, in 1869. Soon after his arrival he received a visit from Liddon. He arrived as Paget was dressing for football:

> I bowed and apologised myself backwards into my bedroom, from which I emerged an altered being. However, yesterday we had a very pleasant and amusing breakfast, and have, I think, settled most of the important questions of the day.[4]

To all this he added a concern for the spiritual welfare of a growing number of people who sought his help, some of whom, as in the Cuddesdon days were troubled with the ever present problem of 'Roman difficulties.' In addition, he used his skills as a pastor and teacher to off-set what he perceived to be the increasingly secularised atmosphere of Oxford, as the reforms made in the 1850s were supplemented by further secularisation. Many years after leaving St Edmund Hall, on 12 November 1882, he wrote about his pessimistic feelings to C. T. Redington, a Roman Catholic friend in Ireland. He informed him that he had resigned his professorship and continued, 'Oxford is indeed to me a sad subject. The effect of the recent changes is to cut out almost by the roots the old religious provisions and associations of the place . . .'[5]

Eventually he began to feel the strain of his multifarious activities and his health suffered. The earlier biographies are always reticent about Liddon's health, except to say that he was not strong, and it is not now possible to get behind his own laconic diary references to discover what was actually wrong. It is apparent, though, that in the summer of 1862 there was some sort of crisis which led Liddon to the conclusion that he should resign from St Edmund Hall. Johnston made an unexplained reference to 'a serious attack of illness,' but also noted that Liddon turned down the Wardenship of Radley College at that time. There was no hint that his churchmanship was the cause of his departure from St Edmund Hall. He had been required by the Principal to remove an altar cloth on the grounds that it was an innovation to the customary furnishing of the chapel, but the candlesticks which he donated remained. He left with his reputation intact and with a growing ministry as a preacher and spiritual director. Once again, however, there was the problem of what he should do with his time. He was not pressed by financial considerations. In addition to his private income, there was a small emolument attached to his Studentship at Christ Church. Nor did he have any worries about his personal security in Oxford. Those who had been appointed to Studentships before the changes of 1867 enjoyed the right to retain the post for life. In later years the number of such men dwindled and by 1885 it was reduced to five, Liddon and his friends R. M. Benson and C. L. Dodgson, and T. J. Prout and T. V. Bayne. When he left St Edmund Hall, the income from the Studentship was a useful supplement to his private means, but when his circumstances improved he stopped using it and gave it away to needy undergraduates. His rooms at Christ Church were not ready when he left St Edmund Hall and he stayed at Pusey's home in Tom Quad for three months. When he did move into his own rooms he lived there, while in Oxford, for the rest of his life. At this time Liddon looked at one or two vacant livings of which Christ Church was the patron. It was at this time that he was also invited to become the first Vicar of St Alban's, Holborn. This was a new church built by the generosity of a Mr Hubbard, later Lord Addington. After taking advice from Pusey and Keble he declined and then recommended his former colleague at Wantage, A. H. Mackonochie. He was pleased when Mackonochie was appointed, and watched with interest and some alarm when he proceeded to make the place famous as a centre of Anglo-Catholic ritualism. In November 1862 having declined the Wardenship of Radley College, he was despondent about his future. Pusey was among those who were anxious that he should stay in Oxford, but Liddon was beginning to long for a wider involvement in the life of the Church, as was indicated by his readiness to look at other possibilities. In 1863 he fulfilled a promise made more than a year before to Swinny, to conduct a retreat for clergy at Cuddesdon. Surviving reminiscences from those attending suggest that it was both appropriate and helpful, but Liddon was not convinced.[6] He felt that it was not his métier, and he never conducted another retreat, despite often being asked to do so.

In 1859 he had made the acquaintance of Bishop W. K. Hamilton of Salisbury. The first priest of Tractarian sympathies to become a bishop, he found in Liddon a congenial companion. Five years before, when Hamilton had been made bishop, Liddon wrote to his Aunt Louisa and told her to say a *Te Deum* at the news. In 1863 Hamilton made him one of his examining chaplains, and the following year he made him a Prebendary, or Honorary Canon, giving him the stall Major Pars Altaris in Salisbury Cathedral; he was installed on 2nd September. His involvement with Hamilton and the work of the Salisbury Diocese did not make many demands on him, although in 1867 he devoted a good deal of time to assisting Hamilton in writing a major 'Charge' to his diocese. This was a document in which Hamilton's theological views were expressed. He defended sacramental confession, the Eucharistic sacrifice and the Real Presence, all of them doctrines to which Liddon adhered. Only two years afterwards, in 1869, Liddon was involved in caring for the Bishop in his last illness. He also helped Bishop Wilberforce in the capacity of what would today be called a 'research assistant,' but again the work was not heavy, and he undertook some similar tasks for Bishop Hamilton. His preaching ministry continued, and in 1861 he preached for the first time in Westminster Abbey at the invitation of Dean Trench. There were several other occasions when he preached at Westminster Abbey, but in later years he declined invitations from A. P. Stanley, who succeeded Trench in 1864, although the two had known one another since Liddon was an undergraduate. The reason, which he explained at painful length to Dean Stanley, was embarrassing; he did not wish to appear to be associated with the new Dean's liberal theology. There was a lengthy exchange of letters which reveal a considerable degree of charitableness on the part of Stanley, and Liddon dined at the Deanery in April 1864. Among the guests were the Archbishop and Mrs Tait and also 'a great "posse" of liberals'. Liddon thought it best to keep clear of 'personalities' as far as possible on that occasion. Liddon's side of the correspondence with Stanley got progressively more petulant, especially when the latter pointed out that T. T. Carter[7] and also Bishop Wilberforce had both accepted his invitation to preach at the Abbey. It was not until 1866 that Stanley finally abandoned his efforts to persuade Liddon to preach at Westminster, but he tried again nearly ten years later, and Liddon preached at Westminster Abbey on 18 June 1876. The sermon was on the parable of Dives and Lazarus. Significantly, when Stanley died in 1881, Liddon was very warm in his tribute to the Dean's personality, but still critical of his theological position. In November 1862 he had the honour of being chosen as a Select Preacher by the University of Oxford. He preached in St Paul's Cathedral on 19 April 1863 at the suggestion of the Bishop of London, Dr Tait, later Archbishop of Canterbury. The sermon, according to Liddon's diary, took an hour and ten minutes to deliver and the Dean,

H. H. Milman, thought he tried too hard to be audible. He was in an anxious state beforehand; 'I was fortified with mutton chops, salvolatile and sherry.' Afterwards he was exhausted and there may be some truth in Pusey's waspish comment, made when he was critical of Liddon's failure with the Commentary, 'You preach sermons an hour long at St Paul's, and nobody hears you, and you are knocked up for a fortnight afterwards.' In 1864, Liddon published his first collection of sermons. It bore the title, *Some Words for God*, but the second and subsequent editions saw the title changed to *Sermons Preached before the University of Oxford*. Later a second volume of sermons preached in Oxford University was published, and the two were distinguished as *First Series*, and *Second Series*. The first volume was dedicated to his friend William Bright.[8] The original title had been chosen because Liddon thought that it reflected the nature of the collection as theological apologetics, but all his sermons, and many others were to be published, were full of dogma and nothing was lost when the less specific title was adopted. Many of the sermons were rewritten for publication. At this stage in his career Liddon was accustomed to preach from notes. He developed the habit of compiling a fuller script or analysis of each sermon shortly after it was preached and the published versions were prepared from these sources. He was embarrassed and distressed when an article appeared in the October 1867 edition of the 'Theological Review.' It came out over the initials C.K.P., a clergyman named C. Kegan Paul. He asserted that Liddon's personal influence in Oxford was higher than Liddon himself believed, comparing him with Newman at the height of his powers. This was one source of embarrassment, another, and also the cause of his distress, was Kegan Paul's allegation that he had plagiarised the 'Spiritual Exercises' of St Ignatius Loyola. Liddon wrote to Kegan Paul on 31 October and explained that the offending sermon was compiled from notes in his own hand writing made some years before the sermon was preached, and that the preaching was some years prior to publication in the book. He assumed that he had made the notes from Ignatius back in 1852 or 1854 and later failed to realise his debt when he prepared and preached the sermon. Kegan Paul was not entirely happy with this not very satisfactory explanation, but accepted Liddon's word and the matter was dropped. He did, however, contest the modesty of Liddon's rejection of the high view of his personal influence as did William Bright who wrote in response to a complaint from Liddon, 'The fact is that you are not the best judge as to the precise extent of your influence . . . you are the best judge on the point of real interest for this particular occasion, *i.e.* that you never do, did, or could, seek influence for its own sake.'[9]

It was William Bright who, in March 1865, initiated the next piece of work which enhanced Liddon's reputation and for which he should still be remembered. He suggested that Liddon should put his name forward for election as the Bampton Lecturer for 1866. John Bampton was an eighteenth century Canon of Salisbury who left an endowment to provide for eight annual lectures in St Mary's church, Oxford. The intention was that the lecturer should expound and defend the Christian faith as expressed in the Fathers, the Creeds and Scripture. The first series of lectures was given in 1780, and in 1895 they were changed to a biennial pattern. As was his customary practice with anything important, Liddon consulted Pusey who advised that he should not put himself forward as a potential lecturer, because a successful application would delay Liddon's work on the Commentary yet again. In this Pusey was also reflecting his personal view, which became almost institutionalised among Anglo-Catholics, that a man should not seek any kind of preferment or recognition. Liddon hesitated, but not for long. On 18 March he sent in his name as a candidate, rejecting Pusey's advice. The electors had already met on one occasion, so Liddon's application was late. A second meeting was held on 16 May and the meeting was evenly divided. Liddon received seven votes, so did the Reverend A. W. Haddon. The chairman of the electors was the Vice-Chancellor, Lightfoot of Exeter College, and his casting vote went to Haddon whom Liddon, fifteen years later, was to describe as 'a true theologian and a profound historical scholar, by whose comparatively early death the Church was deprived of real intellectual maturity and power'.[10] However, the matter did not end there, as Liddon wrote to Bishop Hamilton on 8 November 1865:

> ... It will interest you to hear that Haddon, who was elected Bampton Lecturer in the spring, having been obliged to resign from ill-health, the electors have appointed me to take his place.

What Liddon did not say, and might not have known, was that the electors were unanimous in their second choice. The lectures were to be given in March 1866, so Liddon had a little less than four months to get ready. With some understatement he continued his letter to Hamilton:

> To a certain extent this places me in a difficulty, as I have nothing but the vaguest idea of my subject, and, of course, have not written one line. But one must trust in God and set to work.[11]

His diary for the next few months contains many references to the progress of the work. Liddon decided that the subject of his lectures should be the divinity of Christ, and they constitute his only significant piece of sustained Christological writing which was planned as such. He produced a masterly survey of traditional Chalcedonian Christology. Once again, it seems that he consulted Pusey who discouraged him from providing a survey of modern theology. This time he happily followed that advice. It served his purpose to do so because he hoped that his lectures might draw together Christians of different view-points at a time when, as he believed, liberal theology was undermining the traditional beliefs of the Church. In the course of the lectures Liddon created opportunities to attack such liberalism by setting out to 'reject any notion of development in belief,' according to Peter Hinchliff in his recent biography of Frederick Temple.[12] In preparation, however, he read extensively in the short time available. His diary records his reaction to some of the modern material he had to read; 14 November 1865, 'Read some of Strauss's new *Life of Jesus*, and felt wretched. His cold infidelity chills one's soul to the core.' December 19, 'In the evening read a great deal of *Ecce Homo*,' another 'Life' of Christ, which had been published anonymously in 1865 and which had had a very wide circulation. 'It is, I feel sure, Dr Temple's.' In this he was incorrect, it was not by Temple but by Sir John Seeley of University College, London, although speculation as to the identity of the author included such widely differing individuals as Newman, Gladstone and A. P. Stanley. The diary also records that he found the process of writing the lectures difficult. Words and phrases recur; his beginning, on 17 November, was 'unsatisfactory'; on December 21, he made 'little headway'; a few days later he again felt 'wretched.' And so it went on. In addition to the problems of preparing the lectures, he was not helped by his reputation for speaking at length. The very conservative Vicar of St Mary's, W. J. Burgon, was alarmed at the prospect of Liddon in his pulpit and wrote in January warning him, 'not to make the Bamptons too long,' and in March he received another letter from him which was 'uncomfortable.' Burgon had cause for anxiety for Liddon himself recorded later that the first in the series, delivered on 4 March 1866, lasted one hour and a quarter, 'reading very rapidly,' and the last in the series took one hour and forty minutes to deliver. In between he had to contend with the criticism of his friends, and again his diary is revealing. On March 12, he noted, 'the Doctor [Pusey] told me that Palmer had said that my Bampton yesterday was rhetorical, but that the logical element in it was feeble. He

spoke strongly – from what motive I do not know.'[13]   Despite
Pusey's sharp remarks and despite their length, the lectures were
widely appreciated. The church was very crowded for the first in
the series, and undergraduates and others continued to attend.
Johnston spoke of the 'enormous congregations' which were present.
However, Liddon's sense of achievement as the series progressed
was tempered by news of the death of John Keble on Maundy
Thursday, 29 March 1866.

Keble was one of the greatest influences on Liddon's development
and the suggestion that a memorial be established in Oxford was an
idea that Liddon soon saw as a duty to be carried out. It was at
Keble's funeral at Hursley that the idea of a College in Oxford was
suggested as a fitting form of memorial, and Liddon seems to have
been its originator. He wrote in his diary that, while at Hursley for
the funeral, he and some others had gone to see the Bishop of
Salisbury who was staying nearby, 'and the plan of a College at
Oxford, which I had started the night before at Hursley Vicarage,
was agreed upon. It is to be called Keble College.'[14] As the plans
progressed, Liddon served as one of the secretaries of the fund. With
Keble's funeral behind him, Liddon returned to Oxford to deliver the
remaining Bampton Lectures. Eventually, to his relief, the series was
concluded but then came the task of preparing them for publication.
Once again, he had spoken from an incomplete manuscript, so the
revision work was considerable. He devoted much of the summer of
1866 to the task, staying with relatives at Brislington. Each
completed section was sent to William Bright for criticism and evaluation. Afraid that Bright might complain of their length, Liddon
explained that another friend, a man named Fraser of Oriel College,
had recommended that the footnotes should be kept brief and that
explanatory matter should be included in the text of the published
lectures. Despite this caveat, he told Bright, 'I cannot say how much
I prize your kind interest and assistance.' The book came out in
October 1867 with a preface dated Ascension Day that year. By
1880, twenty-five thousand copies had been sold in eight editions and
Liddon revised the whole book for the ninth. The seventh edition was
translated into German and published in Basel in 1883. The fourteenth, and last, edition was published with a new preface which
Liddon had completed only a month before he died.

Liddon had much appreciated Bright's assistance with his Bampton
Lectures and at the end of 1866 he sought to promote his friend's
career by recommending him for the Regius Professorship of
Ecclesiastical History. Bright feigned indignation when he discovered
what was happening because he had been secretly promoting

Liddon's cause! In the event, the successful candidate was the Reverend H. L. Mansel. He was an incongruous choice, having been previously Professor of moral and metaphysical philosophy. He had given the Bampton Lectures in 1858 on 'The Limits of Religious Thought.' Two years later he became Dean of St Paul's Cathedral and Bright, to Liddon's surprise and delight, was appointed to the Professorship. Bright, however, was not the only man concerned about Liddon's career. On 4 June 1866, Dr Pusey asked him to consider accepting the headship of Keble College. He thought that Liddon would be 'startled' at the suggestion, and so he was. Moreover, Liddon did not feel that he would be an appropriate choice and said so. As the building project continued, others joined Pusey in trying to persuade him, including the Bishop of Oxford, Lord Cavendish and, later, Lord Beauchamp. Despite Liddon's repeated refusal, the Trustees empowered the Archbishop of Canterbury to approach Liddon formally in June 1868, but still he refused. Pusey, in a vexed tone, asked whether, 'apart from his supposed disqualifications, he considered his present work of more importance than the headship of the College.'[15] This was rather harsh of Pusey, who knew that Liddon had no official employment of any kind. Liddon kept to his original decision and it is easy to follow his thinking which he had summarised in his diary as early as 4 June 1866; 'In the evening I wrote to Lord Beauchamp, telling him why I thought it impossible (1) on account of the share I had had in getting up the idea of a College; (2) on account of my not being a First Class man; (3) on account of the Cuddesdon row when I was "blown upon."' It is not difficult to believe that the last of those factors was decisive for Liddon. He repeated and expanded these reasons in a lengthy letter to Beauchamp two years later, on 2 June 1868, but even that did not prove to be final and as late as 1869 the suggestion was still around. By then Liddon was urging that the first Warden, the correct title for the head of the College, should be the Reverend E. S. Talbot, who was appointed and served for eighteen years with distinction. Liddon wrote of Talbot in 1881:

> Keble [College] has been fortunate in meeting with a warden, who combines the faith of a Christian with very high intellectual ability, and the lower but not unimportant advantages of gentle birth and good connections. To ourselves he appears to have given proof of remarkable skill as an administrator; he has, within ten years, made his college one of the four largest in Oxford; while, as an educational success, it altogether now transcends the boldest flights of fancy in which its projectors ever ventured to indulge.[16]

Liddon was well-pleased, but this was far into the future. In the meantime, Pusey continued to press the appointment upon him. Liddon wrote to him on 16 April 1869:

> As to myself, I deeply feel and thank you for all your kindness. You see all your friends and me beyond others, I fear in the light of your love and generosity. But, as you know, my own conviction of my unfitness for such a post has, from the first, been clear and strong. Had it been otherwise, I must long ago have yielded to so much pressure. As it is, I cannot help feeling in all sincerity that, whomever you may appoint, you will appoint a better Principal that I could be.[17]

When he had finished preparing the Bampton Lectures for publication, Liddon went to Russia for two months with Charles Dodgson, who had never been abroad before. Dodgson was an enthusiastic photographer. They travelled via Brussels, where they were given a dinner of seven courses, and Cologne. Liddon recorded in his diary on 15 July 1867 that Dodgson 'was overcome by the beauty of Cologne Cathedral,' which had been only recently completed according to the original design. Liddon found him 'leaning against the rails of the Choir, and sobbing like a child.' Later Dodgson described it as the 'most beautiful of all churches I have ever seen, or could imagine.'[18] A verger came to show them round, but Dodgson made off on his own, 'he said he could not bear the harsh voice of the man in the presence of so much beauty.'[19] The pair spent five days in Berlin and then travelled to Konigsberg, where Liddon was ill for a short while. When they got to Russia, after more than a day on a train, Liddon was entranced by St Petersburg, particularly by St Isaac's Cathedral. The building itself and also the devout behaviour of the congregation during the liturgy impressed him. His humour showed with regard to the people, 'they crossed themselves with a kind of business-like energy, which would be equal to some mechanical labour, such as working a pump.' He seems to have argued with Dodgson as to whether the Eastern Church was as imposing as the Roman Catholic Church. Liddon thought it was, although it reinforced the cultus of the Blessed Virgin Mary in a way that he found unsatisfactory. Nevertheless, 'to call her [the Eastern Church] a petrification here in Russia would be a simple folly.' He repeated the latter point in a long and rather fulsome letter to Bright, although he did acknowledge that his conclusion could be a rash generalisation after only a short visit. By early August, after another long journey on a train, they were in Moscow, and Liddon received some letters of introduction that had failed to arrive before he left England. These enabled him to meet a suffragan Bishop of Moscow, Leonide, a former army officer. Liddon found him to be an attractive character who was well informed about some aspects of recent Western theological writing, including Strauss and Renan and even the work of Bishop Colenso.[20] Leonide did not approve of such theologians, nor of the way that theological thinking was going in the west, but was 'most cordial in his disposition' towards the English Church and wanted to know how the Church of England was dealing with what Liddon called 'German theologians.' It is likely that Liddon's replies to such enquiries were rather partisan, but they seemed to have reassured Leonide who invited Liddon to accompany him to meet the great Philaret,[21] Metropolitan of Moscow, at a humble country house near a monastery about forty miles from Moscow. Liddon described, in a letter to Bishop Hamilton, what happened:

> ... He received us in a room which had no carpet on the floor, and no papering on the walls, but a *prie-dieu* and several Icons and religious pictures. There was also a large print of Canterbury Cathedral, which contrasted strangely (and very pleasantly) with its Oriental surroundings. The Metropolitan spoke Russian, and Bishop Leonide kindly interpreted my remarks; the interview lasted about an hour and a half.[22]

The discussion ranged widely with Leonide translating into French for Liddon, but Dodgson took little part in the theological exchanges. Philaret wanted to know about what he termed the 'defects' in the English Holy Communion service. He also wanted to know about the circumstances of the Roman Catholic Church in England, and whether the University of Oxford was still a Christian place. Later in the conversation he turned to the foreign policy of the British Government and was critical of the welcome that the Sultan of Turkey had received on a recent visit at a time when the Turks were persecuting Christians. The French Government was also criticised for the same reason. Philaret evidently found it difficult to comprehend how avowedly Christian governments could deal in a friendly fashion with such a regime. However, the courtesies were preserved, and Liddon and Dodgson were invited to the liturgical celebrations a few days later which marked the fiftieth anniversary of Philaret's consecration to the episcopate. Liddon ventured to tell Philaret that, had they known of the anniversary, the Bishop of Salisbury, the Bishop of Oxford and the Archbishop of Canterbury would all have wished to send congratulations to the Metropolitan and, in his letter to Hamilton, he asked that the Bishop should arrange for such greetings to be sent.

On their return to St Petersburg, Liddon and Dodgson also called on the English chaplain where, as Dodgson recorded, Liddon had difficulty in recovering his coat, which he had given up to a servant. Eventually, after ridiculous mimes and fruitless gestures, and a farcical response from the maid, Dodgson rescued the situation by taking paper and drawing a figure of a man receiving a coat from a female servant.[23] The two set out to return to England in the first half of September 1867, and Liddon was pleased to have seen more of the Russian Church than he would as an ordinary tourist. At Dresden they seem to have disagreed about the attractiveness of Roman Catholic liturgy, for Dodgson did not share Liddon's appreciation of large scale, formal acts of worship. Morton N. Cohen, Dodgson's recent biographer, thought that they probably quarrelled, because they ended up in different hotels in Paris, and travelled to England separately. However, there was no permanent rift, and the two remained friends. Indeed, it was Liddon who suggested the title for *Through the Looking-Glass and What Alice Found There*.[24] Dodgson continued sometimes to consult Liddon on personal spiritual matters and, on at least one occasion, sought his advice with regard to a serious pastoral problem presented to him by an undergraduate.

Back in England, Liddon's life continued with its customary round of private study, preaching engagements and the Sunday evening lectures. The Wardenship of Keble College continued to haunt him, as has been noticed, but another event caused him some anxiety. He was invited to preach at Windsor before Queen Victoria. He set out on 27 June 1868 and got on the wrong train, 'was carried on to Taplow,' and had to retrace his steps. When he arrived at Windsor he was relieved and pleased to discover that Mr and Mrs Gladstone, whom he had first met in 1853 when he took his M.A., were also staying at the Deanery. Later he told Bishop Hamilton that the presence of the Gladstones had made what he called 'the Windsor episode' very pleasant. The sermon itself went well. He recorded in his diary that an official told him that the Queen was pleased. The rest of his diary entry for 28 June described the day in brief, almost laconic, terms:

Went with the Dean to Matins in the Private Chapel at 10 o'clock. At 12 to Litany, which the Dean of Windsor said, and then I read the Communion Service and preached the sermon on 1 St Pet. v.5: 'Humility' extempore. The Duke of Edinburgh sat next to the Queen.

This entry is important in its own right, not least because it was sometimes alleged in the press, in later years, that Liddon had offended the Queen on this occasion.

Later in the same year he preached at Harrow at the Commemoration service on Founder's Day, 10 October 1868. G. W. E. Russell was a boy at the school and in his biography of Liddon he gave a fulsome description of the occasion which is of interest. The boys knew that Liddon was 'a great Oxford swell . . . [and] . . . the author of the most eloquent Bampton Lectures that had ever been delivered.' He described Liddon: 'the beautifully chiselled, sharply-pointed, features, the close-shaved face, the tawny skin, the jet-black hair, reminds us vaguely of something by Velasquez or Murillo.' He went on to describe Liddon's voice as 'vibrant . . . exquisite,' with an 'almost over-refined articulation.' It seemed to be the 'very note of culture.' The 'restrained passion, which thrills through the disciplined utterance, warns even the most heedless that something quite unlike the ordinary stuff of school sermons is coming.' Russell went on to describe the sermon in similarly extravagant terms. He concluded with the observation that Liddon changed his preaching style at about this time. 'He began to subject his genius to a more rigorous discipline. The exuberance of early manhood was laid aside; he no longer indulged his natural tendency to extemporaneous declaration.'[25] However, his sermons continued to be lengthy affairs; the one at Harrow took an hour, but Russell claimed that the boys did not notice its length!

The twelve months from the autumn of 1868 was a time of sadness for Liddon. He was genuinely distressed on churchmanship grounds when the Bishop of London, A. C. Tait a longstanding opponent of the Tractarian position, was appointed Archbishop of Canterbury in succession to Longley. Tait's successor at London was Jackson of Lincoln, a devout and tolerant evangelical, in whom Liddon also had no faith. At about this time, in December 1868, Mackonochie was condemned for illegal ritualistic practices at St Alban's, Holborn, and compelled to pay the expenses of both sides. Liddon saw this as a blow to the Catholic revival in the Church of England and he linked it in his mind with the episcopal appointments which he described, in a private letter, as 'miserable.' At a more personal level, there was further sadness when Bishop Hamilton of Salisbury became ill. Liddon held him in very high regard and spent as much time as he could with the Bishop in what proved to be his last illness. From London he wrote to C. Wellington Furse a letter which was lost until discovered in 1983 in a second-hand bookshop. In it he declined an unspecified invitation on the grounds that 'the Bishop of Salisbury is very ill here; the end cannot be far off. Remember him ... before God'. In fact the bishop survived for another six months.

On Christmas Eve he wrote to his sister, 'the Bishop does not, I think, improve. He gets sleep by means of opiates, but he is very restless and ill during the day.' Three months later Liddon wrote in similar terms, and it was obvious by then that the Bishop would not recover. He spoke constantly, Liddon recorded, of his death. By the middle of the summer Liddon was also having to come to terms with the pending death of his father. He was at Clifton with his father when bad news came from Salisbury. He set out at once and arrived in time. The Bishop 'was much moved to see me,' he wrote in his diary on 31 July 1869, and continued in a staccato style: 'could not bear to be talked to. Is greatly changed since Wednesday week. In the evening I prayed with him, and on my saying that he would feel the truth of our Lord's promise, "When thou passest through the waters I will be with thee," he pressed my hand and nodded assent. In the morning he had told Mrs Hamilton that he is quite ready to go. He is not today suffering any pain. *Deo gratias*.' The entry for the next day recorded that he was called by a servant, 'at twenty minutes after midnight Mirehouse called me, and I found the Bishop breathing with increased difficulty. Prayed with him at intervals. "O Saviour of the world, Who by Thy cross," etc., and the Passion prayer from the Litany. Breathed short ejaculatory prayers to our Lord in his ear. Said the "De Profundis", and a commendatory prayer as he was dying.'

Liddon went back to Clifton the following day and only returned to Salisbury for the Bishop's funeral, on 8 August, at which he preached.[26] The Bishop was buried in his cathedral, and is commemorated in the nave by a fine canopied monument. Liddon remained with his father for the month of August. Once again the diary records harrowing scenes. However, as was always the case, it reveals relatively little of Liddon's own emotional state. He was gratified when his father asked him to administer Holy Communion to him and was pleased to be told that it had given the sick man the 'greatest satisfaction.' He was distressed at the severe pain which his father had to endure, and prayed with him as he died at 1 a.m. on 31 August 1869. He wrote in his diary:

What a solemn August this has been, beginning on the 1st with the death of my dearest father in Christ, and ending on the 31st in that of my dear father in the bonds of nature! May I have grace not wholly to miss the lesson!'

Pusey wrote to him, on 4 September, a kind letter with a perceptive end:

> I only had your letter today, having been detained on the road. *Requiem aeternam dona ei, Domine.* I will remember him at the altar tomorrow. It is a different world when there is no father on earth to look up to, and to have only to look to those who look up. God comfort you all.[27]

Liddon's discomfort at the bereavements he had suffered was not to end immediately because events took an odd turn. He began to be referred to as Hamilton's likely successor. There was, of course, no truth in the rumour but it did appear in some west country newspapers. Liddon had to deny the veracity of the reports, which he did with a sense of thankfulness. But the embarrassment did not even end at that point. Early in September, the Bishop of Exeter, the old-fashioned and irascible High Churchman Henry Phillpotts, resigned and Liddon's name was also associated with that vacancy. It was not, however, merely newspapers that were interested in Liddon's career. On 5 November 1869 Liddon was surprised to receive a letter from his friend Sir Robert Phillimore.[28] In it Phillimore begged him, in Johnston's words, 'not to decline the Canonry at St Paul's, which Canon Dale was expected to vacate, in case it should be offered to him.'[29] However, nothing seems to have happened for several months. On 6 February 1870 he received a letter from Gladstone, who had become Prime Minister for the first time in 1868. He asked Liddon whether he would accept a Canonry at St Paul's, should he make another appointment which would create a vacancy there. With Keble, Hamilton and his father all dead, Liddon had only one adviser whom he could approach in confidence. He went the same day to Oxford and dined with Dr Pusey. 'He was not at first averse,' wrote Liddon in his diary, 'but gradually he became so, on the ground that I should be taken away from Oxford, and ought to remain to work the Theological School and prevent its getting into the hands of the Rationalists. He became very pathetic and emphatic.' Liddon was distressed by Pusey, and eventually told Gladstone that he would leave the decision with him. He also authorised Pusey to write to Gladstone and turn down the offer in his name. Pusey was deeply touched. 'Thank you for all your loving confidence in me. God bless it to you.'[30] Pusey, despite his own feelings and his loneliness, did not interfere with the decision, and the appointment to the canonry was announced on 16 February 1870. That summer, Liddon was very busy, but he had his customary continental holiday and saw the

Passion play at Oberammergau, about which he wrote home enthusiastically. It was not until towards the end of the year that Liddon moved into number 3, Amen Court. It remained his London home for the rest of his life. His sister, Mrs Ambrose, was his housekeeper, and shared some of the tensions that came his way. Liddon's other companions were his cats. At one time he had two Persians whom he named Tweedledum and Tweedledee. Years later, at a dinner party, a serious-minded priest who was sitting next to a young niece of Liddon's, asked what her learned uncle talked about to her. 'Oh!' she said, 'usually cats.'

Pusey's reaction to his younger friend's good fortune was not entirely due to his stated reasons, nor to his aversion to preferment, but rather because Dr Scott, the Master of Balliol, was about to retire from the post of Ireland Professorship of Scriptural Exegesis, and Pusey hoped that Liddon would be his successor. Liddon was unaware of this. He wrote to Pusey on 8 February, 'I had not heard of the Master of Balliol's resignation,' and he would not promise to be a candidate for the forthcoming professorial election, perhaps because of the pending canonry. However, although his diary was blank for much of the relevant period, Liddon did record on 11 June 1870, 'At 4 p.m. I was elected by the Heads of Houses Professor of Exegesis. Saw Bright and the V[ice] C[hancellor]. A letter from the Dr in highest glee.' As a consequence of his new status, Liddon received the degree of Hon. D.C.L. on 22 June 1870 and was made B.D. and D.D. by decree of the Convocation of the University of Oxford on 22 November 1870. Among his friends, Dodgson was as delighted as Pusey. The latter was always keen to keep him in Oxford because he saw the University as the main aspect of his work. Indeed, he implied that the London canonry should be seen primarily as a source of income for Liddon's professorship. Liddon did not share that enthusiasm to the full. He had been reluctant to allow his name to go forward for election and felt, increasingly as time passed, that his real work was in London. However, he delivered his professorial lectures regularly until 1882, but sadly to a diminishing number of students; perhaps this was an indication that his conservative scholarship had become unfashionable.

While Liddon's future was beginning to be discussed by newspapers and also by individuals whose influence was more significant, the man himself was not only trying to recover from his bereavements, he was working on a major project. It originated in a request from John Jackson, the new Bishop of London whose appointment he had regretted, and came about in the months between the first approach regarding his canonry and him taking up the post. The

Bishop wanted him to deliver a course of sermons on Sunday after-noons in Lent 1870 in the fashionable London church of St James, Piccadilly. Liddon described them as 'lectures', and once again they were lengthy disquisitions, sometimes longer than an hour and a half, which earned criticism on that score just as they earned praise for their subject matter and content. The course ran from the beginning of Lent to Palm Sunday and tackled the fundamentals of the Christian faith, which was what Jackson had requested. Russell described Liddon's fashionable audience of 'Ministers of State, members of the Houses of Parliament, great squires, leading lawyers, and all their contingents of wives and daughters.' Henry Scott Holland wrote an extravagant description of the lectures and the effect they produced on their hearers:

> Was anything ever seen like the sensation which they produced? Those smart crowds packed tight, Sunday after Sunday, to listen for an hour and forty minutes to a sermon that spoke straight home to their elemental souls. It was amazing! London never again shook with so vehement an emotion. 'Society,' in its vague, aggra-vating ignorance, believed itself to have discovered Liddon. How indignant we used to get with the rapturous Duchesses who asked whether we had ever heard of this wonderful new preacher! Why, for years before we had stood ranked thick on each others' toes in huddled St Mary's [Oxford], to catch every word of the ringing voice. Those belated Duchesses, indeed! Yet it was something that, however late in the day, they should all feel it necessary for their reputations to be there at St James's.[31]

It seems that Holland had not exaggerated. Russell also described the crush of people who pushed unceremoniously in the open space in front of the church to gain a place inside from which Liddon could be heard; it was like the 'first night' at a theatre.[32] Every seat was taken half an hour before the services began, and the aisles and passage-ways were also crammed with people. It was a natural consequence that the sermons or lectures should be published, and Liddon made an early promise to do so. However, circumstances made difficult the process of preparing them, and they did not appear until 1872. The title of the book was *Some Elements of Religion*, and it proved popular at once. Many editions were produced, the fourteenth appeared in 1899, nearly a decade after Liddon's death and almost thirty years after they were delivered in St James's church.

Liddon's appointment to his canonry, and the election to the Professorship brought to an end the eight year period which followed his departure from St Edmund Hall. During that time he had had no formal employment and Johnston declared that they were years which 'do not admit of lengthy record.' However, the record does show that he was not idle. From time to time he had been projected into prominence as a result of his sermons or lectures, and the intellectual standard of his publications bears witness to his constant, but essentially conservative, scholarship. His own view, however, was that his more private work as a spiritual director or adviser was of greater significance. He was a man of theological seriousness, who was utterly devoted to the Christian gospel and he sought constantly to commend the faith in its Anglican dress to those with whom he came in contact. His letters and diaries reveal that there were a large number of such individuals, and that work continued in the next and more formal phase of his career.

Chapter Three

Devotion to the Church of Christ

A priest who is almost simultaneously appointed to a residentiary canonry at St Paul's cathedral and to an Oxford professorship is clearly someone with an established reputation in both the academic and the ecclesiastical worlds. That such appointments should have been conferred upon Henry Parry Liddon was remarkable at the start of the 1870s. Although the conservative nature of his scholarship was not seen as an obstacle to his appointment to the professorship, his churchmanship made his appointment to the canonry exceptionable. He was committed to that uncompromising Anglo-Catholicism which tended to disqualify its adherents from preferment in the reign of Queen Victoria.

His theological opinions were so much part of the man that his character cannot be comprehended without them. Liddon was utterly loyal to the Church of his baptism, and it is therefore necessary to study his understanding of the Church of England. In his utterances, both public and private, Liddon used, without any inconsistency, the terms 'the Catholic Church;' 'the English Church;' 'the Church of England' as interchangeable. In this he was, in effect, making the theological statement that the Church of England rightly occupies a place in the catholic firmament. Liddon responded whole-heartedly to the notion that the Church of England, and the whole Anglican Communion, was heir to the truths of ancient undivided Christendom. He accepted that the whole Church

has passed from the prayers and agonies of the Coliseum and the Catacombs to define, under altered circumstances, her unchanging faith at Nicea, at Constantinople, at Ephesus, at Chalcedon; not indeed presumptuously to add to what Apostles had taught once and for all, but to scan, to catalogue, to study the Apostolical treasure of the Divine Words more accurately than before, and in the face of those who would have impaired it.[1]

The theological task, as Liddon interpreted it, was to preserve and to present the gospel within the Catholic Church to each generation and to demonstrate conclusively the right of the Church of England to be considered an authentic part of that catholic heritage. This understanding of the Church included a severe and conscientious spirituality yet was tempered with moderation. Pusey, as he aged, combined principle with good sense,[2] and Liddon's own approach echoed this. Neither man was happy with the rigidity which became dominant as ritualism[3] developed and which became a continuing part of Anglo-Catholicism. It has already been noted that Liddon began his career as an undergraduate in 1846 at the time when the Oxford Movement was suffering the consequences of Newman's secession and seemed to many, of whom R. W. Church was the most eminent, to have failed. Indeed, that the Movement had ended in failure was part of Richard Church's thesis in his *The Oxford Movement, Twelve Years, 1833–1845* published posthumously in 1890. Liddon's early acquaintance with Dr Pusey gave him the opportunity to get behind this apparent failure, to discover that all was not loss, and to reinforce his own convictions about the integrity of the Church of England. He was able to witness the way in which the Tractarian Movement in fact survived the catastrophe of Newman's departure and entered upon 'a period of peculiar richness'[4] which enabled it to continue to influence the thinking of the Church of England. As late as 1884 he could say that the Oxford Movement had 'found itself engaged in the work of proving and reasserting large elements of the Church's creed and system'.[5] This he saw as a departure from earlier practice, which had repeatedly made what he believed to be unwise concessions to what he called rationalism:

> for not a few of the defenders of Christianity in previous years had thought to defend it best by the method of incessantly making concessions to its enemies; like those unarmed travellers who, when pursued by hungry wolves, threw first one and then another of their company to the savage brutes, in the hope that if not sated, they would be appeased, or at least occupied, by what had been so easily surrendered.[6]

However, he continued, the Tractarians had come to see the folly of 'abandoning faith in the grace and presence of Christ in His Sacraments, and in the necessity of an Apostolical ministry'. Those who had abandoned such fundamental doctrines 'had really in ways little suspected at the time made the assaults of scepticism on such central truths as the Atonement and the Holy Trinity much more difficult to resist. For truths are related in numberless ways to each other; or rather, Revealed Truth is a great whole, no part of which can be withdrawn or denied without impairing what remains.'

It is important to remember that the contribution of the Tractarians was not simply a negative desire to return to some 'golden age' of Catholicism. Maurice Cowling pointed out that the Oxford Movement had 'constructive characteristics', and he described Liddon as offering a 'constructive polemic'.[7] When Liddon described Pusey's contribution to the process of stiffening the resolve of orthodox Christians, in the sermon from which the above passage is quoted, he could have been also speaking of himself, for although Pusey remained the leader of the Movement until the end of his long life, Liddon became increasingly to be seen as his spokesman. Liddon's first biographer, Johnston, writing just over a decade after Liddon had died, provided some insights into the original perception of the Tractarians:

> . . . in the early Sixties Oxford was still in the throes of that great struggle for religious truth which ensued after the direct work of the Tractarian Movement in the University had been suppressed. That Movement was, in the minds of its chief promoters, a great effort to prepare to withstand the incoming tide of Rationalistic thought – 'Theological Liberalism,' as it was called – which was already sweeping over Germany in the first quarter of the century, and, before the Tracts began in 1833, was beginning to show itself in England. The popular view of Tractarianism as a mere opposition to Evangelicalism is due to misunderstanding. It was really, as it was in the history of Liddon's own mind, the necessary complement of Evangelicalism and not its opponent. The Tractarians felt that the real defence against 'Liberalism' was to be found in reasserting and insisting upon the whole of the Catholic Faith; this, they felt, would give a basis for a reasoned resistance to Rationalism which the narrow popular Evangelicalism could never supply. But the Evangelicals of Oxford had misunderstood the attempt, treated it as necessarily Roman, and as hostile to their conception of the Christian Faith; and in 1841, when argument failed, they threw in their lot with the 'Liberals,' and used the antiquated forms of the University to crush it.[8]

Johnston also said that, '. . . in 1863 the Church in Oxford was fighting for the maintenance of the central position of the Creed,' and Liddon had thrown himself into this struggle, particularly in the years when he had no formal occupation. Through his learning, his sermons and his willingness to enter upon controversy, and through his friendships with Keble, Pusey and many of their followers, he was enabled to make a unique contribution to the task of re-presenting to English Christians the value of the Catholic faith as perceived by the Tractarians, and also to promote the related claim that the Church of England shares fully in its heritage. Henry Scott Holland, in an obituary published in the *Contemporary Review* in October 1890 (vol. lviii) tellingly observed that Liddon brought to a new generation 'the intensity, the fibre, the moral toughness of the older Tractarians.' To a greater extent than his less well-known contemporaries, Liddon was the *de facto* leader of the High Church revival from about the time of his appointment to St Paul's. In this capacity he enabled the Oxford Movement to continue to exert a powerful influence upon the minds of many people who had no direct contact with its originators. Similarly, he brought it to the attention of many who would otherwise have remained ignorant of the catholic nature of the Church of England, or who would have misunderstood the assertions of High Churchmen. In many respects Liddon was simply carrying forward and making a significant personal contribution to a process which had begun in the reign of Elizabeth I, and which E. R. Fairweather described as a 'quiet Anglican "Counter Reformation"'.[9] Liddon's role as a populariser was, therefore, considerable and by no means as superficial as the word might suggest.

He preached at the opening of Keble College Chapel, on 25 April 1876, St Mark's Day, and naturally took the teaching, piety and example of John Keble as his subject. Liddon described Keble as an orthodox Christian who was 'a sincere believer in all the Truths of Christian Revelation, as understood by the ancient and undivided Church of Christ.' However Keble, like Pusey, had remained within the Church of England because,

> the hierarchical fabric of the Church of England, and the public language of its formularies, and the traditional appeal of its greatest divines to that Christian antiquity which alone could justify them in the block, still remained.[10]

For Liddon, like his Tractarian teachers, the catholic integrity of the Church of England was beyond question. Over the whole period of his adult life a significant proportion of his efforts went into explaining and setting forth his understanding of what he believed to be the true nature of the Catholic Church. However he was always anxious not to elevate the doctrine of the Church to the point at which it might obscure Christ or replace him in the minds of believers. This was a danger to which he made definite reference in a sermon entitled 'Devotion to the Church of Christ' which was preached in 1888, and published in *Sermons Preached on Special Occasions*. It is likely that some such thought was in his mind when he urged ritualists to moderate their practices.

Liddon's understanding of the application of the Tractarian insight concerning the catholicism of the Church of England was revealed in a realistic loyalty to the Church of his birth and baptism. This was eloquently described by Owen Chadwick in *The Founding of Cuddesdon*:

> The purest spring was not so clear of mud as Liddon was clear of disloyalty to the Church of England. He had early in his life medi-tated on the other possibilities and had rejected them – and nothing is so certain as what was once in doubt.

This observation was made in the context of Liddon's early career and is an obvious allusion to his experience in Rome in 1852. It is also true of his reaction to such controversies as that surrounding Gorham and, in his own experience, Golightly at Cuddesdon. Indeed, this loyalty is confirmed by reference to the obituary published in the October 1890 edition of the *Church Quarterly Review* where the unknown writer made a passing reference to the recent death of Cardinal Newman and then said that, by contrast, Liddon was 'ever-faithful to his Church.' More than a quarter of a century before, Liddon had written that Newman's

> *Apologia [pro Vita Sua]* is a wonderful drama; and I love Newman more than ever for his generosity and tenderness towards our friends. But, intellectually, he is the advocate and the preacher of a dilemma, 'Rome or nothing' – which I don't believe [is] warranted by the facts of history, but which, if it were so warranted, would, I am well assured, drive more men of our time into sheer unbelief than we can contemplate without a shudder.[11]

Liddon was sincerely distressed when secessions occurred. He shared the belief held, for example, by T. T. Carter, that they were 'wrong' for the individual and also damaged the prospects for reunion between the Churches concerned. Not only at Cuddesdon, but also in later years, his diaries record that he went to some lengths to help those who were troubled in this way, often spending several hours at a time counselling them. In 1878 he attended a meeting at Keble College on 18 March, which was convened to discuss the matter. He recorded in his diary that he thought 'an association of some kind might do good, but it was discouraged by most of the speakers.' Not everyone, however, appreciated the strength and depth of his personal commitment to the Church of England. His friends had no doubt of where he stood, but it seems that his public position was sometimes misinterpreted. His private papers contain a number of letters and other communications which accuse him of significant disloyalty to the Church of England. Most of them are anonymous, and most were written at the time of the ritualist controversy and do no more than reveal the opinions of their authors. Two examples will serve to illustrate the degree of misunderstanding. One, noted in Liddon's handwriting as received on 2 May 1871, says, 'one thing is clear, that you are a thorough faced infidel . . . that you are a traitor to your God, your country, your conscience and your Church whose emoluments you dishonourably receive.' Another such accusation, but this time not anonymous, was contained in a letter from a man named John Warton, dated 22 June 1874[12] and suggested that 'Popery' was the 'only logical and possible end' for men who held such views as the writer imagined Liddon to hold. Emotive charges of this nature were painful to receive. They completely misunderstood Liddon's position, and that of High Churchmen, most of whom who sought to be true to the Church of England.

To Liddon's mind the statement that the Church is the Bride of Christ and his mixed metaphor that the Church is a 'branch of Christ's Body', could be applied with complete accuracy to the Church of England. He maintained, with Pusey and the 'best Anglican writers . . . that the spiritual endowments of the whole Catholic body belong to the English portion of it no less than to the rest.'[13] His use of the phrase the 'best Anglican writers' reveals his fundamental presupposition that neither his vision of the catholic nature of the Church of England, nor that of Pusey and the other founding fathers of Tractarianism, was merely an isolated aberration. He was sure that it is part of the great community of faith which has maintained intact the sacramental system and the machinery of government bequeathed by Christ to his Church. G. W. E. Russell, in his biography of Liddon, summarised Liddon's theology of the catholicity of the Church of England by saying that 'he believed that the Church of England, possessing Apostolic Orders, holding Catholic Creeds and administering valid Sacraments, offered all that was necessary for the edification and salvation of her children.' He would therefore have willingly accepted, in summary, the definition which Bishop Pearson gave in his Exposition of the Creed in the seventeenth century. Catholicism consisteth generally in universality, as embracing all sorts of persons, as to be disseminated through all nations, as comprehending all ages, as containing all necessary and saving truths, as obliging all conditions of men to all kinds of obedience, as curing all diseases, and planting all graces, in the souls of men.

These factors, which together distinguish the branches of the Catholic Church from Protestant dissent, were not, in Liddon's view, exclusively to be found in the Church of England, although at times his loyalty was such that he seems to have been close to arguing that the Church of England enjoys them in their greatest fullness. In his contacts with Roman Catholics, and with the Old Catholic movement and the Eastern Churches Liddon found, as have others who made similar contacts, that it was necessary to be able to explain and justify the existence of Anglicanism. The Easterns tended to regard Anglicanism as a rebellion against an earlier rebellion, as Liddon himself expressed it in the Preface to the Report of the 1875 Bonn Conference.[14] He went on to counter this by drawing out the similarity of the position between the Church of England at the Reformation and that of the Old Catholics after the Vatican Council. Both bodies were 'forced into separation from the Roman See by its unwarranted and ever-advancing claims.' He did not endeavour to gloss over or ignore the variety of views held conscientiously by members of the Church of England. He did not see this comprehensiveness as a factor which damaged catholicity or could destroy it, but it should be noted that he did not share the twentieth century conviction that comprehensiveness can be seen as an asset or source of strength. Undoubtedly the Church was marred by its internal divisions, but in a letter 'to a lady' quoted by Johnston, Liddon wrote on 23 July 1872:

... admitting the differences observable between English clergymen to be excessive, and such as would not have been tolerated in the early Church, what does this prove? That the English Church is diseased? Yes – *that* no wise and honest Churchman would deny, as he must assert the same thing, though for different reasons, of the Church of Rome. But – that the English Church is dead! No – unless the presence of error in a Church forfeits its life. What does the Apostle mean by saying, 'For this cause there shall be heresies *among you*, that they which are approved may be made manifest among you?' He does not say heresies 'external to the Church, with which you never come into contact.'

The Church is not a monochrome organisation, nor is it dormant, although Liddon accepted and promoted the idea, now somewhat discredited, that the Church of England in the Hanoverian period was virtually moribund.[15] Despite this, however, Liddon was able correctly to identify the Evangelical Revival and the Oxford Movement as two particular aspects of Christian vitality which had made significant contributions to the recent history of Church life in England. Both of them were part of the Church's actual heritage and Liddon recognised their common origin; he was able to say from the pulpit that Christ was 'in them.' Both recognised, as a modern scholar observed, that

> the enemy was dryness, aridity, and indifference in the spiritual life; theologically it was a loss of a sense of God as one who calls and sanctifies human beings through Christ and the Spirit and who has revealed himself and his will in scripture and in the life of the Church.[16]

The Evangelical Revival had brought about a re-emphasis of the doctrine of the atonement. Arising directly from that, Liddon thought, should come a fresh interest in the converting and sanctifying work of the Holy Spirit. To some extent, Liddon was proved right by the emphasis on the doctrine of the incarnation which assumed greater importance within Anglican theology later in the nineteenth century. Noticing the relationship between these phenomena was not unique to Liddon, as has been recognised by modern writers such as Owen Chadwick who observed that 'there is a certain continuity of piety between the Evangelical movement and the Oxford Movement.'[17] Liddon believed that the Oxford Movement, however, was the most important work of Christ within the nineteenth century Church of England, although he was hardly likely to claim less for the movement to which he devoted his best efforts. It was, he said, a spiritual phenomenon which recalled men 'to what He had revealed respecting the nature and constitution of His Body, the Church, and the value of those Sacraments by which we are united to Him.' This belief reinforced his tendency to dismiss the positive aspects of the Church of England in the previous century.

The ultimate foundations upon which the Church of England rested its claim to catholicity had been recognised anew by the Tractarians and were central to the thinking of all High Churchmen, of whom Liddon was, in many ways, both typical and an exemplar. Those foundations were the teaching of Christ enshrined in Word and Sacrament and the establishment and perpetuation of apostolic doctrine and government. This doctrinal corpus is independent of the

capacity of individual believers, in the Tractarian view, being objec-
tively given by Christ as an indefectible deposit. Liddon argued this
in the second sermon in the collection of *University Sermons, First
Series*, preached on 7 February 1864. It had been maintained by the
Tractarians from the beginning that the Church of England, despite
the vagaries of history, particularly during the Reformation period
and seventeenth century and despite the indifference which they
believed to have prevailed in the eighteenth, was preserved within the
Catholic fold and had resisted the efforts of Puritanism which,
Liddon claimed, had 'done its best to destroy the Church of England
altogether.' Liddon perceptively asserted that when viewed in the
light of the great corruption and failures of the mediaeval Papacy, the
Reformation had been a 'corrective and expurgatory action' of
'substantial service to the Christian faith.' This reasoning, however,
was not held by all who constituted the Tractarian Movement,
although few were as vehement as Hurrell Froude had been in the
early days with his declared 'hatred' of the Reformation. Liddon
represented a mature and moderate influence among High Churchmen
with his belief concerning the Reformation and his conviction that
under the providence of God the outcome of this historical process in
England had been the preservation of a properly catholic branch of
the Church which was more free from both doctrinal error and spurious additions than had been the case before the Reformation. In this
sense the Church of England was, to Liddon's understanding, more
accurately a reflection of primitive Catholicity than the modern
Church of Rome.

His confidence with regard to the Church of England was not
blind, however. He was aware of its deficiencies, and at times was
acutely conscious of the problem posed by its status as an Established
Church, not least from his memories as a young man of the furore
surrounding the Gorham judgement. He recognised that there are
strong arguments against the concept of establishment and he recognised and was sympathetic to the desire among some High
Churchmen that it should be ended. Indeed, Keble's Assize
Sermon,[18] which Newman, at least, recognised as starting the whole
chain of events, had been preached as a criticism of proposed legislation about the Irish Church and warned of the possible dangers which
it represented. Although the Bill was not specifically referred to
except in the preface of the published version of the sermon, nevertheless the sermon can be seen as a criticism of the establishment and
Liddon found this criticism congenial, when he encountered it as an
adult. Five years after Keble's fateful sermon was preached
Gladstone had published, in 1838, *The State in its Relation to the*

Church which was the first statement by a follower of the Tractarians to endorse explicitly the concept of an established religion. Gladstone, however, shifted his ground in later years and seems coincidentally to have moved to a position not unlike Liddon's. The problems posed by the existence of the establishment continued to be a matter of debate throughout Liddon's life, and his practical view seems to have been pragmatic. This is at variance with his other theological convictions which were comparatively inflexible. This pragmatism was not due to any compromise of principle, but rather the opposite, for underlying his flexibility was the constant desire to protect the Church from external interference.

Disraeli's plan[19] to legislate about ritualism was an occasion which brought Liddon's combative instincts to the surface, and encouraged some Anglo-Catholics to believe that disestablishment would protect the Church from unwarranted interference by the State. Liddon always knew that controversy had to be faced, and said so in a speech delivered in St James' Hall, London, on 16 June 1874, at the time the legislation was proposed. 'My belief,' he said, 'is that disestablishment is not by any means inevitable, at least for many years to come.'[20] This peaceable observation, however, was followed by a reference to circumstances that would, in his view, make disestablishment inevitable and was an attempt to calm the more hysterical reactions among some High Churchmen to the pending legislation. It also revealed a certain ambivalence on the matter. But his indecision was more apparent than real, for the grounds that would make inevitable a sundering of the Church and State would arise if the secular authority endeavoured to exercise an excessive control of the Church. Liddon, in an Assize Sermon of his own, preached in 1869, allowed himself to explore recent history which had made this danger seem more likely. The Judicial Committee of the Privy Council had been established in 1832 with the right to hear ecclesiastical cases, but probably without the expectation of having to deal with any. But like almost all the followers of the Tractarians who knew about it, Liddon believed that the Judicial Committee usurped the Statute of Appeals of 1533 and the powers of the High Court of Delegates which had had ecclesiastical jurisdiction since its inception by King Henry VIII. The Committee was dominated by laymen and this was a chief objection to it. He quoted an 'eminent authority', in fact Sir John Taylor Coleridge, who had observed that

Even if the committee were necessarily composed of Churchmen, there would be the question whether such matters are properly to be adjudicated on by laymen; but it is well known that among its members may be those who are, conscientiously or otherwise, not only alien from the Church, but opposed to it.[21]

By the late sixties there was ample evidence of the inappropriateness of the arrangement, and Liddon referred to this evidence:

It would be easy to dwell for no inconsiderable time upon the grave consequences of the present state of things to the best interests of religion; and those who know anything practically of the difficulties with which the English Church has to contend in a great many quarters at the present moment, know with what urgency and effect this feature of our actual system is pressed against her.[22]

Liddon, like all Anglo-Catholics, was very unhappy with the Judicial Committee of the Privy Council, and a witty remark reveals that he believed it to be positively harmful. He observed that a spell of cold weather in spring had caused 'the green things which had begun to grow to look terribly pinched, like Christians after a "Judgement" of the Privy Council.'

A few years later, in 1876, Liddon printed, but only for private distribution among his students, what he called an *Explanatory Analysis of St Paul's Epistle to the Romans*. A revised version was published posthumously in 1893, and it might reasonably be expected that his comments on Romans 13.1–7 would contain some discussion of the relation of the Church to the secular authorities. He described the passage as being in the 'Practical Part' of the Epistle; he headed the section as follows: 'Obligations of Christian Morality for the Christian as living under a (pagan) civil government', using the parenthesis himself. Unfortunately, the comments are consistent merely with an intention to provide an analysis, and although he was methodical, his work on the passage reveals nothing of his opinions. Charles Gore, by way of contrast, in a commentary of his own, devoted about half of his remarks on this passage to its application to modern England, reaching conclusions that were not dissimilar to those held by Liddon thirty years earlier, but for which one looks in vain in the *Analysis*.

The problem of the Church of England as a national church was a real issue during Liddon's lifetime, although disestablishment was not a serious threat to it. The question of the disestablishment of the Church in Wales was discussed from the 1850s but did not occur until 1920. The situation regarding the Irish Church, which was disestablished in 1871 during Gladstone's first term as Prime Minister, gave the whole debate a fillip. Proposals to disestablish the

Church of England were raised in Parliament by Edward Miall in 1871, 1872 and 1873 but were dismissed. To claim, as did Donaldson, that Liddon 'did not approve of disestablishment or of the secularisation of the Church's revenues either in Ireland or in England' is an over-simplification, and indeed is less than accurate. Chadwick noted that 'men like Pusey, or Liddon, or C. J. Vaughan, or Roundell Palmer, were not so enamoured of establishment as to think that the Irish Church could not well do without it.'[23] and Liddon's biography of Pusey does not even mention it. Government concern about the Irish ecclesiastical situation had, however, been a reality for many years. As a loyal son of the Oxford Movement Liddon knew that Keble's Assize Sermon had borne the title 'National Apostasy' and that Keble had seen the proposals of Lord Grey's Government to rationalise the Irish bishoprics as Erastianism. It is important to notice that Keble, back in 1833, did not think of himself as stirring up a conflict between Church and State, although his view of the matter was somewhat radical. He believed that he was simply drawing attention to a conflict that already existed. This was exactly Liddon's position. He wrote to Lord Carnarvon, 'my own line would be to accept Disestablishment for Ireland, and to endeavour by doing so to secure two advantages, or so much of them as possible.' These were the preservation of the Church's endowments, 'or as much of them as could be saved,' and also 'in particular, freedom from the doctrinal jurisdiction of the Judicial Committee of the Privy Council.'[24] In so far as conflict was being 'stirred up,' it was the State which had been the initiator by usurpation even if its proposals were, in themselves, reasonable. From the beginning, the catholic revival in the Church of England believed itself to sit somewhat askance to the old High and Dry Tory establishment type of Churchmanship found in the previous century, although recently Peter Nockles has drawn attention to the Tractarians' largely unacknowledged debt to their predecessors,[25] and done much to correct earlier impressions. If the logic of Keble's stance in 1833 had been carried through, then the Oxford Movement and its followers in later generations would have gone on to seek disestablishment as essential to the freedom of the Church of England. That this did not happen must, in part, account for the ambivalent attitude of men like Liddon and, indeed, Richard Church and those who followed their lead. In the next generation men such as Charles Gore[26] and Henry Scott Holland,[27] did oppose establishment, but it never became a serious subject for debate outside Anglo-Catholic circles.

To Liddon's mind the State, like the Church, was of Divine origin. This was a conventional theory which saw the Church as exercising spiritual authority and the State as exercising secular or physical authority. Since the conversion of Constantine the Church had been in a special relationship with the State whereby the latter recognised and enforced the Church's laws and admitted its officers to a place in the civil constitution. In his speech at St James' Hall in 1874 Liddon amusingly described how he had, 'the other day' come across a writer who indulged in what he saw as 'a species of archaeological pedantry, who termed the Parliament of the English People "the Sacred Synod of the English Church"'. The report of the speech inserts, in brackets, the words 'great laughter' at this point. But Liddon went on to be serious and gave a brief résumé of the *prima facie* grounds in history for this assertion. He did recognise that the highest development of the identity of Church and State in the British Isles had been at the time of the Elizabethan settlement when, for Richard Hooker, the two were 'strictly co-extensive,' a view which Liddon summarised in the following trenchant statement: 'The State of the Ecclesiastical Polity is only the Church acting in a civil capacity, among a people which wholly belong to it.'[28] He also maintained:

> But this I do say, that since Hooker's time, circumstances have changed so fundamentally and so vitally that it is absolutely impossible to quote him or any of the precedents which stand in his rear as applicable to our time.[29]

Liddon therefore did not believe that historical precedent could provide much help to nineteenth century Churchmen. This was an interesting, but not inconsistent, position for him. It is noteworthy that he republished Keble's lengthy review article of Gladstone's important but difficult book. He was one who looked to the history of the primitive Church as a guide for modern believers, but who interpreted that history by the teaching of the Tractarians. This interpretation was rather one-sided, despite his recognition that both Church and State had changed since Hooker's day, and that what was entirely appropriate in the sixteenth century would not do for either Church or State in Victorian times. Gladstone, according to Perry Butler, 'had jettisoned Hooker's identification of Church and State and argued that both were separate, independent and sovereign bodies.'[30] Liddon took this a little further and insisted that the State should not be able to interfere with the Church's right to self-government. Dr Alec Vidler in *The Orb and The Cross* described Gladstone in terms that could also be, to a lesser extent, applied to Liddon, 'he is a symbol of the fact that no satisfactory doctrine of the relations of the State with the Church or of a Christian politics was found in the Victorian era to take the place of the older doctrines.'[31]

In an Advent sermon Liddon referred to the distinction between the State and the Church in the following terms. Both are 'societies of men'. But the Church was 'immediately founded by God for purposes higher than and beyond this present life'. The State, however, was merely 'instituted by Him through the medium of human wills, and the causes which work in human history, with a view to man's well-being in this present phase of his existence.' In this sense the State, whatever its coercive powers and strengths, is theologically the junior partner in a joint enterprise. He stated this view clearly in an unpublished letter of 1874, which is retained in the Keble College archive, 'the Church is just as much a public interest as the State, and I, as a Christian, think it the higher and more sacred public interest of the two.'

The development of non-conformity and the recognition by the State of its right to exist as a legitimate phenomenon in English life, together with the removal of constitutional disabilities from Dissenters and Roman Catholics at the beginning of the nineteenth century, had altered the earlier and idyllic picture, although as Edward Norman trenchantly observed, 'those who defended the Establishment sometimes ignored the difficulties which the existence of a real denominational pluralism interposed.'[32] This was a reference to men such as Archbishop Tait and Dean Stanley of Westminster. Liddon, whose support for the Establishment was of such a qualified nature and who distrusted both men and much of what they stood for, did not fall into this trap. His acceptance of the existence of non-conformity acknowledged that the Church of England had 'deeply wronged them' by a 'reliance on an arm of flesh, as shown in our Erastianism,' a sentiment which Charles Gore was to echo after Liddon's death. In addition the recognition that even, taken together, the Churches did not command the allegiance of the whole of the population of nineteenth century England was also a factor with which Churchmen had to come to terms in their reflections upon the relationship of the Church and the State.

As might be expected from someone of his fierce integrity, Liddon was far from happy with the idea of adapting the established Church into an all-embracing phenomenon, an idea which surfaced occasionally. Thomas Arnold was the most important proponent of this unlikely idea in the middle of the nineteenth century with his 'design for comprehending the Dissenters within the pale of the Establishment,' which he put forward in a pamphlet, *The Principles of Church Reform*, published in January 1833, just six months before

Keble's Assize Sermon, and when Liddon was only a child, but its proposals would have been an anathema to him, as they were to Newman at the time. Liddon's strictures in later years fell, not upon Arnold's radical concept as such, although he vehemently disliked it, but upon the idea that the Church of England could be, or already was, sufficiently tolerant to accommodate without fuss those who held unorthodox convictions or even very few convictions at all, for Arnold's idea rested ultimately on a rejection of dogma. Liddon firmly rejected the view of those who said that the Church of England existed to provide a home for all the religious opinions which are found within the nation. This idea does not ask for 'loyalty to the revealed truth of Christ so much as practical attachment to the Establishment'. Such a concept, he believed, would falsely make such a Church 'a much greater and more sacred thing . . . than any creed or conviction.' He claimed that he did not undervalue the Establishment:

> but to ask support for it, while professing indifference to the truths which it represents, is, with all serious minds, to do it deep and lasting injury. After all, the Faith of Jesus Christ does not exist for the sake of justifying the existence of an Established Church; the Church exists for the sake of teaching the Faith. Mere support of an institution, combined with indifference to the truths which it represents, can only rest upon motives which religion may not recognise; and is likely, in the long-run, to defeat the object of its enthusiasm.[33]

However, he was at his most scathing in criticising the concept of a 'national church' in the biographical *Sketch* or memoir of Bishop Hamilton which he wrote in 1869. He revealed a rather journalistic style when he wrote that 'the leading journal' [he meant *The Times*] of 1 November 1866, had published an article critical of Hamilton which contained some discussion on the nature of the 'ministerial commission' of the clergy of the Church of England. The consequent exchange eventually contained the thoroughly erastian statement, which Liddon quoted disapprovingly in his little book, that 'the ministers of a national Church are bound to consider the nation. Every clergyman is invested with a political character; he is distinctly a servant of the State.' It is likely that this was no more than a rather forceful expression of a view widely held among the non-theological public. But it filled Liddon with horror.

   Liddon's comments in the Hamilton biography revealed as much about his own view of the establishment as it did about Hamilton's:

if the real scope and contents of the Gospel Message of Salvation is an unsolved matter, to be decided, not by the ministers of Christ collectively, not even by a believing laity, but by 'the nation', that is to say, by a multitude of Christians and unbelievers combined; then, beyond question, the Bishop has no right to appeal to documents of the Church of England, however solemn and authoritative they might be. But also, if these principles could be admitted, the bare use of the formularies of the Church of England, – the morality of publicly addressing them to Almighty God, or in His Name and Presence, to man, – are matters surely open to challenge. Nor is it difficult to conjecture how long any man who feared God, and respected the sanctities of his own conscience, would care to minister in a Church capable of so prostituting the truth which created it, its very *raison d'être*, to an ambitious effort to be comprehensive. Doubtless every Churchman must desire to see the Church co-extensive with the nation. But no sacrifices, whether of money or position, would be too great to be accepted, if the nation should insist upon demoralising the Church, by forbidding her to proclaim truths which are part of her inalienable treasure, or by insisting on her condoning errors which have been condemned by Christ. The Church would never have conquered the world if she had attempted the task in the spirit of a clever newspaper, embarrassed by no fixed principles, and aiming, above everything, at a large circulation; nor, if in her old age, she could postpone all care for Truth to a reckless determination to be 'national', would her 'nationality' be worth ten years' purchase.[34]

In the same way that he shied away from this concept of a national Church, so Liddon was also anxious to preserve the integrity of the Church of England in relation to unacceptable interference on the part of the legislature, and once again there is a similarity of view between him and Gladstone. In a speech on the Jewish Disabilities Bill in 1847, Gladstone had noticed that

there are several senses in which a legislature may be called Christian. For example: either because all its members profess a known and definite body of truth constituting the Christian faith; or because they all adopt the designation of Christians; or because from the great preponderance of Christians in its composition . . . a Christian spirit pervades their legislation.[35]

Liddon's later reaction to the Christian (or otherwise) nature of the legislature was well illustrated in the St James' Hall speech of 1874, but it was also discussed in correspondence with a Miss Stopford. In his replies to the letters, which are to be found in the Keble College Archive, Liddon refuted an unidentified report which claimed that he had described the House of Lords as 'a body of infidels':

> it is, I think, a matter of fact that both Houses of Parliament do contain some 'infidels'; as well as a great many others who without being 'infidels' are bitterly opposed to the doctrine and well-being of the Church of England ... The Church of England will not be severed from the State in our day as it appears to me unless persons in high position insist upon treating her as a mere 'branch of the Civil Service', and the British Parliament as an assembly of divines.

Both of these points were made publicly in the speech. Since the days of Hooker, he said,

> first of all the Protestant Dissenters, then the Roman Catholics, then the Jews, then any sort of person who repudiated the name altogether of Jesus Christ our Lord, have taken their seats in the National Parliament. As a consequence of that, Parliament, however it may have increased its titles, and I do not deny that it has done so, to the loyalty of the English people in its entirety, has most certainly in a precisely exact proportion diminished its capacity for dealing with strictly theological questions.

The enthusiastic response which he received in St James' Hall reveals that Liddon was well in tune with the opinion of High Churchmen, but later in the speech his appeals for moderation of ritual were not so welcome to his hearers. These appeals were an important part of his address and should not be ignored; they will be considered in detail in the next chapter.

Parliament, however, did contain a number of divines in its assembly. Until 1847, when the see of Manchester was formed, all diocesan bishops sat in the House of Lords. Liddon would have liked to see them removed. He said so in a private letter to C. L. Wood on 24 September 1880 but sadly gave no detail and did no more than refer to the matter. In a letter to his brother-in-law, Richard Poole King, written six years earlier at the height of the controversy over the Public Worship Regulation Act, he was very outspoken. It seems probable that, of Liddon's earlier biographers, Johnston knew of this letter, but decided not to quote from it because it showed a more radical side of Liddon's nature. He wrote:

> I am seriously considering . . . to write a pamphlet for turning all
> the bishops out of the House of Lords. They do <u>no</u> good there;
> they betray every spiritual interest that they are there to uphold;
> and this process of eternally paying court to irreligious lay opinion
> ends in making them – well! – what the two archbishops [Tait and
> Thomson] appear to be![36]

The pamphlet, however, was never written, and history does not have
the benefit of his considered reasoning on a matter which continues to
divide opinion.

The important exchange of letters with Miss Stopford also took place
at the time when the Public Worship Regulation Act was passing
through Parliament. This was a major issue and will be discussed later;
it did, however, cause Liddon to articulate a sentiment that summarised
his fears concerning the relationship between Church and State. Because
of the hostile elements in Parliament, he stated with more perception
than was shown by the Archbishops at the time, 'it does not seem
prudent, on the part of the friends of the Church of England, to introduce into such a Parliament, measures affecting her closest interests. A
man need not be a prophet to foresee the result of doing so in days like
ours.' Liddon was convinced that the Church should have the freedom
to regulate its own affairs. This was an opinion which gathered support
among High Churchmen at the time when the Act was being passed. In
his little book of sermons, *Thoughts on Present Church Troubles*
(1881), the title of which he feared hinted at more radical thinking than
the contents expressed, he rejected the charge, which he reported as
having been made although he did not say by whom, that 'Ecclesiastics
have often shown themselves unfit to be entrusted with power.' The
grounds for his rejection were sweeping and astute; that, on the basis of
the accusation, 'there is no institution in the country which does not
merit condemnation.' It is true that there is a certain ambivalence in
Liddon's evaluation of the establishment, but his view can be reduced to
a simple principle. As long as the Church is free to order its own affairs
then he was prepared to countenance the continuation of the Church-
State relationship. But his regard for the gospel was such that if he had
become convinced that the continuation of the established relationship
was a hindrance to the mission of the Church, then he would not have
regarded disestablishment, and possible disendowment, as too high a
price to pay for the preservation of freedom and integrity.

One of his few references to disendowment is to be found near the
end of the long introduction to the collection entitled *Thoughts on
Present Church Troubles*. He wrote:

Few, if any, Churchmen desire to see the Church disestablished and disendowed; but if it be a question whether it is better to be turned out of house and home, without any clothes, and even on a winter's night, or to be strangled by a silken cord in a well-furnished drawing room, what man, or Church, will have any difficulty in arriving at a decision?

This nicely-phrased rhetorical question echoes a passage from a dozen years before which, in 1869, he wrote in the preface to his re-publication of Keble's review of Gladstone's *The State in its Relations with the Church*. In response to the suggestion that the Irish Church should be disestablished and disendowed but remain under the restraints of ecclesiastical courts, he wrote that it was a 'cruel proposal to turn her out in her old age, famished and bare-footed, into the cold; and withal in a spirit of jealous suspicion, worthy of the narrowest and least religious species of Erastianism, to load her enfeebled limbs with rusty irons that were forged by extinct despotisms ...' These were courageous sentiments in an age when few Anglicans argued for disestablishment and even fewer would have accepted disendowment.

An external matter which demonstrated the potential for harm which Anglo-Catholics like Liddon saw within the existing arrangements of the Establishment was the long-running problem of the Jerusalem Bishopric, a scheme 'doomed from birth.'[37] This had started in 1841 when Liddon was a schoolboy, with an agreement between the government in England and the Chevalier Bunsen, representing Frederick William IV of Prussia, to set up a joint Anglican-Lutheran bishopric in Jerusalem. The politicians involved in the original scheme had political as well as religious motives. The leading Anglican layman, an ardent Evangelical and a cousin of Pusey, was Anthony Ashley Cooper, later the seventh Earl Shaftesbury. He was attracted to the phenomenon of nineteenth century millenarianism. Among the hopes and expectations of this theological movement, which caught the imagination of some evangelicals in the Church of England, were the restoration of the Jews to Palestine and their conversion to Christianity as a necessary prelude to the second coming of Christ. Ashley Cooper (Shaftesbury) believed that the establishment of what he perceived to be a Protestant bishopric in Jerusalem, although such an adjective would have been unacceptable to the Tractarians, would be a 'portent of the Second Coming. . .'[38] This aspect of the affair has been largely neglected by historians but the Jerusalem bishopric proposals cannot be understood without due weight being given to such views. Ashley Cooper also hoped that it would assist the expansion of evangelicalism, and it has been claimed that he rejoiced in the appointment, in which he had been involved, of Michael Alexander as the first bishop 'because it was a slap in the face for the Tractarians.'[39] The Archbishop of Canterbury at the time was William Howley. He was persuaded to agree to the scheme, as was Bishop Blomfield of London, and an arrangement was made which stipulated that the holder of the see would always be in Anglican episcopal orders but would be appointed alternately by Britain and Prussia. The scheme was erastian in origin, and its unsatisfactory attitude to episcopacy represented a failure to respect Catholic order. However, it did not, at the time, arouse the opposition of all High Churchmen. Pusey saw the scheme as a means of introducing episcopacy into German Protestantism and believed that to be a good idea. Liddon noted, in a lengthy description of events in the second volume of his *Life of Pusey*, that he 'strangely failed at first to see what principles were involved, but eventually joined in condemning it.' Newman, however, was deeply distressed by the proposal. Gladstone was later to claim that the scheme had finally driven Newman from the Church of England, a view that Newman himself encouraged in his *Apologia Pro Vita Sua*. Liddon was more clear-sighted than either Pusey or Newman had been when the scheme became a renewed source of difficulty in the eighties. His theological attitude was closer to Newman's, although without the same result. He recognised that the scheme did not undermine the Church's credentials, although it did besmirch them. When the see became vacant upon the death of its third occupant Bishop Barclay, in 1881, Liddon was pleased that the scheme appeared to lapse. The reasons for his relief were two-fold. First it seemed to mark the end of an unwelcome protestant compromise of catholic order and of an unwarranted interference in the affairs of an authentic part of the eastern branch of the Church. Second, and just as important was the demise of a particularly erastian arrangement whereby the Church of England appeared to be controlled in its relations with other Christian bodies by the Government and by senior bishops acting without even consulting their colleagues.

Consequently, Liddon was among the Anglo-Catholic objectors to the revival of the scheme. Archbishop Edward Benson's biographer implied that Liddon was the most articulate of those who, the Archbishop recorded in his diary, had 'been moving quietly to oppose the [new] appointment.'[40] G. K. A. Bell in his biography of Randall Davidson, stated that Richard William Church, who became Dean of St Paul's soon after Liddon took up his canonry, shared the leadership of the opposition with Liddon.[41] However, Dean Church's daughter and his first biographer nowhere mentioned her father's involvement. The matter gets only two brief mentions in the later biography by A. B. Smith who maintained that R. W. Church approached Prime Minister Gladstone and urged that the bishopric be left vacant in 1881.[42] It does appear that Liddon was the real initiator of the public protest. Liddon went on his extended tour of the Middle East in the winter of 1885 before the controversy broke, and reached Palestine in April 1886. To imply, as did Bell, that Liddon 'went out to Jerusalem' with the specific intention of assessing the situation regarding the Bishopric is not true. While he was there he did have at least two private meetings (13 April and 22 April) with Nicodemus, the Orthodox Patriarch of Jerusalem. He struck up a friendship with the Patriarch which led to him receiving permission to celebrate the Holy Communion in the Chapel of Abraham in the Church of the Holy Sepulchre on Easter Tuesday, it being the Patriarch's wish 'that all Catholic Christians should share at this season this sacred spot.'[43] Liddon also attended some public events including the Easter Eve liturgy of the new fire. From his sister's letters it appears that he and the Patriarch did relate well to each other, but there is nothing in the correspondence to suggest that there was any truth in Davidson's opinion that Liddon 'tried when at Jerusalem to force an unfavourable opinion, first into, and then out of, the Greek Patriarch.' Liddon certainly did not feel as Davidson said a few months later in a letter to Archbishop Benson, that he was one of those 'outsiders' who were 'in no way concerned' with a matter 'for which nobody asks them to be responsible.'[44] During the conversations with the Patriarch the question of the vacant Anglican-Lutheran bishopric had been discussed and, as Liddon subsequently reported to Archbishop Benson, he had rather incautiously but perhaps in the hope of promoting his own views,

> ventured to say to the Patriarch that, so far as I knew, no new successors to Bishop [Samuel] Gobat would be appointed. And he was pleased to express his great thankfulness and satisfaction at the news.

The Patriarch felt aggrieved because when Samuel Gobat had been appointed bishop back in May 1846, he had incautiously and inappropriately allowed his clergy to proselytise among the Greek Orthodox in Jerusalem, and this had not been forgotten.

The letter to Benson was written in October 1886 because, after his return to England in June of that year, Liddon discovered that plans were being made for a new appointment. In that first letter to the

Archbishop, Liddon emphasised that it was inappropriate to appoint a bishop to a see 'already occupied by a Bishop of an ancient Church, with which we desire to be at least on friendly terms.' This was despite his recognition of Pusey's assertion that 'the rule of antiquity allowed people who spoke different languages, although living together, each to enjoy the blessing of a bishop.'[45] Bishop Gobat's proselytising policy had created a rather different situation. Liddon, in a letter to Charles Gore, was more forthright than he had been to the Archbishop of Canterbury: 'One had hoped that that unhappy result of Bensen's meddling and pedantic influence on English religion had been allowed to die quietly.' Liddon's opinion reflected, and in fact helped to form, the opposition of High Churchmen to the whole concept of the scheme. He wrote to Gore requesting that he should use his influence with E. S. Talbot, the Warden of Keble College, and get his support in opposition to the bishopric, but Talbot's biographer did not refer to the matter. Also involved in the protest was J. M. Neale, the key figure in the Eastern Churches Association which had tried to stop the proselytising. Archbishop Benson's biographer summarised well the reasons for the opposition of Liddon and his friends: the bishopric was 'on the one hand, an intrusion into the Orthodox Patriarchates, and, on the other, a compromising alliance with German Protestantism'. The question of millenarianism does not seem to have been a factor at this later stage, perhaps because Shaftesbury had died in 1885, and Liddon did not mention it.

An address was drawn up, probably by Liddon himself, signed by a number of leading High Churchmen and sent to Archbishop Benson in March 1887. In it was a request that the new appointee should be instructed 'to check all proceedings on the part of English clergy which infringe on the rights of the Patriarch and his clergy' and a further request that future appointments to the bishopric should only be made with the concurrence of the ruling Patriarch. The full text of the address was published in *The Times* on 22 March 1887. Naturally the second of the requests was not accepted, but when the new appointment was made, Benson wrote introducing the new bishop, and also seeking the approbation of Nicodemus and the Patriarchs of Constantinople and Antioch. The new bishop was required to forbid proselytising among the community of Eastern Christians and the Lutheran element of the scheme was quietly dropped. Liddon, in leading the opposition to the scheme, had, as his 1886 and 1887 diaries and the press cuttings he collected reveal, devoted a great deal of time and effort to the problem; he was right to feel that he had failed in his endeavours to get the scheme abandoned. He remained keenly alive to the objections that could be levelled at it from the point of view of the Patriarch. He was also aware of the ambiguity of the Anglican bishop's role, particularly as it had been interpreted by Samuel Gobat. Third, he endorsed, despite Pusey's theory, the theological reasons for not duplicating unnecessarily an episcopal ministry in a particular place. Liddon was entirely accustomed to the erastian manner in which episcopal appointments were made and his unease at this underlay part of his opposition to the scheme. Of greater significance to him was the conviction that 'the Archbishop had yielded the position to "the Puritans,"' by which he meant Ashley Cooper and his friends, and had thus compromised Catholic order. The withdrawal of the Prussians partly met this objection, but he was left with the knowledge that he had been unwittingly sanguine when talking to the Patriarch Nicodemus. All that remains is to note that Bishop George Popham Blyth, formerly Archdeacon of Rangoon, was appointed to the see in March 1887, and in the face of this *fait accompli,* Liddon's involvement with the scheme came to an end.

Finally, with regard to his opinion of the established nature of the Church of England it is to be regretted that he left almost nothing about his perception of the Church's role in relation to the British Empire. All that can be said is that Liddon seems to have shared the commonplace Victorian conviction that the English nation had some sort of God-given vocation. He alluded to this in his first lecture on Buddhism, published posthumously in *Essays and Addresses*, 'no man who believes in a Providence can suppose that we, the inhabitants of a small island in the remote West, have been introduced to these high [imperial] destinies for nothing, or only for commercial or political ends.' Unfortunately, he did not develop this line of thought, but it is useful to know that it was there.

Despite the inevitable vicissitudes of history, the Church was still established in nineteenth century England and the traditional situation had not changed so far as what Liddon called the 'earthly side' of the Church was concerned. The Church, he said, 'enters into human history, and her annals are intertwined with those of the kingdoms of this world.'

Chapter Four

'Prejudice and experience,' Ritualism

R. M. Benson observed that Liddon, in his Cuddesdon days and before, had been concerned with 'little ritualistic frivolities,' but his involvement in the development of a more advanced ritual in the Church of England arose partly as a result of his convictions about the intrinsic authority of the Church to govern its own affairs and, specifically, to regulate its own practices. So, an important area of concern in the nineteenth century Church-State relationship in England was that surrounding what became known as 'ritualism,' although Liddon would have liked the 'whole question of Ritual relegated to its true position of relative insignificance.'[1] At the simplest level he was convinced that ritual is the servant of dogma. A. B. Donaldson accurately noted that 'he was a true Tractarian in placing doctrine first, and symbolicism [sic] second.'[2] Liddon had a greater awareness than many of his contemporaries of the potential divisiveness of ritual, and, although he appreciated the richness that it added to worship, he maintained an independent attitude even when ritualism became a dominant aspect of the catholic revival. He was more concerned with the theological basis of the Oxford Movement and in this respect he seems to have remained closer to the old, pre-Tractarian, High Church tradition and also to the attitudes of Keble and Pusey than did many of his, and the next, generation. He said, in a long-winded remark which explains both his espousal of a more elaborate ritual, and also his views about furnishings and fittings in church,

> It seems to be the true and generous instinct of an earnest piety to deem no measure of artistic beauty too great for the embellishment of the temples and of the service of Christ.[3]

This was made in a sermon preached in 1867 and echoes one made seven years earlier; it is to promote 'the Master's glory' that

Christians 'fill [churches] with the voice of prayer and the grace and presence of Sacraments,' and beautify them for the same reason. These are no more than hints of his views about ritual but he seems to have been careful not to be explicit in the pulpit regarding such matters. Some of his contemporaries were much more outspoken, and engaged in ritual controversy even to the extent of involvement in litigation and, in a few cases, imprisonment for their views. He agreed with Pusey's sentiment that 'love of ritual for its own sake is ... [a] ... weak point,' and even in the preface to the sermons published as *Thoughts on Present Church Troubles* Liddon remained circumspect, maintaining 'that, as a rule, matters of contemporary controversy are better excluded from the Christian pulpit,' although he allowed himself considerable liberty of expression in the Preface. This little collection of sermons was produced as a result of the imprisonment of two ritualist priests, T. P. Dale and R. W. Enraght,[4] in 1880, and appeared the following year. That action was taken by Lord Penzance in response to the contempt of court by the two, a contempt which revealed to Liddon that

> There is occasion for considering whether some error in legislation may not ... have made obedience to the law of the land inconsistent with some higher sense of duty in the case of unquestionably good men, who are not demonstrably unreasonable.

This statement, in the same preface, reveals that the heart of Liddon's view of ritual was to do with the question of authority. Legislation by the, as he thought, secularised Houses of Parliament was regarded by him as a possible threat to the integrity of the Church; and it was a threat which did materialise. The core of the matter was not the problem of whether Parliament could legislate; 'Parliament, we know, can deal with anything it likes, but the question is whether Parliament is fitted to deal with it,' he said. To his mind, as he often made clear, it was a prerequisite of liberty that the Church should be free to order its own affairs, and this included the regulation of its expressions of worship. The insistence of the State upon a right to control the forms and ceremonies of public worship confronted Churchmen, at least in theory, with the painful choice between a national and compromised Church and one that was properly catholic and which retained its integrity. Dale and Enraght had been imprisoned by a secular court which, to Liddon and his friends, was manifestly unqualified to deal with such matters.

This is not to say, however, that he gave uncritical support to all ritualistic priests. Johnston accurately observed that Liddon's position 'was not a little difficult.' 'On the general principle he was entirely in agreement with those who were being attacked, and on that ground openly supported them. But he was far from agreeing with all the actions of those whose main position he was ready to defend.'[5] The ritualistic changes in the worship of the Church of England were usually imitations of Roman Catholic practices. This was not entirely due to a mere imitative spirit but was thought by its proponents to have a sound theological basis. Some clergy, Enraght among them, argued that, if the Church of England claimed to be part of the Catholic Church, then it should resemble Roman Catholicism in its liturgical practice. W. J. E. Bennett, the ritualist vicar of St Paul's, Knightsbridge, from 1840 who built St Barnabas, Pimlico, in 1850, held a similar view. This element had been present to some extent in the early days of the Oxford Movement but it had never been supported by Pusey or Keble and had, to some extent, temporarily died back after the secessions to Rome led by Newman. To Pusey the teaching and practices of the Romanizing group were unacceptable, although he was careful in his use of 'temperate language' in order to reduce the provocation that had so often led to bitter rows and also to further secessions. Liddon, similarly cautious, was no slavish follower of Rome in his own liturgical behaviour, preferring to follow the Tractarian theological concept of a patristically-based catholicism, not a modern Roman one. Despite this, however, he recognised, in a letter to Newman in 1875, that 'hard things' could be said of some Ritualists 'because they say and do that which is it is hard to defend on the score of consistency in several particulars.'

The divergences in Anglican practice had been forced upon his attention in 1874 by two very different incidents. One was a newspaper controversy. At the end of the year Liddon was out-manoeuvred by a Roman Catholic priest named T. J. Capel in a controversy that caused him considerable work and embarrassment. Capel was born in 1836 and ordained by Cardinal Wiseman in 1860. The two men had met in 1865 when Liddon was on his continental holiday. He described the occasion to Bishop Hamilton:

> Father Capel is an active, tolerably well-informed, and very gentlemanly man, and does all he can for the 'English Mission'. He came here to luncheon yesterday. After luncheon I had an argument with him of two hours and a half; it was impossible to allow some of his statements to pass unchallenged. The argument ended as such arguments generally do, in leaving both of us much where we were at starting . . .'[6]

Capel had a chequered career, working for some time in a school he had founded and then as Rector of a newly-formed college of higher education. His controversy with Liddon was but one among many. He died in 1911 in California, where he had moved to avoid financial difficulties. In 1874, however, as Johnston's biography described the situation, he charged 'the Ritualists in general and Liddon by name, with disseminating doctrines peculiar to the Roman Church, and causing a continuous supply of converts to Rome.'[7] Liddon refuted each of the charges but he overstated his case by denying not only the claims about his own teaching but also by denying the claims made against other High Church clergy. And so, as Johnston said, 'he fell into a trap.' Whether Capel was trying to snare Liddon or just criticising High Churchmen was immaterial. He responded to Liddon's incaution by writing to *The Times* on 8 January 1875 where he listed four particular doctrines: the invocation of the saints; the doctrine of Transubstantiation; the Roman doctrine of absolution and 'the doctrine of the Incarnation [as] it finds its expression in Devotion to the Precious Blood, to the Five Wounds, and even to the Sacred Heart . . .' He supplied quotations to support his charges, not only from anonymous High Church publications but also from T. T. Carter's *Treasury of Devotion* and the *Catechetical Notes* of John Mason Neale. Liddon was thrown on to the defensive. In his diary, on 8 January 1875, he described the opening of the controversy as 'a long attack on me in *The Times* by Mgr Capel. I sat down to answer this at length.' He began his answer, which was published in *The Times* the following day:

> Perhaps I may be of the opinion [sic] that Monsignor Capel, before writing the letter which appears in your impression of today, would have done well to ascertain that I am personally responsible, either as author or as editor, for any one of the sentences upon which he comments. It would not be difficult to present him in turn with a long list of *curiosa,* collected from Roman Catholic books of controversy and devotion, the explanation or justification of which, even in skilful hands, would take up more space than you could allow. But, as he will say that he is justifying his attack upon English High Churchmen, I pass this by; and I thank him for the opportunity he has afforded of a more thorough discussion of the issue which he has thought fit to raise.

He went on to answer each of Capel's four points, but it is clear that he found it uncongenial to have to defend views which he did not hold and which he believed, in some cases, to be unnecessarily provocative and contrary to the concept of catholicism to which he was personally committed. Towards the end of his letter he made an unflattering reference to

> the two great additions which the Church of Rome has made to her creed within the lifetime of the present generation. The Vatican Council has taught us that her claim of *semper eadem*, [roughly, 'always the same'] unwarranted before, can only now be admitted by those who close their eyes to the plainest facts of Church history.

And he ended by claiming,

> Not for the first time in our history, Rome and Puritanism, forgetting their irreconcilable hostility, appear willing to play into each other's hands, if only they can silence the voice of true Catholic teaching within the walls of the Church of England. But if we are resolutely true to the guidance which God has given us in our English Prayer Book, with its appeal to Scripture, as interpreted by Catholic antiquity, we need not fear for the result.

This letter did not, however, settle the controversy which rumbled on into the early months of 1875. From a journal called *The Hour* for 5 February 1875, he preserved a cutting in which an anonymous writer who simply signed himself 'Laicus' accused Liddon of being 'disingenuous' if he expected other people to believe that he was not 'cognisant' of the contents of such devotional books as those referred to by Capel. This writer went on to fuel the controversy with further examples. The amount of correspondence which Liddon received was large and it forms a modest but significant proportion of the material preserved at Keble College. It includes an aggrieved sounding but obscure note from Archbishop Tait, and an almost illegible letter from T. T. Carter as well as many others from clergy and laity who felt impelled to take one side or the other. Unfortunately, apart from the material published in *The Times*, nothing by Liddon appears to have survived, and the diary references merely record the various exchanges without giving details of their content. However, Liddon had undoubtedly tried to defend an untenable position with regard to the activities of some other High Churchmen, even if he was able to acquit himself. This incident serves to illustrate his occasional tendency to precipitate himself into a controversy without checking all the facts before-hand. He was 'worsted in battle. The wily Monsignor ... caught him off his guard more than once.'[8] But perhaps more importantly, it also illustrated the difficult position in which he found himself. He was an advocate of moderation and caution in matters of ritual and devotional practice, but had gained the reputation for being an extremist. This was at a time when moderation was increasingly being rendered irrelevant as the controversy developed along lines of open provocation by some ritualists in the face of sometimes literally violent opposition. Years later, in 1883, Liddon produced, at the instigation of Bishop Forbes,[9] an English translation of Rosmini's *Five Wounds of the Church*. Rosmini was, Liddon said, a 'conscientious' ultramontanist, so in his preface he was careful to point out that Rosmini was not an author which members of the Church of England could accept 'unreservedly.' He had learnt a hard lesson.

The other incident was much more serious and began earlier in 1874. It was the proposal that eventually issued in the passing of the Public Worship Regulation Act which, Liddon felt, 'lodged a barb in the Church of England.' Disraeli had defeated Gladstone in the 1874 General Election and Liddon looked to the immediate future with foreboding. He was right to do so. The Act grew out of the persistent perception that the Church of England was under threat from clergy who wished to undermine what had been achieved at the Reformation. Liddon, in a sermon preached while the Bill was going through Parliament, called the protestant reaction an 'unreasoning panic.' Ritualism was thought by staunch Protestants to be a tool of the subversives and Disraeli, whom Liddon so profoundly distrusted, described the Public Worship Regulation Bill, as it then was, as an Act to 'put down ritualism.' Other extravagant allegations were made about ritualism, which in fact was a preoccupation of only a minority of clergy. Lord Shaftesbury, with his penchant for over-statement said, 'the very fate of the Church of England was trembling in the balance.'[10] This was untrue, but it fuelled the controversy. The Act was designed to simplify proceedings against contumacious clergy but, like much hasty legislation, it was not entirely successful. It is well chronicled in James Bentley's *Ritualism and Politics in Victorian Britain*. However, Liddon's involvement in the matter has never been properly assessed. Already the activities of Liddon's erstwhile colleague, the Reverend A. H. Mackonochie, at St Alban's, Holborn, were seen by many to epitomise the ritualist position. A prosecution of Mackonochie in 1867 had been initiated by the Church Association[11] on the grounds that he had introduced coloured vestments in 1865 and incense at Epiphany 1866. Liddon had visited the church and had attended a service in January 1874. He noted in his diary on the 11th of that month, 'the ceremonial [was] more elaborate than I ever saw before. Stanton [the curate who served the church for over fifty years] in a cope sat on a stool in the middle of the choir – censed the altar at the Magnificat . . .' When the proposed legislation became public knowledge Liddon, with Pusey, wrote to Mackonochie urging restraint and suggesting that it might be possible to 'take some early opportunity of considering how much of recent additions to customary ritual could be abandoned without doing harm?' Mackonochie's reply was lengthy and relatively unhelpful, for he maintained that he did not wield any influence over other ritualists and he was more than reluctant to make concessions, believing that they would be interpreted as signs of weakness,[12] which was probably true at that time.

Faced with what amounted to a rebuff from Mackonochie, Liddon did not despair. He had written to the Honourable C. L. Wood, later Lord Halifax, on the same day as he wrote to Mackonochie, 14 March 1874, suggesting that a meeting of ritualists be called 'with a view to minimising points of offence, and so removing the excuse (so far as it might be done lawfully) for such legislation as that in question,' this proposal gained Wood's support and was persevered with. Although there is no evidence of a direct link between Liddon's suggestion and the gathering, it is likely that the St James' Hall meeting, held on 16 June 1874, arose from this correspondence. Towards the end of his long speech, he once again counselled restraint:

I venture to address such of my reverend brethren as may be present here with all humility as an equal. Let us consider if it be possible anything we have done, even with simple sincerity of purpose and for the glory of God, let us ask ourselves whether there may not be among what we have done some features, some elements, some details which may profitably, and in the interests of the general Church be retrenched. We are quite sure of the purity of our motives. We resent with utter indignation the notion that we are other than loyal to the English Church. We say that even if previous to the late Council of the Vatican the thing was impossible, since that Council there can be no doubt whatever about our duty to ourselves and to the English people by making it quite plain that we are not, in any sense, Roman Catholics. We do not wish for one moment to introduce the cultus of the Blessed Virgin as it exists at Rome. We do not for one moment wish to be committed to the extraordinary and unhistorical dogma of the simultaneous infallibility of fourteen or fifteen self-contradictory Popes. Since we believe we can be, in the ancient and historical sense of the term, Catholics without in any sense committing ourselves to positions like these, it seems to me that a grave crisis of this kind imposes upon us the solemn duty of considering carefully and before God whether there is anything in our public or private actions which may possibly be misunderstood and to act accordingly.[13]

This sensitive and irenic aspiration would have been encouraged, for instance, by Dean Church who was on the side of those who urged toleration and patience towards the ritualists and who wished to avoid conflict within the Church of England. However, the ritualists felt themselves to be under threat, they were not feeling particularly accommodating, and Liddon's advice was not acted upon to any recognisable extent. In fact events soon moved to a point which was beyond his reach. J. G. Lockhart's biography of Lord Halifax quotes a significant letter from Queen Victoria to Archbishop Tait, whom Liddon distrusted almost as much as he distrusted Disraeli, which included the statement 'something must be done' to combat 'the liberties taken and the defiance shown by the Clergy of the High Church and Ritualistic party.' The letter also contained the suggestion that laymen should be included among the bishops in the latters' new endeavours to prevent what were described as 'these Romanising practices.' The Queen did not specify whether such laymen should serve as judges in ecclesiastical courts, nor did she offer any sort of analysis or description of their role, apart from that of giving 'aid' to the Bishops. This letter no doubt reinforced Tait's dislike of the ritualists and strengthened his resolve to co-operate with Disraeli.[14] In March 1874 Tait had leaked to *The Times* the news that legislation was intended. Liddon confirmed that the report was true by contacting both Lord Salisbury and Sir Robert Phillimore; at one point he hoped that the storm might be avoided if they, as people of influence, could be persuaded to oppose the legislation even in draft form. But his private endeavours were no match for the combined forces of the Queen, the Prime Minister and the Archbishop of Canterbury. Part of the problem, according to Edward Carpenter, was that Disraeli had not expected to win the election and came back to power 'minus a fully articulated legislative programme. Tait stepped in with his Act to fill the vacuum.'[15] Liddon's diary for 1874 contains many references to the progress of the legislation and one entry indicates that he went to listen to the opening of the debate on 20 April, 'heard the debate in the House of Lords on the Archbishop's Bill.' He received a letter, dated 21 July 1874, from E. Francis Smith concerning Disraeli's challenging remarks in the Commons about the Bill and asking, 'Will not you, Sir, as the acknowledged Champion and Leader of the Catholic Movement in this country, take up the gauntlet.' Obviously this correspondent could not have been aware of Liddon's contacts with Wood and Mackonochie, nor of his political enquiries to Phillimore and Lord Salisbury. Liddon's role was that of a leader, but not of the type that mans barricades or requires others to do so, and events were soon to prove that his moderate approach to the legislation was the most appropriate. He had some influence through his political contacts but was unable to do more than encourage them to resist at least the Bill's most aggressive clauses. His widespread contacts among the Anglo-Catholic clergy gave him the opportunity to counsel caution and common sense, but here too he was not particularly successful as the clergy involved believed that they were fighting to protect first principles and Liddon himself believed the Bill to be thoroughly erastian. In the circumstances that prevailed it is doubtful whether anyone could have done anything effective to defuse the situation. Certainly his correspondent's wish that he should 'take up the gauntlet' was asinine, and the way in which Liddon did try to deal with the problem would not have met with Smith's approval. The Bill became law on Christmas Day 1874 and, in the vestry after the afternoon service at St Paul's on that day, Liddon spoke strongly against the Archbishop and the Bill to Dean Lake of Durham who 'deprecated what I said; but I spoke my mind, as fearlessly as I could.' Liddon's last phrase is interesting when his customary willingness to enter upon controversial matters is remembered. His remarks soon led to an interview with Archbishop Tait, which Dean Church also attended. Liddon wrote to Halifax on 28 December:

> The Archbishop of Canterbury has written to beg me to come to Addington to talk freely on Church matters. This grew out of a conversation I had last week with the Dean of Durham . . . [who] reported this conversation to the Archbishop, who certainly shows a Christian spirit, in asking me to see him, after hearing what I said about him . . .

The interview took place on 30 December 1874. As Liddon recorded in his diary, the main points made by Tait with regard to the Act were:

> that the new Court of appeal, should, if possible, be improved and then obeyed – some courts must be obeyed –. He dwelt greatly on 'the Courts' as if that was the true instrument for governing Christian

Churches. Incidentally, he expressed a conviction that Vestments would never do in the present temper of the English people: that, however, the Purchas decision[16] must be reconsidered.

However, Liddon became less concerned as time wore on about the consequences of the new law, and in this respect his judgement was correct. He had written to Charles Wood in July 1874:

> The question is whether it [the Act] will be at once put in force on any considerable scale. I am inclined to hope not. Numbers of [Members of Parliament] have been supporting the Bill in order to prove to their middle-class Protestant constituents that they wish to be doing something; and before the exact value of what they have done can be appreciated in the light of experience, a new combination of colours, we may hope, will be presented by the political kaleidoscope. I have written to Mr (or rather to Mrs) Gladstone to thank <u>him</u> for so generous a speech; ... I wish we could have a church party in Parliament which would make purely political issues of secondary importance to religious ones.
>
> Of course, there is no reason for despondency. No legislature can really destroy a religious conviction, except by exterminating its holders.[17]

This last remark contains a note of grim humour which was repeated a few months later in a letter to his friend Miss Muirhouse 'As to the Ritualists, first of all, they cannot be put to death, however desirable that consummation might appear. That being so, they have to be reckoned with.'

In his evidence to the Royal Commission on Ecclesiastical Courts in 1882, which will be considered below, however, Liddon did identify two consequences of the legislation with which the Church had to deal. The first was relevant to the status of the Church of England in relation to the wider world, and reveals an aspect of Liddon's pastoral work which will also be discussed later. The Act had, in Liddon's opinion, made it more difficult to refute the long-standing and popular Roman Catholic charge that the Church of England is, as he described the view, 'an Act of Parliament church'. The Court established under the Act was, obviously a creation of Parliament. Personally he thought that the inference was answerable, but he felt that it was an answer 'which it is extremely difficult to persuade persons to accept who have an inclination towards Roman Catholicism.'[18] His other point, which came earlier in his evidence, was concerned more with the effects of the Act upon individuals and only secondarily with its effect upon the whole Church. Liddon said that he could recall specific individuals who had decided against proceeding to take holy orders because of the erastian nature of the Act. This 'diminution,' as it was described by the Archbishop of York, had occurred according to Liddon on two occasions, the last 'about six years ago'; that is to say in the years immediately following the passage of the Act into law. He did not identify the earlier occasion, but he was almost certainly referring to the years after the Gorham case. Questioned further he gave this reply:

> If it were allowable to do so, I could give the names of young men of great promise who would have been in holy orders at this moment in the Church of England, but who are not, on account of the passing of the Public Worship Regulation Act.

This point incidentally reveals that for Liddon the legal administration of the Church was inescapably bound to its spiritual life and its pastoral ministry, something which might have escaped those who acquiesced in the erastianism that Liddon deplored. This second consequence of the 1874 Act was probably only observable by someone who, like Liddon, had teaching and pastoral responsibilities for undergraduates who were potential clergymen. Despite these consequences, the victory which the Act seemed to promise the anti-ritualists was soon to prove to be pyrrhic, 'there are victories which are fatal to the conqueror; and the Ridsdale Decision is likely to be one of them' he wrote in 1877, referring to the ruling of the Judicial Committee of the Privy Council over ritual at St Peter's church, Folkestone and the Reverend C. J. Ridsdale its vicar. But the Act was not left unused and despite the bishops' right of veto, five priests were imprisoned under its provisions. The imposition of custodial sentences arose because of a legal anomaly; an early nineteenth century Act of Parliament had changed the earlier punishment of excommunication for contempt of an ecclesiastical court to imprisonment. The anonymous notice of Johnston's *Life and Letters* in the 'Church Quarterly Review' thought that Liddon's biographer should have suppressed 'nothing of interest' and regretted that much was omitted concerning the prosecutions brought under the Act,

> The imprisonment of the clergy . . . filled his heart and mind to a far greater extent than this volume shows. He grieved for their distress; he grieved yet more that no personal challenge availed to bring him into the same predicament; he admired, almost to envy, those who were suffering for conscience sake.

The first priest to be imprisoned was Arthur Tooth, of whose practice of celebrating the Holy Communion without the required minimum number of communicants Liddon was critical. Tooth was the Vicar of St James' church, Hatcham in east London. Liddon and his sister visited him in prison on 24 January 1877, as he recorded in his diary:

> Went with Louisa to Horsemonger Gaol to see Mr Tooth. He walked up and down with us in the part of the gaol which is closed in with bars. His brother, Mr Alfred Tooth, was there with tears in his eyes. I thought Mr Tooth's manner and bearing very quiet and dignified.

The Keble College archive also contains two brief notes from R.W. Enraght, imprisoned in 1880 in Warwick prison, under the Act, thanking him for his 'kind wishes.' Neither of these men were known personally to Liddon, and it is therefore possible that he also established some sort of contact with T. P. Dale, who was also condemned in 1880 and with S. F. Green who was imprisoned under the Act in 1881–2. The last priest to be imprisoned under the Act was James Bell Cox, Vicar of St Margaret's, Toxteth Park. Cox and the parish were both known to Liddon. His important sermon *Edward Bouverie Pusey* was first preached there, in aid of the Pusey Memorial Fund, on 20 January 1884. The prosecution took place in 1887, but the procedure began much earlier and there is an extant letter of February 1885 in which Cox thanked Liddon for his 'kind and helpful letter' and promised that he would not 'give in' but would do his best 'to be as calm and discreet' as possible. He concluded that he was helped by knowing that he had Liddon's sympathy. It seems that Liddon deliberately supported and encouraged those who were penalised by the Act. This fact probably gave rise to the reviewer's comment noticed above, for there is nothing in his diaries or unpublished letters to indicate that Liddon envied those who were imprisoned.

Liddon did not live to see the completion of the trial of Bishop Edward King for ritual practices, despite a claim in G. W. E. Russell's biography of Liddon, that he found the outcome an 'immense relief.' He was, however, involved in the opening movements of the case. Edward King had been appointed Bishop of Lincoln in 1885 and Liddon had preached at his consecration. King was denounced to Archbishop Benson of Canterbury in June 1888 for illegal ritual acts in a celebration of Holy Communion in Lincoln Minster on 4 December 1887 and another celebration in the parish church of St Peter-at-Gowts, Lincoln, at 8 a.m. on 18 December.

King had, in fact, followed the customary ceremonial of that church and had used 'altar lights, the commixture, the eastward position, the sign of the cross, the ceremonial ablutions at the end of the service, and . . . the Agnus Dei,'[19] all of which he found entirely congenial to his own views.

King was already revered for his saintly life and, as Chadwick noticed in his pamphlet, *Edward King, Bishop of Lincoln 1885-1910*:

> Several people thought that the circumstances might prove to be a blessing in disguise. If these fanatical prosecutions were to cease, it was better that a bishop should be prosecuted than a priest; that that bishop should be prosecuted for some exceedingly moderate customs, more moderate (as was observed) than were practised in London churches attended by the prime minister and the Prince of Wales.

Liddon would not have shared this optimism. He was alarmed that the prosecution should take place, believing that it was a 'serious misfortune to the Church – much more serious than to the Bishop himself'. This was a sentiment which was shared by Dean Church, and Liddon feared that 'anything like a condemnation would be followed by consequences which I do not venture to anticipate.' Although he did not specify them it is likely that the consequences he dreaded were either a further spate of secessions to Rome, or schism within the Church of England. To add to his anxiety, Liddon also thought that perhaps King did not realise 'the historical importance of the case' and how, should it proceed to a judgement by the Judicial Committee of the Privy Council as he thought likely, King would establish a precedent if he even appeared to recognise the Committee's jurisdiction.[20]

A novel element in the pending case was Archbishop Benson's personal involvement. Earnest de Lacy Read, the Church Association's petitioner, had requested that the Archbishop should himself put King on trial. For a short time Benson doubted whether he had the jurisdiction to act, but his son and biographer noted that the idea appealed to him, and he entered into even the 'minute points' of the case with a 'microscopic eagerness, which betrayed that they possessed a remarkable attractiveness, antiquarian and aesthetic, for his mind.' Liddon, with King's lawyers and other friends, tried to exploit this unusual aspect of the case and on 25 July 1888 he wrote to his friend and former colleague at St Paul's, Bishop Lightfoot of Durham, urging that the case was 'frivolous' and asking him to use his influence to get Benson to dismiss it. Lightfoot did not do so and the case gradually developed. Faced with legal advice that the Archbishop could not act alone, King went to Oxford and called a meeting, on 5 February 1889. Liddon took part in this, but it is not known who else attended. In his diary Liddon recorded that he put forward four reasons for 'objecting to an Archbishop's Court of Advisors in favour of Convocation,' but unfortunately, he did not record what those objections were. There is no evidence in the biographies as to the nature of them, but an incomplete and partly illegible note in the St Edmund Hall archive does survive; headed 'Trial of Bishop of Lincoln,' it states in Liddon's hand-writing:

Reasons for preferring Upper House of Convocation to the Court of . . . [incomplete].
1. It is more in accordance with the Primitive Church that a Bishop should be tried by a Synod of Bishops than by a Metropolitan acting with assessors who have no vote.
2. It is <u>less</u> clear in the former than in the latter case that an Appeal lies to the Crown.
3. The <u>Definitum fidei</u> is likely in the long run to be safer in the hands of a Synod than a single primate [the rest of this objection is indecipherable].
4. To recognise [?] so much power in the Archbishop will have a retrospective [?] as well as a prospective [?] effect . . ..

He wrote on 6 February,

The more I think of it, the clearer it is to me that, as a broad question of principle, and in view of his example upon the future of the Church, the Bishop is right in making this appeal to the Comprovincial Bishops, with the Primate.[21]

King thus found that the advice from his lawyers was in agreement with that of his friends. He decided to follow it and challenge the Archbishop's right to hear the case on his own. On 12 February 1889 the opening legal moves of the trial began. Eventually the Archbishop sat with five episcopal assessors, having been assured by the Privy Council that he did have the power to proceed. None of the assessors were to have a part in making the judgement, so Benson was effectively acting alone. One assessor was William Stubbs who owed his life to Liddon's prowess as a swimmer, and who had been one of his fellow canons at St. Paul's from 1879 to 1884. He had been consecrated Bishop of Chester in that year and was to be translated to Oxford in 1889. He pointedly observed, 'it is not a Court; it is an

Archbishop sitting in his library.' Liddon shared this cynicism; still doubtful of the legitimacy of the proceedings he wrote that

> The Archbishop somehow seems to bury great issues out of the sight, at any rate, of his own mind, beneath a mass of drapery and phrases; and the great ecclesiastical ladies who flit about in the surrounding atmosphere add an element of grotesqueness to the whole thing which makes it difficult to keep its great seriousness steadily in view.

After twelve months the actual trial began on 4 February 1890 and continued until 25 February. By the time the Judgement was announced Liddon was two months dead, but he would have rejoiced that Benson's verdict, delivered on 21 November 1890, substantially vindicated King. This decision, which was summarised in the biography of Archbishop Benson, was supported by the Judicial Committee of the Privy Council on appeal on 2 August 1892.

This was the last in the series of actions for ritual heard by the courts and was, in Dean Church's opinion, 'the most courageous thing to come out of Lambeth for the last two hundred years.'[22] Liddon's part in it, although necessarily small because of his failing health and the gathering storm over *Lux Mundi*, was significant in that he was able to keep before King and his advisors the seriousness of the matter in regard to the authority of the Church as a spiritual body in its relation to the State. Although he would have been gratified that King was largely vindicated by the Judicial Committee of the Privy Council, he would have held to the Anglo-Catholic belief that the decision was, in the final analysis, irrelevant. As Benson's biographer put it, 'for the High Church party of course the trial ended with the Archbishop's Judgement.'[23]

The emergence of ritualism and the reaction against it in both the Church and the State focused the attention of many upon the forensic relationship of the two aspects of the establishment in England. By the end of the seventies it had become apparent that the Public Worship Regulation Act, was proving unsuccessful in putting down ritualism. It had, however, drawn attention to the fact that a different method of achieving discipline within the Church was necessary. In May 1881, several years before the accusations against Edward King, when Gladstone was Prime Minister for the second time, a Royal Commission on Ecclesiastical Courts was set up. It consisted of twenty-five members, including Archbishops Tait and Thomson, and Canons Westcott and Stubbs. Liddon was requested to give evidence and was reluctant to do so but acquiesced. He was one of fifty-six witnesses, including Dean Church, William Bright, A. H. Mackonochie and C. L. Wood. Liddon appeared before the Commission on the afternoon of 16 March 1882, although Johnston incorrectly it dated three years later. His examination lasted about an hour and three quarters with Archbishop Thomson of York in the Chair, and seventeen members present. Part of his reluctance to participate in the Commission's work arose from his conviction that the bishops should be allowed to exercise, unhindered by State-formulated legislation, their God-given responsibilities for governing the Church. In the speech in St James' Hall back in 1874 he had alluded to the theological reality of episcopal authority in terms that would have been uncongenial to some ritualists:

... if Church principles mean anything they mean, not merely the sacramental necessity, but they mean also the living authority of the Episcopate – not merely of an Episcopate in some bygone world, but of the actual living Episcopate which confronts us week by week and day by day.

A month earlier, in a letter to his sister Annie Poole King, he had analysed the current situation with regard to episcopal authority in relation to the Public Worship Regulation Bill:

Ideally, of course, and in a healthy state of things the bishops ought to have much more power than they actually possess. They are 'judges' by virtue of their office according to the oldest law of the Church; and the 'discretion' which is to be allowed them is ecclesiastically speaking their due, if indeed they have not a right to something beyond.
But practically we know that this is merely a case of invoking Church principles for anti-Church ends.

In the address at St James' Hall, he argued that if the State felt any need to influence or control the activities of the bishops, it already possessed two ways of achieving this. The first was described in ironic terms by reference to part of a conversation he had had some years before with a 'distinguished Liberal layman,' who remained unidentified, and who said that bishops should continue to sit in the House of Lords, because 'it is of the greatest possible importance to the country that the bishops should be brought from time to time under the influence of a healthy lay public opinion.' The record of the speech says that this was received with 'great laughter' and Liddon went on to exploit his advantage with further criticism of the

Bill. The second means by which he felt that the State could influence the episcopate is described in the preface to his little book of *Thoughts on Present Church Troubles*. Its publication early in 1881 is closer in date to his evidence to the Royal Commission than is the St James' Hall speech. He claimed there, and again he was not entirely convincing, that the State effectively retains ultimate control of the bishops and their decisions because 'they would all have been nominated to their Sees by the Crown.' But part of the problem which led to the establishment of the Royal Commission was due to the fact that the bishops could not exercise their proper authority when it came to the matter of clergy discipline. At one level the State had, in his view which was typically that of High Churchmen, interfered with and reduced that authority, and at another level that authority was often ignored or rejected by the clergy, in part because it was seen to be prejudiced by State interference.

The Minutes of Liddon's evidence provide, despite his own belief that he could add nothing to the material before the Commission, a very thorough statement of the High Church view of the problem, and the fact that he slipped into using plural pronouns on at least two occasions suggests that he saw himself as in some sense a representative of a point of view. So it seems that he did at least unconsciously, sometimes accept what he often denied: that he was a leader among High Churchmen. This makes his evidence to the Royal Commission particularly worthy of study and comment. An additional reason why his evidence was so valuable, as the summary of the Commission's recommendations by James Bentley reveals, was because Liddon's ideas won significant, although unacknowledged, approval. Bentley summed-up the recommendations as follows:

> The Commission 'proposed entirely new courts, distinguishing doctrinal and ritual cases from cases of misconduct; ritual matters were to be tried by the archbishop or bishop, along with his theological and legal assessors, and the final court was to consist of five lay judges, all of whom must be members of the Church of England. The Public Worship Regulation Act was to be repealed.[24]

These recommendations, as will be seen, bear a considerable resemblance to what Liddon said, and if legislation on these lines had been implemented, then Liddon's ultimate importance to the history of the Church would be more apparent. Predictably, his evidence reveals yet again the conservative nature of his thought patterns. However, this characteristic, which took him back behind the controversies of the day, issued in suggestions which evidently struck some of the

members of the Commission as being radical. As might be expected
from Liddon, he felt that the best way to deal with the problems
before the Commission was in a historical manner;

> in throwing ourselves upon the historical constitution of the Church
> of Christ we had done our best, and we could hope then, as we
> could hardly hope otherwise, that we should be assisted from
> above and that the inevitable risks would be lessened or avoided.[25]

In this he was adhering to a principle which, he said, had been enun-
ciated by the Emperor Constantine in addressing the bishops at
Nicea, 'Ye indeed, are overseers of those things which are within the
Church; I of those things which are without it.' But this was to
presume upon the whole reason for the setting up of the Commission,
the brief of which was to enquire into the constitution and working of
the Ecclesiastical Courts in England. At the beginning of his examination, the Archbishop asked Liddon for his opinion on whether
dissatisfaction within the Church with regard to the courts was a
recent phenomenon. Liddon thought that it went back to the Gorham
case of 1850 and that such eminent men as John Keble and Bishop
Hamilton had believed that the Judicial Committee of the Privy
Council was not an appropriate court for ecclesiastical matters which
included judgements concerning doctrine.[26] He did not deny that the
Church needed a court to advise the Queen, a function fulfilled at the
time by the Judicial Committee. Such a court, however, should
confine its activities to ensuring that justice is done to individuals,
and should not be concerned with dogma. With regard to the constitution of such a court, Liddon would have preferred it to consist
entirely of bishops, who might have with them as expert advisers
either 'canonists or theologians'. But if such a court proved to be
unacceptable to either the Crown or the State, his second choice was
for a court composed entirely of laymen. 'There would be no mistake
as to its character; and it could not possibly be invested with spiritual
attributes which did not belong to it.'

The worst form of court to his mind, and to that of ritualists who
might have to appear before it, would be a mixed court of laymen
and bishops, he told the Commission. Such a body would not,
because of its lay element, be qualified to legislate on points of
doctrine but, he shrewdly observed, because of its episcopal element
would expect to be able to do so. Liddon was merely anticipating his
later comment that there is a tendency inherent in the very existence
of a final court 'to create doctrine', to use a phrase of the
Archbishop's. Liddon, as an Anglo-Catholic convinced of the

adequacy of the creeds, did not want to think of any court as creating doctrine but, if such a process was unavoidable, then an episcopal court would be the only one that could hope to do best 'what you cannot avoid doing somehow.' If such powers 'to make new doctrine' are recognised as an unfortunate but consequential and even a legitimate part of the function of an ecclesiastical court, then Liddon felt that they should only be used in exceptional circumstances. Such 'legislative authority would naturally be held in reserve; it would only be exerted when the documents before the court are not clear enough to furnish materials for a decision,' and such power would not be unlimited, 'the formularies and canons would be there to govern its decisions.' As far as Liddon was concerned, the vital issue was that no lay final court of appeal should be permitted to deal with matters of doctrine; and, if such a court did stray into theological areas, it should not have the power to impose its decisions.[27] The contention of those who fell foul of the courts, as of all other Anglo-Catholics, was that ritual represents doctrine, and that attempts to curtail the former were, in effect, regulations about the latter. It is at this point that Liddon's views came most acutely to bear upon issues of ritual in the nineteenth century Church of England. The discussion about ecclesiastical courts had arisen as a result of the post-Oxford Movement liturgical developments. Liddon was asked by Archbishop Thomson whether, in ritual cases, 'the first decision should be a process as inexpensive as the process before the Bishop?' Liddon's reply was oblique yet also unequivocal, 'certainly that it should be as inexpensive as possible, and that it should be entirely before the bishop.'[28] He took the subject further and made the typical Tractarian claim that 'Our Lord Jesus Christ has given no authority to laymen to rule authoritatively on questions of Christian discipline and doctrine.' His inclusion of 'discipline' with doctrine went unchallenged by the Commission and he thereby scored a debating point. Shortly afterwards he also managed to slip in his conviction that bishops are the natural rulers of the Church of England and even cited Archbishop Grindal of Canterbury (1575–83) as a puritan-minded advocate of his theory, claiming that a quotation from Grindal which he offered 'shows how mistaken it is to suppose that the sensitive feeling about the transfer of purely ecclesiastical duties to the Crown or to laymen began with the High Church Caroline reaction.'[29]

The evidence which Liddon submitted to the Commission was not merely historical, nor was it just a statement of the inadequacies that prevailed at the time. He had thought ahead and it is clear that at the heart of his conviction, even at this date, was a perception of the need for an entirely episcopal ecclesiastical court, and he provided the Commission with what the Archbishop described as a 'sketch': 'for ordinary cases seven bishops, five to form a quorum, elected to serve for a given number of years by the whole episcopate of Canterbury and York.'[30]

Questioned as to whether he envisaged 'a kind of rota of bishops', he claimed to be reluctant to go into too much detail, but did speculate that service for a limited number of years would be 'wise' on the ground that 'certain members of the episcopate would be obviously marked out by antecedents and accomplishments as best fitted to undertake this particular work.' Also 'the two primates would be elected to sit as a matter of course.' Although he had specified certain numbers of bishops for his proposed court, he also envisaged that for 'cases of great gravity' the entire episcopate of both provinces would serve. Interestingly, as has been discussed, Bishop King's lawyers in 1889 as well as his friends urged that, when he was arraigned before Archbishop Benson, the case should be heard before King's metropolitan and his comprovincial bishops. In this respect Liddon's evidence to the Royal Commission suggests that he might have been the one who made that proposal to King. To support the feasibility of his suggestions he cited examples from the Churches of Greece and Russia, quoting from what he called the 'Canonical Code' of the latter as follows:

> We do command all orders of the clergy and laity to hold this as a sacred and powerful Government, to seek from it all final decisions and sentences in matters spiritual, to be content with its judgements, and in everything to obey its enactments.[31]

By implication he accepted that the situation was, at least temporarily, different in England because the Church has 'not yet recovered from the effects of the long-enforced silence of her sacred synods', the Convocations which had been suspended since 1717. Liddon made no other reference in his evidence to the Convocations, which had been revived in 1852 (for the Province of Canterbury) and 1861 (for York). But because of the inactivity of the Convocations for such a long period, the Church was not, he said, 'ripe' for legislation. This was in response to questions from the Bishop Mackarness of Oxford, and this exchange concluded with a positive and somewhat surprising assertion, which seems to be unique to Liddon that the existing system should continue to be used, although he would have liked improvements introduced by Parliament along the lines he suggested. The explanation can only be that he feared the situation might be made worse if new and more erastian legislation should be the outcome of the Commission. In the end nothing was done to change things, as Bentley pointed out, 'none of the Commission's recommendations became law; the ritualist conflict was not over, and the Public Worship Regulation Act remained.' Bentley gave as the reason for this the diverse nature of the membership of the Commission.[32] Liddon was certainly astute enough to recognise the crippling nature of this diversity, and he probably suspected what the outcome would be. In the short term he thought that the Church of England might revert to the situation which prevailed before the Public Worship Regulation Act was passed. He was willing to accept a two-tier arrangement with the Dean of Arches as Judge in a first court but for recourse, in a second court, to the Official Principal, an official to whom bishops delegated the exercise of coercive jurisdiction, beyond whom no appeal can be made to the bishop.

On the question of the coercive aspects of jurisdiction Liddon was again unusual in his opinion which showed a willingness to be flexible, recognising the State's right to ensure that injustice did not occur. To this end he was able to envisage a system of ecclesiastical courts which would retain its integrity even though appeals to the secular authorities would be permitted solely on the matter of sentence. He was asked by B. F. Westcott, Regius Professor of Divinity at Cambridge and later Bishop of Durham,

> if the highest ecclesiastical court gave a sentence and expounded the reasons in the sentence you would think it a reasonable thing that a person condemned might appeal to the State in a matter of that sentence? [He replied:] 'In the matter of that sentence.[33]

It is likely, however, that this was a tactical concession offered in the hope of securing a greater freedom with regard to the regulation of ritual practices.

Liddon, in the course of his evidence to the Commission, made a number of references to the consequences of the Public Worship Regulation Act which are relevant to his views of the relationship of the authority of the State to that of the Church. First, with all High Churchmen, he was very unhappy with the choice of Lord Penzance as the necessary Judge which the Act required. Penzance was not an ecclesiastical lawyer and much comment was excited by the fact that he had previously worked on divorce cases. Liddon's criticism of the appointment was rather more profound, although he did agree with the opinion that Penzance was not personally a suitable choice. His main objection, however, concerned the manner of the appointment of the judge and was made on grounds that bear considerable theological weight:

... the real character of the judge, as conceived by the framers of the Act, appears to be shown by the provision that if he is not appointed by the two archbishops within six months, the Crown shall appoint. That seems to show that from the point of view of the framers of the Act the Judge is a person who will possess no powers other than those which he might derive immediately from the Crown, without any delegation of power from the archbishops.[34]

Liddon illustrated this point further by the use of irony. He drew an imaginary comparison with a hypothetical and fanciful piece of legislation which might require the magistrates to administer the Holy Communion in the absence of a priest; the inference would be that there was no significant difference between the two services and that, by extension, the argument would be that the clergy had no special powers or commission.

His evidence to the Commission, despite this last and slightly absurd point, was carefully thought out in advance and provides a useful summary of his convictions as representing the more theologically-minded High Churchmen. It is a rare example of an extended statement of his views expressed in a manner not restricted by the contingencies of preaching, nor in response to a specific controversy, and it is a valuable commentary on his own liturgical practice at that time when such matters were likely to be under scrutiny. Indeed, the history of the Church of England in the decades following the emergence of the Oxford Movement amply illustrates the widely-held Victorian conviction that the ritual employed in the public worship of the Church was of proper and fundamental interest to the State. At a time when any ordained man who questioned this assumption could expect his own practices to be the subject of interest, a priest with such a high profile as Liddon could not expect to be exempt from such enquiry. Indeed this point was well made by Henry Scott Holland who observed that Liddon occupied a position in the Church of England that was historically between the later ritualistic movement and the old Tractarians. Holland was correct in both parts of this observation. Liddon's place in the ritualistic movement is historically important precisely because he was able to relate both to the original Tractarian generation, with its greater concern for doctrine, and also to his younger contemporaries some of whom were captivated by the idea of the expression of doctrine through ritual. As has been noticed, this enabled him to work behind the scenes, although not always successfully, in attempts to reduce provocation by both sides. However, Holland's assertion has not previously been explored, and there seem to be two likely reasons for this. First was Liddon's conviction as a theologian who held that ritual, although significant, was secondary to the task of proclaiming Church principles. He seems to have been careful to limit what he did, preferring to give greater emphasis to teaching doctrinal truth rather than to its expression in ritual practice. In addition, he was not very explicit about his own ritualistic practices and relatively few clues have survived as to what they were. A second reason for this apparent reticence may, again, be found in the very fact of Liddon's close relationship to the earliest Tractarians. He was fully aware of the concept of 'reserve' in communicating religious knowledge, as put forward by Isaac Williams in *Tracts for the Times, no. 80* in 1837, and in *Tract no. 87* in 1840, and although this was set aside in the fervour of Liddon's preaching, vestiges of it may have remained before his mind when he thought about rites and ceremonies. But not all High Churchmen believed that ritualism was entirely secondary; indeed William Bright in a letter to Pusey in 1873 claimed that the development of ritualism was 'within limits ... the providential outcome of the Movement now just forty years old.'[35] But Liddon remained very aware of the need to understand the limits. In this he was more perceptive than many of his contemporaries.

Liddon had, indeed, been guilty of those 'little ritualistic frivolities' but he did not like the word 'mass' which he said 'alienated thousands,' and there were 'no genuflections' at Cuddesdon. His mature attitude was that of a love of beautiful and dignified ceremonial. This was somewhat fulsomely described by George Russell who said that Liddon:

> brought [ceremonial] to the test of the Church of England; what she taught he believed; what she prescribed, he practised; what she forbade, he eschewed. He mistrusted all such vague phrases as 'the whole spirit of our liturgy' and 'the living voice of the Church'. He made his constant appeal to the written word of the Prayer Book as the authoritative guide of English Church-people, both in faith and worship.[36]

A description of Liddon's attitude as a celebrant of the Eucharist has survived from the pen of V. S. S. Coles:

> There was something about his manner of performing this, as he realised it, the greatest act of his life, which was all his own, although he was as far as possible from any intention of intruding his own feelings or personality.

Both writers also confirm that he attended celebrations of the Holy Communion where the full eucharistic vestments were worn, and also that he frequently wore them himself. There may be a contrast here with Pusey's practice which was 'very cautious about their introduction, [although] from 1868 he occasionally wore them himself in private chapels.'[37] The most explicit of the very few references in Johnston to Liddon's opinions about vestments is a letter of 16 December 1881 to an unnamed recipient referring to the Privy Council decision made in 1877 on the Ridsdale case:

> So far as I understand the subject, I have no doubt that the Decision against Vestments was a bad Decision, and that those who wear them are obeying the true law of the Church.[38]

However, almost exactly a year before he wrote that letter, in Advent 1880, he had revealed in a rhetorical flourish sentiments that demonstrate his fundamental belief that there were more important issues facing the Church:

> Maintain, if you like, that your Bible is honeycombed with mistakes and legends, provided only that you do not maintain it too coarsely and too provokingly. But beware, oh! beware – of the crime for which our modern wisdom practically reserves its sternest condemnations, the crime of wearing a vestment too many or a vestment too few . . .[39]

In this his concern as a dogmatic theologian can be seen to outweigh the more commonly encountered concern with ritualism as such.

Greater clarity can be gained with regard to Liddon's views and practice concerning the eastward-facing position of the celebrant at Holy Communion. This is, of course, a ritual stance which was seen to express a doctrinal conviction about the sacrificial nature of the Eucharist. Liddon shared in the common, and ultimately successful, High Church desire to establish it as normal, or at least, acceptable. The practice had ceased to be used in the Church of England at the Reformation because it was felt that its sacrificial connotations were unacceptable, although it had been at least partially revived in the seventeenth century. However, it began to be a contentious issue in the nineteenth century and Liddon was committed to the practice. It was used by him for most of his time as Vice-Principal of Cuddesdon. It was discontinued on the instructions of Bishop Wilberforce even though Liddon had the support of Keble in his efforts to retain it. Despite this setback, Liddon reverted to his favoured practice after leaving Cuddesdon and recorded in his diary on 14 April 1861 'cel[ebrated] in St E[dmund] H[all] Chapel on the new altar for the first-time and facing east'. Bentley has described an interesting exchange of unpublished letters between Liddon and Gladstone in 1871 after the Purchas Judgement had declared it illegal:

> Liddon asserted initially that in attacking the eastward position the decision went 'the whole length of proscribing any adequate expression of Sacramental belief in the ritual of the Church of England'; he added that the position was used by many 'old fashioned and well-educated High Churchmen' and that the judgement 'would have condemned Mr Keble, had he still been among us.'

Liddon might also have added the name of Isaac Williams (1802–65), the author of the *Tracts for the Times* on 'Reserve in Communicating Religious Knowledge,' who also had been an advocate of the eastward position. Gladstone was not particularly sympathetic, for this seems to be an example of Liddon's tendency sometimes to push his arguments too far. However this particular aspect of the Purchas Judgement did cause considerable alarm to many High Churchmen. In the Diocese of London, Bishop Jackson commanded his clergy to obey it. Liddon, with Robert Gregory his senior colleague at St Paul's, declined to do so and they dismayed the Bishop by informing him in writing of their decision. Gregory, in his autobiography, declared that the offending letter was written by Liddon and signed by them both. The Bishop was unable to persuade them, either by letter or by speaking to them, to change their minds. Their motives were two-fold. First, Liddon and Gregory wanted to seize the initiative, so that the Church Association, which sought to enforce Protestant doctrine and practices in the Church of England, 'should not be left to choose its own battle-grounds.' This arose not from a desire to seek notoriety, but from a charitable and far-sighted wish to protect parish clergy, who could be more vulnerable to prosecution than senior cathedral clergy. In this respect their behaviour was similar to that of Pusey, who had occasionally offered himself as a 'mark' for others 'to shoot at.' Second, they wanted to call the Bishop's bluff and perhaps re-establish a liberty which the judgement had endeavoured to take away. This unique action led to an exchange of letters which caused the Bishop to interview Gregory and Liddon on 22 March 1871, an event which the latter described:

We have had our interview. The Bishop evidently expected concession, and talked of how much depended on our decision. We argued the matter at length, and I hope put most of its bearings before him. He was very patient when I told him that the Judgement was unjust somewhat emphatically. In fine we said that, for various reasons which we stated, we could not submit; that we hoped he would take proceedings against us, before doing so against any of the parochial clergy, who might be less able to defend themselves; and that, as we both adhered to the same practice, we wished our names to go in one indictment. We had evidently anticipated a threat. The bishop 'had thought that it would be his duty to deal with us first;' it 'would give him the greatest pain.'[40]

Both men left the interview with the feeling that the bishop would not proceed. Liddon then went on holiday without having heard anything, but they were right in their assumption that Jackson would take no further action. Even so, the affair did not end immediately. Two months later, in May, Jackson sent a letter to all the clergy of his diocese announcing his intention to act in accordance with the Judgement. Liddon and Gregory replied in a published *Letter to the Rt Hon and Rt Rev the Lord Bishop of London by the two senior Canons of St Paul's Cathedral.* They publicly repeated their refusal to comply and Jackson was forced to resort to a simple ploy to release himself from the dilemma:

he stated that he would prosecute the two Canons of St Paul's if they broke the law in the way they claimed the right to do, if he was 'duly called upon, by the authorities of the Cathedral to which we belong, to take cognizance of the offence'.[41]

Jackson knew that relationships within the Chapter of St Paul's Cathedral were such that, despite differences of temperament and outlook, there was no possibility of such cognizance being called for. Consequently, the manoeuvre by Gregory and Liddon was successful; no further prosecutions were brought within the London diocese by Jackson. It had been a calculated risk. They recognised that their position was strengthened because of the unwillingness of the civil authorities to imprison them, although Liddon did observe, 'if I was shut up it would give me time for a great deal that I have no chance of doing now, besides answering all applications about preaching for a long time to come....'[42] Liberty was preserved and Liddon's fellow clergy had cause to be grateful for the determined action of the two Canons. A few years later, on 7 December 1875 Liddon recorded in his diary that he and Gregory had urged a clergyman named Ashwell 'to hold firm' if attacked for using the eastward position. This entry is the last of several in that year which refer to this matter, although Jackson did order that his rebuke of another clergyman for the same offence should be recorded in the London Diocesan archives. Liddon tartly remarked that it was more important to have one's name in the Lamb's Book of Life than in any diocesan archive!

The following year he felt the necessity to discuss with his sister, who lived with him, 'as to what is to be done in the event of an adverse decision in November about the Eastward position by the Privy Council.' He had a similar discussion with Dean Church, but did not record the details. It seems that the judgements which had ruled the eastward position to be illegal had upset Liddon, and it appears from this diary entry that he contemplated resignation. However, this was never made public as a threat and could have been no more than a passing moment of despair. Gregory, by contrast, was such a robust character that no such thought would have entered his head. An ironic note was struck during this period when Liddon and Gregory defeated a proposal which arose as the result of a ruling by the Privy Council, that the Dean and Chapter of St Paul's should buy a cope for the Bishop to wear in his own cathedral. They opposed it on the grounds that acquiescence would have appeared to recognise the authority of the Privy Council.

A final point of interest regarding the eastward position is revealed when Liddon's practice is compared with that of Pusey. As has been stated, Liddon used the position from his early days as a priest. Pusey, however, was less uncompromising. Donaldson described the situation:

> Dr Pusey's own practice had been to refrain from the Eastward position at Christ Church, out of deference to two of the older Canons. But after his practice had been quoted against that of Liddon at St Paul's, he made it his rule only to consecrate at the north end when either of these two Canons were present.

The reference to 'two older Canons' is itself interesting, because Pusey himself was almost seventy when Liddon went to St Paul's. The fourth volume of the biography of Pusey, which Liddon did not live to write, merely says that he did not adopt the eastward position in Christ Church Cathedral, although he did so elsewhere, because 'two of the Canons . . . would be pained by such an action,' but Pusey like Liddon, who was bolder than his master in this matter, 'was extremely anxious to throw in his lot with those who contravened the Privy Council's interpretation of the law.'

Further information regarding Liddon's personal ritualistic opinions can be gleaned by noticing some of the things which he recorded. These provide a picture of a priest cautiously trying to change standards of worship. Occasionally, as has been noticed, contemporary observers have suggested that Liddon was not as irenic as his biographers have claimed. It seems, however, that there was sometimes an unfortunate divergence between Liddon's day-to-day conversations and the written material which has survived in the archives. Illustrative of his conciliatory approach is a polite letter from Liddon to the Principal of St Edmund Hall, dated 26 May 1861, only five weeks after he had recorded that he had celebrated facing east, when he promised to remove the offending altar cloth the same day. The cloth had been given by a former pupil. Liddon regretted that it had caused offence but wrote 'had there been anything theological at stake, I should have of course asked your permission.' Years later, when he was installed as a Canon of St Paul's Cathedral in April 1870 Liddon supplied another deficiency, this time a liturgical one, which, incidentally, reveals that he had considerable liturgical expertise, a fact that gives greater value to his opinions concerning ritual, but which has been largely over-looked. He was asked by Robert Gregory, whose own installation two years earlier had not been at all satisfactory, to provide a form of service. Gregory said to Liddon:

> The gas was turned out, the congregation dismissed after Evensong; and then the Residentiary (Archdeacon Hale), by the light of what looked like a farthing dip, said one or two Prayers and put me into my seat, and all was over.[43]

Gregory believed that this dismal and unsatisfactory start to his canonry, which he described at length in his *Autobiography*, was due to hostility on the part of the existing canons to his appointment. Liddon's installation was a much happier affair. It took place after the second lesson at Evensong, in the presence of the entire Chapter, on 27 April 1870. The installation was according to the form of service which Liddon supplied and which he described in his diary as 'the Sarum Use.' Those present might have suspected that a new era in the life of the previously somnolent Cathedral was dawning with Liddon being installed so soon after the energetic Gregory and then, a few months later, the arrival of Richard Church as Dean.

During Liddon's twenty years at St Paul's the cathedral suffered a number of what he called 'outrages'. These were physical protests by men who objected to the degree of ceremonial used in worship in the cathedral, or who objected to the forms of service. They merit description because Liddon's accounts of them in the diaries reveal his feelings and also the standards that were introduced by the cathedral's vigorous administration between 1870 and 1890. The first occurred on Good Friday, 19 April 1878, and Liddon described it in his diary:

> H. C. Shuttleworth [a Minor Canon] gave the Three Hours in St Paul's Cathedral. Mr MacClure of the Protestant Working Men's League went out of the Cathedral after the First Word and attempted to address people on the steps of the N. Porch. But he was warned off by the police.

Liddon did not mention that this service was an innovation in 1878. Five years later, at Easter 1883, MacClure and his friends were active again. This time the protest was more specific, and Liddon also recorded it graphically in his diary:

> at afternoon church today an outrage occurred. A well-dressed man advanced during the anthem, into the choir and after passing the choristers, put his hat on, rushed at full speed to the altar, jumped on it, threw cross and candlesticks to the ground, and began clearing away the flowers. Gregory, two others [plus] Kelly and Shuttleworth ran after him and with difficulty laid hold on him, and gave him up to the police. He shouted 'Protestants to the rescue!' But Gregory with great decision put his own pocket handkerchief into his mouth. He was taken out, struggling violently, by the S. E. doorway, and will be brought before the Lord Mayor, and a full bench of magistrates on Monday morning.

The damage was quickly repaired 'and everything was made to look as if nothing had happened.' A letter in the Pusey House archive, written by Liddon, said that two thousand people were attending the service but there was 'not a panic.' The incident was referred to in the diary entry for the following day, Easter Day and the feast of the Annunciation, 25 March 1883:

> Mr MacClure of the Protestant League was at morning service and (Green [the head verger] said) was astonished at seeing that everything at the altar had been put right after Mr Campion's 'outrage' yesterday afternoon. He seems to have been an emissary of the Protestant League.

Easter 1885 saw another similar protest. On Good Friday (3 April) the Dean was celebrating Holy Communion at 8 a.m., an interesting fact in its own light when later Anglo-Catholic tradition is recalled. The protester 'dashed the cruet from the credence table – swept the paten from the altar and poured the wine all over the sanctuary. It was happily during the Church militant prayer' and before the Prayer of Consecration. Once again the man was seized by the clergy present, the redoubtable Gregory among them. Liddon was not at this celebration, although he recorded the event. He never attended Holy Communion on Good Friday.

Another episode which it is appropriate to discuss at this point concerns the erection of the reredos at the east end of the choir of St Paul's. This, although obviously not a question of ritual in the usual sense, was to do with the embellishment of the cathedral and attracted the sort of attention that was being given to matters of ritual at the time. The initiative came from the Chapter and not from the indecisive Decorations Committee. Probably Liddon was behind the Chapter's intention, for he had a few years earlier initiated a similar scheme with William Bright at Christ Church Cathedral, Oxford.[44] Liddon in his diary recorded the decision to commission the work from G. F. Bodley RA, the same architect as that employed at Christ Church, on 13 November 1883, and on the last day of December, 'saw Mr Bodley in the Vestry about the reredos in the choir of St Paul's. Hope to get it in hand at once'. Prestige, *St Paul's in Its Glory*, recorded that 'the novelty of Bodley's ideas demanded some degree of acclimatization. Liddon's first inclination was for a simpler design. But the more he studied Bodley's proposals the more he liked them.'[45] The proposals never ceased to be controversial; the reredos was damaged in the Second World War and Dean Matthews wrote of it then:

> A feeling existed in knowledgeable circles that the reredos was a Victorian blunder and, though in itself it was a good example of 19th century sculpture, it was out of harmony with Christopher Wren's conception.[46]

The following letter, by Liddon to an unnamed person, described the process of self-persuasion, and in its reference to Wren reveals, when contrasted to Dean Matthews' observation, the subjective nature of artistic taste:

> Referring to the two points which you mentioned . . . Bodley is, it seems to me, right in asking that two of the columns should be

twisted and wreathed. He forcibly urges that Wren contemplated this; and such columns do give a great impression of richness – not to speak of their association, even in popular art, with the fittings of the Temple. Then he has almost, if not quite, made me a convert to his statues on the top of the Reredos. They belong, as it seems to me, to the general conception of the work, and indeed to Bodley's theory of a religious effect in Art.

His idea is to take captive the mind of the spectator by some composition of great beauty in detail – beauty in detail which extends throughout the composition, and does not allow the mind to escape from its effect by anything on a lower level than its own. It seems to me that the exquisite treatment of the background of the Crucifixion, and of the frame of the picture, and of the columns adjoining, demand something not less elaborate than Statues would be at the top. In short, I credit Bodley with an instinct for symmetry which I trust; and I trust it at the cost of sacrificing a more simple ideal of the general frame of the Reredos. For this simple idea, however beautiful independently or in other hands, would not be natural to Bodley; and I doubt whether it would be in keeping with the central feature of his work. He is eminently a man who has a good reason for what he suggests; and I shrink from the attempt to modify his proposal if it be accepted at all.[47]

Johnston dated the letter from which this long quotation is taken 4 September 1883, more than two months before the diary entry which records the decision to commission Bodley. However, Liddon's diary records that the Chapter voted £11,000 for the work on 24 January 1884. This must have been an interim sum because, according to G. L. Prestige, it was not until November 1884 that Gregory produced 'a statement of the cash available to pay for its execution' and the final cost of the reredos 'and its accompaniments' was nearly £40,000. The work was finally completed in 1891 with the installation of a new high altar given by Liddon's sister. The Jesus Chapel which was formed in the apse behind the reredos, and which ultimately contained Liddon's monument until it was removed to the crypt, was dedicated at the end of that year. Another apparent discrepancy regarding dates is to be found in Prestige where it is recorded that work on the new reredos began in August 1886. Liddon, however, noted in his diary on 17 December 1884 that he went to see the reredos under construction and 'observed that the workmen laughed immoderately when I came in; but tried, poor fellows, not to let me see it, from a spirit of courtesy'. This may, however, refer to some of the necessary work prior to the erection of a 'cartoon' of the reredos in 1885 and if Prestige's assertion applies to the commencement of work on the actual reredos itself, this discrepancy in the information is resolved.

In addition to the representation of Christ upon the Cross, the topmost statue was of the Virgin nursing the infant Jesus. These two elements of the reredos, combined with its general elaborateness, provoked considerable controversy as objects of 'superstitious regard,' and proceedings were instituted under the Public Worship Regulation Act, by the Church Association, which raised a petition with 9,000 signatures. The Bishop of London, Frederick Temple, exercised his right to veto the prosecution, basing his decision on the outcome of an earlier case when he was Bishop of Exeter. However, the promoters of the suit applied successfully to the Court of the Queen's Bench to proceed. This time Temple turned to the Court of Appeal which, on 17 December 1889, unanimously reversed the Queen's Bench Judgement. Liddon preserved an undated and unidentified press cutting describing the hearing in terms which suggest that the lawyers took it with less than full seriousness. But he took it very seriously himself, as is revealed by the large collection of press cuttings that he compiled. However, Temple demonstrated his solidarity with his Cathedral by personally conducting the Three Hours devotion in St Paul's on Good Friday 1890. The Church Association continued the battle, and at least two pamphlets were published with their sanction. The Association was not defeated until after Liddon's death. In July 1891 the House of Lords upheld Temple's right of veto and the now completed reredos was permitted to remain. There are various inconsequential references to the suit in Liddon's diary, but perhaps the most significant is that for 12 June 1889 when the Chapter voted £500 to Bishop Temple 'towards his expenses in the Reredos case.'

Liddon's concern for structural beauty in cathedral churches, which he shared with the Tractarians who applied it also to parish churches, was not, however, confined to St Paul's. As early as 1851, when he visited Scotland, he had been critical of the internal arrangements of St Giles' Cathedral, Edinburgh, as well as the theological views of those who worshipped there. 'I left the church feeling a deep and unutterable aversion for a system whose outward manifestations are so hatefully repulsive.' A similar sentiment, although less forcibly expressed, about the interior of Salisbury Cathedral is to be found in the *Sketch* of Bishop Hamilton, although on that occasion Liddon acknowledged that 'the best of intentions' had motivated the re-ordering: 'neat, cold, unmeaningly symmetrical, the interior of Salisbury chills the soul more cruelly than does the roofless nave of Tintern.'[48] Many years later Gloucester Cathedral earned much the same criticism, recorded in his diary on 15 October 1884, 'the contrast between the beauty of the shell and the bareness of the fitting up and furniture truly appalling.'

The comments upon church architecture that have been singled out for mention refer to different churches in England, but the diaries contain very many references to the condition and arrangements of continental churches, both Protestant and Roman Catholic. The existence of such notes serves to witness to the comprehensive nature of Liddon's interest in everything to do with the Church. He enjoyed and was anxious to preserve its aesthetic integrity; he was also anxious to promote what he believed to be reverent, prayerful and meaningful worship, and he believed that in order to achieve this goal a proper concept of authority in the Church and its ministry, as well as in the Church's relationship to the State, was essential. He was not alone in holding to these insights which, in large part through his influence, became more widely held in the next generation, but he was almost unique in possessing both the ability to proclaim them and also the opportunity to do so in both Oxford and London.

Chapter Five

Liddon's preaching and pastoral ministry

It was as a preacher of powerful, dogmatic and memorable sermons that Liddon achieved fame in his life-time and that is how he was remembered, although his work on the biography of Pusey over-shadowed so much. However, he preached as he lived, as a man of faith for whom the reality of God's final judgement was close to his mind. It found expression in his public utterances from the pulpit as well as in private advice to individuals. These complementary aspects of his ministry will be explored in this chapter.

Archbishop Benson commented on the way Liddon concentrated his physical and intellectual energy into his preaching, and that his 'spiritual earnestness' was very apparent. As will already be clear from the use of quotations in this study, Liddon brought his theological convictions to his preaching and expressed them with lucidity and force. It was this combination of clarity of expression and inner conviction that established his pulpit reputation. By common consent he was one of greatest Anglican preachers of the nineteenth century, if not the greatest, and it is his preaching ministry which provides the key to his influence. Indeed, the bulk of his published work, with the exception of the large but uncompleted biography of Pusey, consists of sermons. This is not merely a reflection of the nineteenth century habit of often publishing sermons, but indicates his genuine appeal as an individual. Liddon's sermons were so popular that unauthorised versions were sometimes published to his distress and annoyance. In 1872 a publisher proposed to bring out some of Liddon's sermons without having sought his consent. Remarkably he had the audacity to ask Liddon to correct the proofs! He declined and also refused to authorise the publication, whilst acknowledging his helplessness:

I know that I cannot help what is done by another publisher; my only resource is, to say that I am in no way responsible for the details of language which is printed as my own.

People write to me and ask what I mean by particular expressions which I have never used, and which convey ideas more or less erroneous. I can only reply that I cannot help being paraphrased by reporters ... and that I am not responsible for what I would do anything to prevent.[1]

In seeking to analyse his ministry as a preacher it is necessary to remember that Liddon was also active as a lecturer and professor in Oxford, and that his sermons do not embody the totality of his teaching, although they do represent those aspects of it which reached the largest numbers of people, both at the time they were preached and subsequently in printed form. Liddon preached at a time when 'sermon tasting was both a duty and a delight.'[2] His 'were well constructed, full of intellectual depth and power, and were characterised by passionate fervour ...'[3] They were also rich in dogma. As many of the sermons already have been, and will be, quoted in order to illustrate his dogmatic position, this chapter will concentrate on the phenomenon of Liddon's preaching rather than the content of his sermons. It was by no means unusual in those days for members of congregations to go to some lengths to be present when a favourite preacher was to be heard, and it was reputed that some people took a holiday in London each August when it was known that Liddon would be the Canon in residence and preaching regularly at St Paul's. For that reason he did not change his periods of residence after resigning his Professorship, as he would have been free to do. The Victorian period was also a time when oratory was appreciated for its own sake. In the Houses of Parliament and in public meetings as well as in pulpits, good oratory was expected in an age which was more verbal than visual in the dissemination of information and opinions. Another fact of history that contributed to his success as a preacher was that he worked in a generation which could still appreciate the impact of the Evangelical revival, and 'preaching characterised the prophetic interpretation embraced by the Evangelicals.'[4] Earnest worshippers of more profound conviction than shallow 'sermon tasters' expected to learn about the Christian faith, and its application to nineteenth century life, through the medium of the gifted preacher. Sermons were published for three main reasons. First, in the days before broadcasts and sound recordings, printed sermons had their own popularity. Second, they served as a devotional guide. The third, perhaps not always intended by the preacher, was that less able preachers or less competent ones would use the published material in their own pulpits. Some of the volumes in the present author's collection have been marked with dates, suggesting that they may have been used in this way. The most recent date is 1949.

It will be remembered that like John Henry Newman before him and, to a lesser extent, Charles Gore in the next generation, Liddon's own background of conventional Evangelical piety meant that he brought to his sermons at least some aspects of this way of thinking. In his own person he combined the role of a preacher more usually identified with the Evangelical tradition than with that of an apologist for the High Church insights rediscovered by Tractarianism. The result was remarkable and perhaps unique: an Anglo-Catholic preacher whose appeal was very wide-spread; one who operated at a time when the principles of the Oxford Movement were rapidly gaining followers in the wider Church. By the mid-eighties, when Liddon had been at St Paul's for well over a decade, the devotional and pastoral dynamic in the High Church revival began to have an important place in the Church of England, a process to which Liddon (not least through his preaching) made an important contribution. As Holland recorded in a characteristically eloquent contribution to Mary Church's biography of her father, the Dean of St Paul's:

> No one could suppose that the changes in the services and ritual at St Paul's were superficial or formal or of small account, so long as his [Liddon's] voice rang on, like a trumpet, telling of righteousness and temperance and judgement, preaching ever and always, with personal passion of belief, Jesus Christ and Him crucified.

In addition to Biblical and historical illustrations in his sermons, Liddon drew upon his own experience and that of his hearers and also on matters of contemporary national or international concern. An example of a matter of national importance is to be found in the second sermon in Liddon's collection of Advent sermons, with a reference to 'public anxiety on account of the illness of the Prince of Wales' in December 1871; the essential equality of all men before God was an aspect of the doctrine set out in the sermon, and Liddon spoke of judgement which 'will be more readily understood by us in these solemn hours, when the whole nation is watching with breathless suspense at the bedside of the Prince whom it has long learned to look upon as its future Sovereign.' Industrial disputes such as the match-makers demonstration in 1871 and the strike by gas stokers in 1872 also served as illustrations in his sermons. The Franco-German war of 1870–1 and the prospect of war with Russia in 1877 were used by him, as was the installation in 1879 of a new window in St Paul's in memory of Dean Mansel who had died very soon after Liddon was appointed in 1871.

On occasion, as happens to any preacher, his attempts at relevant illustration went wrong. The most spectacular instance of this for Liddon occurred on 7 December 1884. On the question of moral courage in relation to the defence of the Christian faith he said:

> Somewhat more than fifty years ago there was a small dinner-party at the West End of London. The ladies had withdrawn, and, under the guidance of one member of the company, the conversation took a turn of which it will be enough here and now to say that it was very dishonourable to our Lord. One of the guests said nothing; but presently asked his host's permission to ring the bell, and when the servant appeared, he ordered his carriage. He then, with the courtesy of perfect self-command, expressed his regret at being obliged to retire, but explained that he was 'still a Christian' – mark the phrase, for it made a deep impression – 'still a Christian.' Perhaps it occurs to you that the guest who was capable of this act of simple courage must have been at least a Bishop. The party was, in fact, made up entirely of laymen. And the guest in question became the great Prime Minister of the early years of the reign of Queen Victoria. He was the late Sir Robert Peel.[5]

Liddon did not mention the name of the offending guest, who was a young man, for reasons of delicacy, yet also because it was not in his style to do so. His aim was not, as he was subsequently accused when the man's name was revealed, to make a political point and embarrass the Conservative Party. He simply desired to illustrate his sermon by reference to Peel's Christian courage, and he was distressed when his passing illustration became the centre of a dispute. His use of the anecdote, however, was somewhat naïve because, as was the custom, his sermon was reported in the press and the culprit was soon identified as Disraeli, who had died three years earlier. This caused Liddon considerable embarrassment. He had 'a great many letters on the subject from persons on both sides in politics' and at least one angry caller. His friend Malcom MacColl, from whom it seems likely that Liddon obtained the anecdote, tried to mitigate the harm it caused by writing to *The Pall Mall Gazette* on 17 January 1885, claiming that Disraeli had merely quoted something said by Voltaire; but Liddon was unconvinced and his critics were not silenced. For his own part Liddon consistently maintained that his 'object was not to tell a story with a political moral, but to cite an example of Christian courage, which might well be imitated in the society of our own day.' The incident, which arose simply out of his desire to use a telling anecdote in a sermon, helps to illustrate his lack of a keen political sense.

As with the less contentious reference to the Prince of Wales, illness and death, in addition to being a real factor in his pastoral work, provided Liddon with many illustrations for his sermons. An Easter sermon, 'The Lord's Day', recalled three victims of violence who died in the service of their country, 'brave men whose bones were laid two days ago in the vaults of this Cathedral . . . We buried them on Friday, looking, as Christians should to His Cross Who redeemed them; and now Sunday sheds upon their new made graves the light and comfort of the Resurrection.' The men were professor Edward Henry Palmer, Captain William John Gill and Lieutenant Harold Charrington. Liddon did not name them but referred to them in a rather journalistic fashion as 'the accomplished engineer, the gallant sailor, the Arabic scholar . . .' They had been 'murdered by being thrown over a cliff while on a secret service mission to the Arabs of the Sinaitic Peninsula for the purchase of mules, at the outbreak of the Egyptian war of 1882. The remains were discovered and brought back eighteen months later by Sir Charles Warren.'[6] Some of the Christmastide tide sermons also contain, as illustrations of the transitoriness of human life, references to individuals who had been prominent in public life but who had died in the preceding twelve months. Their names were invariably omitted from the sermons, but were included as footnotes in the published versions. A sermon in the Advent series contains a reference to the death of Archbishop Tait which had occurred on the morning of the day it was preached, 3 December 1882. The text which Liddon used was 'Looking for and hastening unto the coming of the day of God' (2 Peter 3.12). It served, he said, as a 'motto for the Christian life' for people who would 'be definite and practical' in face of such a loss. The same sermon refers to the planned opening the next day by Queen Victoria of the new Law Courts in the Strand which could serve to remind Christians of the reality of the final judgement by God.

A commemorative sermon that got Liddon into trouble was preached on 2 November 1875 at Graffham church in Sussex. Bishop Wilberforce, who had been translated from Oxford to Winchester in 1869, had once been its Vicar. In July 1873 he had been killed instantly in a riding accident whilst, Liddon (who was not a horseman) said, 'cantering at a quiet trot.' Liddon felt the tragedy intensely, 'since my father's death, I have had no such personal sorrow.' One of Wilberforce's brothers, Reginald, arranged for Liddon to preach at the service and Archbishop Benson, who was in the congregation, wished for the sermon to be published. Benson's name was not quoted, and the pamphlet merely said that it was published 'by desire.'

Unfortunately the appearance of the sermon re-opened a controversy surrounding the character of the late bishop, and Liddon had to defend himself both in public and private. He refused to admit that Wilberforce had a streak of inconsistency in his character. The most that he would concede was in fact expressed in a letter to Dean Stanley of Westminster. He explained that the Cuddesdon controversy had left him with 'no temptation to indulge in insincere eulogy about him, or to close my eyes to the faults in his character.' However, he would do no more than acknowledge that

> the Bishop was very distrustful of himself, very impressionable, and constantly liable to sudden changes of opinion on points as to which he thought he had made up his mind. This may have been an intellectual infirmity; and it was certainly, at times, a source of practical inconvenience. But it is strictly compatible with general integrity of purpose, and my 'eulogy' only amounts after all, to a denial of the proposition that the Bishop was grossly dishonest.[7]

More than a century after Liddon's death it is difficult to assess the extent to which he was successful as a preacher, but our knowledge of the size of the congregations who heard him does provide some sort of clue. Chadwick has summarised his impact, 'the nave service at St Paul's Cathedral became with Liddon's preaching one of the great services of England. Not less than 2,000 attended, sometimes up to 6,000.'[8] There is an interesting contrast between Liddon's established reputation and an isolated incident from early in his career when a mob turned up to prevent him from preaching in London, at St George's in the East, at the height of the ritualistic troubles in May 1860. The numbers of people who crowded into St Paul's a decade later are such that there is almost no one with whom he can be compared among his contemporaries, although it should be noted that in London were the Baptist preacher Charles Haddon Spurgeon (1834–1892) and the Congregationalist Joseph Parker (1830–1902), both of whom attracted very large audiences. They did not offer Liddon's intellectual depth nor his catholic theology, as was recognised at the time. An unidentified press cutting at Liddon House contrasted the theological content of Liddon's sermons favourably with that of both Spurgeon and Parker. It is recorded that, shortly after he became a Canon of St Paul's, during only his second month of residence, he began by preaching in the choir according to custom on the first Sunday, but that he moved the service out 'under the Dome' for the following week where it remained. S. C. Carpenter, in *Church and People 1789–1889*, said that when Tait was Bishop of

London there had been 'some Sunday services under the Dome,' but it seems that this had not become the habitual practice. The inference about Liddon, although it is not explicitly stated, except by William Sinclair, in *Memorials of St Paul's Cathedral*, is that the size of the congregations compelled the change on a permanent basis. Indeed the inference is not questioned by Holland, who, as Liddon's colleague in the Chapter of St Paul's from 1884, would have known whether it was true. It was during the last few decades of the century that nave services began to be an element in the life of English cathedrals, following a pattern set by St Paul's and Westminster Abbey. Prior to the appointment of Stanley, Liddon had preached at the Abbey on 2 June 1861 to between two and three thousand people; the following day he noted in his diary 'very hoarse . . . after yesterday.' Many years later, on Easter Day 1879 in his own cathedral, he preached to a congregation which he described as 'immense', and a fortnight later he preached on the imitation of Christ to a 'very large' congregation. In addition to his ordinary sermons, there had been, in 1870, the significant series of lectures (both their content and length meant that they were not really sermons) preached in St James' Church, Piccadilly, and which were noticed above in Chapter Two. G. W. E. Russell concluded his description of the scenes at the church by pointing out that fashionable London had 'heard the greatest of English preachers and heard him in the fullness of his physical and mental vigour.'[9] It is clear that the published version of the sermons, *Some Elements of Religion,* did much to confirm his growing reputation outside London and Oxford.

After his appointment to the London canonry it became relatively unusual for him to preach at venues other than the cathedral or Oxford. But occasionally he could be persuaded; the diary records that on 23 May 1880 he 'preached in the afternoon at the Guards' Chapel in Birdcage Walk on 2 Tim 2.12. The Prince of Wales and Mr Gladstone there . . .' If the London congregations ranged from the poorest to the greatest in the land, at Oxford they were composed very largely of people associated with the University. His reputation was once again such that large numbers flocked to hear him. As an anonymous obituary, published in an unidentified journal, recorded 'there were always serried ranks of undergraduates at St Mary's and the floor was as crowded as the galleries.' His Bampton Lectures added to his reputation, but less prestigious occasions such as the courses of Lenten sermons which Bishop Wilberforce had organised each year in his Oxford episcopate, were also assured of excellent attendances when it was Liddon's turn. As he noted in his diary on 29 February 1860, 'preached to a crowded congregation . . . in St Giles'.

To establish an understanding of Liddon as a preacher it is necessary to look at the manner of the man and his delivery. Several descriptions survive, so it is possible to reconstruct something of the nature of his impact. A significant factor was his personality because, as with every preacher, it affected his delivery and how those listening interpreted what they heard. In an obviously biased obituary notice in the October 1890 edition of *The Contemporary Review*, Holland wrote that Liddon had 'that which we might call "distinction" . . . his presence was felt with a distinct and rare impression.' When he spoke, even in an ordinary room, 'his voice, manner, style, articulation arrested you; you wanted to listen to him, whoever else was speaking: his phrases, his expressions caught your ear.' This was also true when he preached. He had, as Darwell Stone, the Principal of Pusey House, recalled as late as 1929, an 'extraordinary skill as an orator' and he concentrated all his powers on preaching. The manner of his sermon delivery was consciously different from that of Pusey, Keble and even Isaac Williams,[10] all of whom believed that sermons should be delivered in an even monotone in order that the personality of the preacher should not obtrude upon the word of God that was being preached. In an unidentified obituary notice in the Liddon House archive, an unknown writer described Liddon's voice as 'not really . . . very strong, . . . but he trained it carefully and made the most of it. He spoke upon a high note and his voice was singularly distinct and penetrating.' William Sinclair used the same adjective, referring to 'that high silvery tenor voice, ringing in impassioned tones through every corner of the building.' Another, and this time contemporary, note is found in the report of an Easter sermon in St Paul's published in *The Echo* of 3 April 1888. The unknown journalist employed a tone of ironic hostility for most of the report, but there is a reference to Liddon's pulpit manner which reveals the personality of the preacher:

> . . . a short, slight figure moves with rapid, silent steps up the pulpit stairs. So quietly and unostentatiously does Canon Liddon take his place that scarcely anyone observes him do it. Then he bends his head very low, and is completely lost to view. It comes, therefore, almost as a surprise to his congregation when he rises, apparently from the depths. There is a momentary pause, and as he arranges his Bible and notes before him an expectant hush falls over all. The broad, thoughtful brow, the slightly sharp nose and chin, the fringe of grey hair, and the flash of keen eyes, are the primary impressions of the pulpit orator. Then in an exquisitely clear musical voice, more charming even by contrast with the drawling and monotoning that have preceded him, he gives out his text.

This description of Liddon entering the pulpit is reminiscent of Pusey, but his manner of delivery, as has been noted above, was significantly different. The reporter said that the sermon proceeded on lines of 'beautiful orthodoxy. The phraseology was faultless; it was splendidly eloquent,' but concluded, however, with more general observations and criticism. Although this writer did not much like Liddon, the newspaper was not as outspoken as the writer of an anonymous letter which Liddon received on 31 August 1886 'telling me that my sermon of last Sunday was a stone instead of bread.'

Part of the difficulty in dealing with Liddon as a preacher lies in the length of his sermons, which to the twentieth century mind seems to be excessive. Anthony Russell has pointed out that in the Victorian period long sermons were customary, and he cited various authorities who, between them, recommended between twenty and forty-five minutes as the optimum. But Liddon's were longer and even his friends did not always approve; Pusey was critical on at least one occasion in the early days. 'You preach for an hour in St Paul's . . . and you are knocked up for a fortnight afterwards.' Indeed, he even seems to have had some qualms himself, for he sometimes noted the length of his sermons in his diary. The following are chosen from different points in his career: on 29 February 1860 he noted that he had preached for an hour and a quarter the sermon in St Giles' Church that has already been noticed as attracting a crowded congregation. It was a sermon in one of these series that E. S. Talbot noted as having 'lasted little less than an hour and a half.' Twenty years later he recorded after the sermon in the Guards' Chapel that 'the Prince [of Wales] looked bored at the length of my sermon' (23 May 1880), and on Christmas Day 1884 in St Paul's he 'celebrated [the Holy Communion] at 8.00, and my sermon at 10.30. Not out before 1.30 and very tired.' There are many references by others to the length of his sermons. Not all of them are complimentary, and it is clear that Liddon's practice was unusual even in an age when long sermons were customary. One of the most plaintive complaints is a letter written in the middle of Liddon's career. It was from a man named Dunn; he was in the habit of attending 'the special services held on Sunday evenings under the Dome.' He had seen an announcement in a newspaper 'that the pulpit of that sacred edifice be occupied by you on the evening of the approaching Easter day.' Very respectfully he addressed a 'few lines on the extreme length of your sermons' and he asked Liddon to limit his sermon to 'fifty or sixty minutes at the outside.' Apparently the doors of the cathedral opened at five forty-five to admit those waiting, in Dunn's view, two or three hundred people. He cited two examples of Liddon's preaching; 'one

hour and fifteen minutes, and one hundred and twenty-five minutes
. . .' Dunn was distressed because on the earlier occasion the service
did not end until after 9 p.m. and, on the latter, not until 9.45 p.m.

> The ill effects attending sermons of such length on a congregation
> like that of St Paul's are these; the people arriving . . . so early and
> waiting such a time until the service commences naturally get very
> tired and a great number leave the Building before it is finished
> which besides being a great nuisance to those who remain does not
> look at all seemly for a religious service.[11]

Dunn's letter is courteously phrased and was written more from a
sense of distress than of anger; there is nothing to suggest that his
references to the lengths of time involved were exaggerated. On the
assumption that his observations were accurate, then it must be
admitted that Liddon's sermons were excessively long even by the
standards of Victorian pulpit oratory.

Turning from his style and the length of his sermons, it is appropriate to look at the opinions which of some of his contemporaries
had about what he said. The general view is that his sermons
contained much of theological weight and significance. It is interesting, therefore, to notice that Darwell Stone, writing in *The Centenary
Memoir* in 1929, thought that

> Dr Liddon's greatness as a preacher did not always mean that his
> words were more satisfying or more permanently valuable than the
> teaching of any other of his time. It was the union of oratorical
> power and skill with knowledge and thought and character which
> gave him his unique position.

As a young man, Hastings Rashdall, who later became Dean of
Carlisle, was 'very anxious' to meet Liddon. He also heard him
preach and remarked, 'really I don't think he said in the course of
one hour and five minutes anything that one could remember' about
his chosen subject, 'though what he did say was very oratorically
expressed.' But Stone, who was theologically more in sympathy with
Liddon than Rashdall, went on to compare Liddon with Dean Church
and concluded that Liddon was superior in 'effective force' although
Church was the greater theologian. Dean Church would have denied
Stone's second point, because he regarded Liddon as the Church of
England's greatest preacher and also 'her most learned theologian.'
Whatever the truth of Stone's remarks, Liddon's preaching did exer-
cise a considerable influence, as his ministry as a whole testifies.

There are records, in the Keble College material, of ordinary individuals who acknowledged the effect of his sermons upon their lives. One such was a soldier, a corporal Lawson, serving in Ireland but who expected to be sent to India. He said that he always tried to hear Liddon preach whenever he could get to London and he wrote, on 31 January 1882, asking for copies of some of the sermons to replace ones that he had lost, 'I should be sorry to leave Europe without being in possession of something to remind me of the most earnest preacher I know.' An acknowledgement of more specific help from a sermon is to be found in a letter from one Elise Morgan, dated 25 April 1883, where the writer told him that a sermon of his 'on doubt' had brought her back to Christianity. A third example is a letter from W. S. Dracon who wrote on 17 April 1888, requesting a copy of a sermon for a bereaved friend. The friend's father had died at the time when Liddon was preaching and the writer and his friend were together in the congregation.

The Oxford sermons were sometimes thought to be of a rather different type from those preached in London. This is accounted for by his consciousness of the different types of congregation. One modern commentator has said that the Oxford sermons 'often became exhaustive treatments of theological topics in a closely didactic and scholarly manner.'[12] It is a mistake, however, to press too hard this distinction, for Liddon did not shrink from presenting the more heterogeneous congregation at St Paul's with what he believed to be the essential truths of the Catholic faith. In terms of his London ministry the lecture-like sermons, *Some Elements of Religion*, go furthest in this direction, but it is possible to find many examples of his theological learning put at the service of the congregations to which he preached. Indeed, it may be that part of his appeal as a preacher lay in his willingness to trust the intelligence of congregations and not to present them with mere pious platitudes. He was, however, aware of the danger of being too technical as he noted in his diary on 20 October 1878, when he heard Dr Westcott[13] preach, 'his sermon was too ideal and Platonic to be of much practical good. There were some beautiful bits in it, but as a whole it went over everyone's head.' The size of the congregations who listened to Liddon are testimony to the fact the he did not fall into the same trap. The unidentified obituary notice in the Liddon House archive went so far as to claim of his preaching generally, 'it is not too much to say' that Liddon's sermons in their published versions 'form a monumental library of theology. They are sermons which demand and repay repeated perusal. We believe that they will have an increasing value, and that no man will be considered a well-equipped theologian who has not mastered them.' This is a rather flattering assessment especially as the unknown author went on to claim that Liddon was a highly systematic preacher. This latter claim cannot be substantiated if the writer was referring to anything more than the way in which he compiled individual sermons. Liddon himself denied it on more than one occasion. In a letter to his Congregationalist contemporary R. W. Dale in 1879, in reply to Dale's acknowledgement of receipt of a copy of Liddon's *University Sermons, Second Series*, he wrote that the contents of the volume 'have no relation to each other, and no pretensions however loosely compacted.' A similar, if less forcible, disclaimer is to be found in the Preface to the first edition of his *Advent in St Paul's*. Liddon, like most preachers, frequently responded in his sermons to the contemporary situation and this militated against any serious endeavour to be systematic in his treatment of theological subjects; he was more concerned to speak about matters of actual concern of his audience. However, the exigencies of his regular periods as Canon in residence in St Paul's meant that over the years he had the opportunity to produce series of sermons on common themes, such as Advent and Christmas in the December residences and Lent and Easter during the April periods. Thus there are many sermons about judgement, the incarnation, the passion and the resurrection. The August residences also add to this general impression of system because, although given over to more general subjects, they follow his tendency (which was unusual at the time) of preaching on one of the Prayer Book lessons. Thus it is more accurate to say that Liddon was a disciplined preacher, rather than a systematic one.

In *The Centenary Memoir*, Stone looked at 'Dr Liddon as a Preacher', but although the essay is very useful, he made no reference to the sources that Liddon drew upon in learning his craft as a preacher. However, any attempt to assess this part of his ministry should notice the sources of his inspiration. H. S. Holland, in the original article in *The Dictionary of National Biography*, said that the 'passionate fervour, much motion and great length' of Liddon's sermons produced in the country folk to whom he ministered immediately after his ordination a conviction that he was 'somewhat "foreign."' The opening words of the biography by G. W. E. Russell are, 'Liddon is half a Frenchman.' The author said that this was how 'the world summarised its impressions of a new and astonishing force' that Liddon brought to London in 1870. The simple truth was that Liddon was an Englishman who had studied what Holland called 'the great school of French oratory.' Pusey had studied theology in Germany as a young man, but it is unlikely that this had any advantageous effect on his preaching. Liddon, who did not have any similar experience, had, however, become aware of the flowering of pulpit oratory in France and had deliberately studied it in written form in order to develop his gifts as a preacher. Consequently he became the first great Anglo-Catholic preacher and retained this reputation despite the length of his sermons and the emergence of other powerful preachers, such as Charles Gore and Henry Scott Holland, from within the High Church tradition towards the end of his life. How Liddon came to know about the French models is not revealed, but he admired Louis Bourdaloue, a seventeenth century Jesuit, and also Lacordaire, an older contemporary of his own who eventually became a Dominican Friar (The Order of Preachers). In addition, Liddon's contemporaries saw that he had been influenced by Jean Baptiste Massillon, Bishop of Clermont from 1718 and by Jacques Benigne Bossuet, a preacher at the French Court who became Bishop of Meaux, whose church Liddon visited on 30 September 1885. He climbed into the pulpit, noting afterwards in his diary, 'but this alas! is a very different thing from catching his inspiration.' Bossuet had been acclaimed by his own contemporaries to be among the greatest preachers of all time. The 1885 diary contains, in an envelope, a sprig from a yew tree under which, Liddon noted, Bossuet often sat to compose his sermons. Liddon's skill was not dependent merely upon those whose example he admired and followed. It was hard-won through perseverance, and occasionally the strain showed. Pusey's exaggerated observation that he was 'knocked up for a fortnight' has already been quoted. It is stated in the biography of Henry Scott Holland that after Liddon had preached in the cathedral he returned home for a warm bath as soon as the service ended and then went to bed;[14] he also offered a bath to visiting preachers who were his guests at St Paul's. On 16 February 1878 Liddon himself confided to his diary that he was 'getting very uncomfortable' about a sermon he was preparing and he expressed similar disquiet about a pending University Sermon in May of the same year. On Sunday 25 July 1886 he had 'a very depressing day, found preaching difficult,' and Johnston who knew him better than most said, 'preaching had always been a great strain to him.'

It is possible to trace an interesting development in Liddon's approach to sermon preparation. In his early days he, with Dr Pusey's encouragement, preached extempore. Liddon distrusted the practice of extemporary prayer in church services, so it is remarkable that he acceded to Pusey's suggestion regarding sermons. Commenting on Liddon's early preaching, Johnston felt it necessary to point out that

> Liddon's extempore preaching was no device for avoiding hard work. To the hearers it may have sounded like the natural, easy onflow of the full tide of the preacher's great gifts; but the style, as well as the matter, was the result of exacting work.[15]

It was probably Pusey to whom Liddon was alluding in a revealing comment which he made in passing in the essay *The Priest in His Inner-Life*, which was a product of that earlier phase of his ministry:

> Earnest men are pretty generally agreed as to the value, almost as to the necessity, of extempore preaching, uniting as it does the advantage of popularity to that of accordance with Catholic instinct and ancient prescription.

Later he changed his practice and followed his earliest instincts and wrote his sermons out in full. This change was chronicled by Johnston who said that the sermons at Cuddesdon and St Edmund Hall were 'mostly written out' although 'for most of his other sermons he made a few notes on an ordinary sheet of note-paper.' When he went as a Canon to St Paul's, however, Liddon

> gave up preaching without notes, as had for very many years been his regular habit except when he was preaching before the University; and he carefully wrote out every word of his sermons, and delivered them as a rule exactly as they were written. A comparison between his manuscripts and his sermons as printed in newspapers from the shorthand notes of reporters, show how clearly he adhered to what he had written.[16]

The Donaldson biography made exactly the same point but gives the additional information that the change was made because Liddon 'felt the great importance, in such a place as St Paul's, of being free as possible to give sufficient care to their delivery and to the management of his voice, without the anxiety of having to give form to his thoughts at the moment.'[17]

Archbishop Frederick Temple preferred extemporary preaching, but he approved of Liddon's technique, describing it as 'the ability to preach . . . a written sermon as though it were not written.' The man destined to be the next Archbishop of Canterbury also heard Liddon preach and liked it. E. W. Benson had written to his wife, back in 1876, that Liddon's

> 'beautiful look and penetrating voice are powerful over one – and then his reasoning is very persuasive. He does not make leaps, and dismiss one with allusions, or assume that one knows anything. He tells it from beginning to end . . .'[18]

The sermon that Benson heard was written out in full. It may be that

Liddon's change of practice was partly due to a reaction between his Evangelical background with its greater reliance upon immediate inspiration, and his catholic convictions which included a higher regard for order in worship. Whatever the reason, it is interesting to note the ultimate rejection of Pusey's advice. Another practical reason for his change of practice may well be found in the fact that, after his fame grew, Liddon expected to have his sermons published, and the process would have been easier if a full and reliable script was to hand. Also, like any other preacher, he would sometimes have appreciated the value of being able to refer easily to the exact words he had used. In the letter to the unauthorised publisher, Liddon had made the point that 'the publication of a sermon is, on a clergyman's part, an act of much responsibility.'

The Donaldson biography claims that Liddon made considerable alterations when preparing his sermons for publication. That he undertook such editing is supported by G. W. E. Russell who claimed that Liddon excised from the published versions the casual and humorous comments that apparently crept into what he said. Russell, in a footnote, observed 'a friend writes; "He put in bits and hits that are not in print".' This is in keeping with H. Davies' note that 'wit and humour' was often characteristic of Victorian preachers.[19] It is more than likely that this practice of editing has robbed Liddon's sermons of some of their immediacy and made it more difficult for those reading them a century later to understand the fascination that they exercised over so many who heard them and originally bought the published versions in their familiar blue covers.

In drawing conclusions about Liddon's preaching ministry it is helpful to recall a remark made by Paul Welsby in *Sermons and Society*. What many preachers 'said in judgement upon the society of their day becomes in turn a judgement upon themselves and the Church of which they are the mouthpieces.'[20] In this sense Liddon and his contribution to the Church of his day are to be judged by his intense personal seriousness. This is a quality that is apparent in every aspect of his life, not least in his sermons, where it is revealed by their length and by their theological content. It was, in turn, reflected in the eagerness and acclaim with which his preaching was received by his contemporaries. This shows a willingness on the part of congregations to work at their faith for sustained periods of time at an intellectual level that was often demanding. This fact is itself a testimony to the quality of Church life in the nineteenth century. In Liddon's day, it was customary for Anglo-Catholics to generalise about the failings of the eighteenth century Church, and Liddon sometimes did so himself. Indeed, Peter Nockles, in *The Oxford*

Movement in Context, went so far as to claim that Liddon was one of the originators of what Nockles argues is this over-statement by the Tractarians and their disciples.[21] Even so, it is true that the Evangelical Revival and the Oxford Movement both helped to create new interest in the Christian faith and also a greater vitality in living according to what were perceived to be its precepts. Liddon was a beneficiary of both aspects of this process of improvement. He also made his own contribution to the re-awakening of English Christianity during the second half of the century. It was through his preaching that he brought his influence to bear upon the largest numbers of people, but it was a process in which his whole ministry was involved.

In addition to his remarkable skill as a preacher, Liddon also had considerable gifts of perception which were well-exercised in his pastoral work. He used them willingly and was unstinting in the help which he gave to many. In this he reflected those qualities that have always been a mark of the clergy of the Church of England at their best. For Liddon, as for so many who accepted Tractarian teaching, this pastoral commitment was enhanced by a strong sense of the vocation of each priest and a deep perception of the Church's calling to serve the people among whom it is set. The settled nature of his convictions released his intellect to cope with the many pastoral problems that were brought to him. His freedom from heavy administrative responsibility which Bishop Francis Paget regarded as a disadvantage,[22] also increased his availability and his pastoral effectiveness. A third factor that enhanced his pastoral ministry is that for many years it was exercised from within two quite different institutions: Oxford University and St Paul's Cathedral. Far from competing for his time, they were complementary in that his periods as Canon in residence at St Paul's Cathedral came mostly in the University vacations. In the early days his periods of Residence were May, September and January, but they were altered to April, August and December in order to fit better with his Oxford responsibilities. The lack of similarity between the two posts meant that his pastoral skills, as well as his preaching, were stimulated by and were available to two different congregations and circles of acquaintances. In this respect he differed from Pusey who although pastorally active with many people, exercised an official ministry only within the University. In addition, Liddon was free from the restrictions of parochial responsibility. His pastoral ministry was, therefore, developed and exercised in an unusual combination of circumstances and this accounts, at least in part, for his wide influence.

His fundamental approach to pastoral work was founded upon the conviction that what he called the 'primal' duty of the ordained man is 'the declaration of the whole counsel of God.' This work required both courage and perseverance, as he believed the early martyrs had demonstrated, but it also required that those charged with carrying it out in each generation should be properly prepared. This conviction that future clergy should be appropriately trained for their ministry had not only provided the motive for his work as a young man at Cuddesdon, it was also present in his mind in later years when he prepared his ordination sermons and when he preached at the Cuddesdon Festivals. Indeed, it was behind all his Oxford work. He was keenly aware that the ministry of a priest is to all who hear his words and this truth influenced his whole preaching ministry, but he well knew that much which is pastorally important is achieved through personal contact with individuals and he drew upon this insight when he preached an Advent sermon in 1881 on a text from Philemon (verse 15: 'For perhaps he therefore was parted from thee for a season, that thou shouldst receive him for ever') 'we may note here how entirely, for the time being, St Paul's interest is concentrated on a single soul.'[23] A little later in the same sermon he made the point that St Paul's priority in the Epistle to Philemon is a priority for each age of the Church, 'all the real good that is ever to be done in the Church or in the world must begin with individual characters, with single souls.' This was a guiding principle in Liddon's own pastoral ministry, as it always has been for conscientious priests in every generation. Liddon exemplified the Tractarian ideal of a dedicated pastor, and although this may have seemed remarkable to those of a generation which had often accepted lower standards uncritically, he was not exceptional when judged by the energetic criteria which he and his friends applied to Christian ministry.

His assertion that such work is in accord with the practice of New Testament times suggests that he was not simply prey to the generalisation about the parochial clergy made by Anthony Russell, in *The Clerical Profession*, that the growth in population during the nineteenth century led inexorably in the direction of the counselling of the few 'in some depth.'[24] One of Liddon's ordination sermons, 'The Moral Value of a Mission from Christ,' caricatured the concept of the 'clerical office' as merely an official lecturer on Scripture or an official philanthropist, and reminded the congregation that 'we are more, because we have duties towards our fellow-men considered as immortal beings, duties for which we are fitted by a special mission and by a supernatural grace.' The concept of ministerial priesthood, he continued, is 'embodied in the word Pastor' and requires enthusiasm and fervour as well as a 'Divine stimulus.'[25] The channelling of

this commitment was described in the verbal sketch of the clergyman's diary in the final section of Liddon's still useful pamphlet, *The
Priest in His Inner Life*. It is also given a specifically theological
expression in the sermon 'The Work and Prospects of Theological
Colleges' where he identified the pastoral work of Christ with that of
his priests in later generations.[26] Another important factor for effective pastoral work which Liddon recognised in the same sermon is
the need for a priest to have a good grasp of the many-sidedness of
human nature. This, he said, is of secondary importance only to the
pastor's study of God himself. Only if he is adequately equipped in
this way can a priest hope to make the most of every opportunity,
even after long periods of waiting. Part of the 'legacy' of power[27]
which every priest inherits through his ordination is revealed by the
sympathy which he can show towards the human condition. This was
not seen by Liddon as mere 'fellow-feeling', but resembled that
which is described by the modern use of the word 'empathy'.

Liddon's pastoral ministry reveals that he had grasped these generalisations and made them his own. Many glimpses into his work have
survived, and it is clear that his influence as a pastor was considerable, and his skill in this facet of priestly work can only have added
to his influence as a leader in the Church of England. Unfortunately
its essentially ephemeral nature has also meant that little in the way
of a full and detailed description of his effectiveness as a pastor has
endured. This was compounded by his earlier biographers, who were
naturally anxious to deal in a discreet fashion with his ministry to
people who were still living. Unfortunately, the lack of such information has strengthened the view, suggested by his conservative and
comparatively rigid temperament, that Liddon was somehow a rather
one dimensional personality. In reality the descriptions which do
survive of Liddon in a pastoral role, reveal a warm-hearted and
compassionate human being.

It was natural that Liddon's ministry should reflect something of a
general tendency in the nineteenth century Church of England which
saw a considerable increase in the amount of counselling which was
undertaken by the clergy and to which Anthony Russell has drawn
attention. This was in part an outcome of the development of the relationship between client and practitioner that came about within many
of the professions, but it was also due in Liddon's case, as in the case
of any conscientious priest, to his personal willingness to enter into
pastoral relationships. Perhaps the most remarkable of them all was
the series of events surrounding his care for the condemned man,
Beale, in 1858 and to which reference has already been made. The
incident made such an impression on Liddon that he drew upon it in a

sermon almost twenty years later in the *Advent in St Paul's* series, on 9 December 1877.

Not all his pastoral work was confined to contacts derived from his personal contacts. As a result of his preaching and teaching he became widely known. Combined with the Victorian penchant for letter writing, this inevitably meant that Liddon received a considerable number of letters, many of which sought pastoral advice or help. They came from people in all walks of life, but it was only comparatively infrequently that he made copies, or retained drafts, of his replies. It appears that he tried to reply by return of post and this means that what he did write may not always have been as well-considered as might be hoped. There are frequent references in the diaries to the writing of large numbers of letters, and the following are almost a random selection of typical entries. On 11 January 1858, the day before Beale's execution when Liddon visited Bristol gaol in both the morning and in the evening, he also wrote seven letters; a few days later (16 January 1858) he wrote six. In later years the numbers increased greatly; on 30 June 1880 he wrote eighteen, and on 31 March 1887 he wrote what he described as 'a great quantity of letters'. Sometimes his correspondents were clearly unbalanced and the archive at Keble College for 1877 contains several letters of this type. One was from a clergyman suffering from acute depression, another was vituperative, and the third was from someone named Perrins who claimed to be the Holy Spirit. In 1885 a man named Henry Parsons wrote and asked Liddon's opinion of an enclosure, a 'copy of a letter supposed to have been written by our Saviour.' These items represent rare occurrences, but serve to illustrate some of the bizarre aspects of a pastoral ministry exercised in the public eye. The vast majority of correspondents were genuine enquirers. Some sought Liddon's help in temporal matters. Clergy occasionally sought preferment and, even more occasionally, rejected it when it was offered. An interesting example of this occurred in the summer of 1882. The parish of Friern Barnet needed a new incumbent. The Dean and Chapter of St Paul's were the patron, and it was Liddon's turn to suggest candidates. He chose a priest named Frederick Hall who declined it for several reasons which Liddon believed to be good. On 9 August, Hall wrote again to Liddon and quoted him as having said in one of his letters:

'I shrink from saying anything to induce you to reconsider a decision which has been arrived at for reasons such as you state, although these reasons make me regret all the more that Friern Barnet must look elsewhere for its new parish priest.'[28]

Correspondence of a similar sort took place in 1885 and concerned a priest named Robinson who asked Liddon for help regarding the technicalities of simony. Robinson had been ordained for sixteen years and was anxious to have his own charge. In a well-meaning endeavour, his father had offered to buy an advowson and present his son to it. The scrupulous priest wrote to seek Liddon's opinion and advice, but unfortunately no copy of the reply was retained. A third example of Liddon's ministry to parish clergy is to be found in the diary for 1888 where there is preserved a letter from W. J. Sparrow Simpson, one of his clerical penitents, and later Succentor, Librarian and Minor Canon of St Paul's, asking for advice on how to get on with the work of his new parish.

Other pastoral difficulties concerned moral problems. Sister Frances Ruth of the Community of St John the Baptist, Bovey Tracey, sought advice concerning what she described as a 'moral and spiritual' lapse by her brother-in-law who was vicar of Tredunnock, Monmouthshire. Another slightly unusual request for advice came from the Reverend Darwell Stone in 1888 who wrote about the case of a Jew who had been divorced from his wife after experiencing a conversion to Christianity and being baptised. The man was subsequently seeking ordination. Stone asked Liddon to advise on the situation if the man were to remain unmarried or if he were to marry. Unfortunately, there is once again no copy of Liddon's reply to these perplexing questions, although the fact that they were asked indicates the esteem in which his pastoral acumen was held. However, when he felt that the circumstances merited it Liddon did sometimes retain either a copy or a draft of his letter. This was the case with regard to an exchange of letters, in 1873, with a Mrs Coghlan, the wife of the Vicar of St James', Halifax. The letters concerned his pastoral care for Mrs Coghlan's daughter who had told her mother that she went to Liddon for spiritual advice. It seems that the young woman had decided to enter a religious community. Her mother was dismayed and wrote a courteous letter to Liddon claiming that her daughter

> has abundant opportunities to glorify God in parochial, domestic, social or even married life – if her heart were not morbidly disposed to seek other scenes and to mark out for herself what she calls a 'higher life'.

Liddon's reply was understandably cautious:

> It is a matter of much satisfaction to me that your daughter Miss Coghlan has told you that she has asked my advice. I need not add

that I did not seek the responsibility of giving it – so far as I have given it, it has been, probably, upon imperfect knowledge – but according to the best of my judgement.

He recorded his surprise and distress at hearing that Miss Coghlan had apparently rejected the God-given parental bond, and he continued

If she asks me whether I think that a single life, chosen not for reasons of selfish ease, but in order to do more work for God, is a higher life than a married one, I must tell her that I do. ... But this does not suspend the claims of her parents upon her loving service so long as they desire to keep her at home. These claims, I should hope, she would never ignore. But parents have no right to oblige a child to marry (I mean in the way of moral compulsion) ...*... although it would be natural for any right-minded child to pay great deference to their opinion, and if her conscience allows her to obey it. This matter is however a part of her own inalienable responsibility, of which as I believe, no clergyman or parent, can possibly relieve her.'[29] (the * indicates a gap in the original which suggests it is a draft).

This judicious pastoral statement was written by Liddon so that the young woman's mother would know exactly the advice 'I gave your daughter or anyone else who ever asks my opinion on such subjects.' It expresses similar sentiments, although in stronger language, to those of Keble who was consulted by 'a young lady ... as to her wish to join a sisterhood.'[30] There is no reason to suppose that Liddon knew of this advice which had been offered many years before.

In addition to the evidence for Liddon's pastoral ministry which has survived in his own papers and diaries, a significant proportion of the large numbers of letters which he wrote to the Hon C. L. Wood, later second Viscount Halifax, were to do with his role as Wood's spiritual director.[31] Much of the early material in this collection is to do with fasting. Liddon, although more rigorous than Pusey concerning fasting before Communion, was anxious to moderate Wood's practice not least because Lady Halifax was worried about her son's health. Liddon said 'fasting is not intended to interfere with health or usefulness'. He asked Wood to limit his abstinence from meat to the first Friday in each month and the three last days of Holy Week, and 'never to receive H[oly] Communion in the middle of the day', if necessary limiting himself to 'attend without receiving, and make a careful act of Spiritual Communion. In other words *always* eat a good breakfast on Sunday at 9 o'clock, at the latest.' Another letter, written earlier in the same year (1873) makes the unequivocal statement that '*vox medici vox Dei* in these matters' and again there is a similarity here with the teaching of John Keble. But six years later, in 1879, he had to 'throw' himself on Wood's 'indulgence' and point out that 'the object of fasting is to keep under our bodies and bring them into subjection, but not to impair their usefulness as instruments with which to serve God.' Other examples of Liddon's pastoral relationship refer to the fact that Wood was one of his penitents, and there are also letters written by Liddon on the occasion of the death of each of Wood's parents and a sad little note in September 1890 when Wood's son, Liddon's godson, died. The Halifax papers contain about four hundred letters from Liddon to Wood and, together with the other examples of his advice that have survived are sensible and moderate, and reveal a priest possessed of a high degree of common sense and a considerable pastoral sensitivity.

Liddon's ministry to the sick and dying, as to the bereaved, was another aspect of his work which he discharged conscientiously. The diaries record a number of occasions when he sat with people who were sick. A typical example is the entry for 4 February 1860 when he sat until 4 am with a man named Lingard who had had fits and a 'seizure'. Another example can be taken from October 1889, a few months before the start of his own final illness, 'went to see Lathbury in the morning; found him much better but not yet able to move from bed. Long spiritual talk.' It seems, however, that Liddon had a particular gift for ministering to those whose illness was likely to prove fatal. This may, in part, be due to the pessimistic element in his character which was expressed theologically in the many references to the transitoriness of life and also the inevitability of judgement that are to be found in his published writings. It has to be remembered that the reality of death was not concealed and was a common Victorian preoccupation. It may be that this made the ministry of a priest a little easier. At Cuddesdon Liddon produced seven meditations on death, with the collective title 'The End of Life,' as part of a collection of thirty-eight. They remained unpublished, and are now in the Bodleian Library. As D. G. Rowell accurately observed in *Hell and the Victorians*, to 'modern taste, [they] seem morbid and repulsive.'[32] But for Liddon this was a real aspect of his personal spirituality which spilled over into his pastoral work. The series of forty-nine sermons, originally published in two volumes, but brought together with the title *Advent in St Paul's* is Liddon's most thorough exploration of the theme of judgement and death, but references are found almost everywhere. A sermon in the series with the evocative title 'The Song of the New Kingdom,' preached on 22 December 1872, has a fine description of the way in which illness and death should be faced.

> One of the most searching questions that a man can put to himself, if he would discover his real spiritual condition, is this: How does he look forward to death? With indifference? That can hardly be, if he ever really thinks. A man can know but little of the mysterious being which he carries about within him, which is himself, if he has not a certainty, prior to speculation and confirmed by it, that this self will not perish at death, but will live on. What will become of it? Does he, then, look forward to death with secret terror, which he would not avow except to a very close friend, but from which he cannot escape? This too is natural enough if, believing in his immortality and conscious of his sin, he feels the years slipping away, and has had more than one warning that his bodily frame is breaking up. But it need not be . . . There are thousands of Christians who look forward to death as, indeed, the gate of life. Not, indeed, we may be sure, without some measure of awe; awe at entering on an untried sphere of being; awe at beginning to exist under altogether new conditions; awe at seeing, for the first time, God, souls, the universe, as they are seen in that other world. But certainly without terror, because terror is cast out by love.

And he continued by offering a reminiscence:

> It was my privilege to witness a deathbed in which this triumph of faith over death was conspicuously manifested. Relations and friends were standing round; it was evident that all must soon be over; and some of those present could not control their grief. The dying person summoned up strength to speak: 'I cannot think why you should be distressing yourselves as you do; if it were not for leaving you all for a short time, I should not have a single regret at what is going to happen. For between thirty and forty years, every morning and evening I have been preparing for this solemn moment . . .[33]

Advent 1873 drew from Liddon's pen another sermon in which the subject of death was considered, and on this occasion he offered an interesting pastoral illustration:

'You have suffered long and greatly,' said a Bishop to a distinguished statesman, whom he was visiting on his sickbed. 'Yes', was the answer; 'but, knowing what I know now, I would not for all that this world can give have been spared one hour or one pang of my illness.'

The statesman, he added in a footnote to the published sermon, was Lord Liverpool, and Bishop Lloyd[34] told the story to Dr Pusey 'from whom I heard it'. He also used this story in specific situations where he himself exercised his ministry as a priest. On 30 June 1888 he sat with a man dying of cancer who said to Liddon that 'he had only been anxious to be able to will entirely what God willed for him, in His Wisdom and Love. I told him the story about Lord Liverpool.'

In his pastoral work there were many occasions when he ministered to the sick, but there is nothing to compare with Pusey's work in London among the victims of the cholera epidemic in 1866. Sometimes the person to whom Liddon ministered was especially dear to him, and one such case provides an insight into Liddon's own feelings as a man as well as illustrating his priestly ministry in action. In the early part of 1858, as the clouds gathered over his work at Cuddesdon, he was often at the bedside of his Aunt Louisa who was suffering a great deal of pain. His Aunt was also his godmother, they were especially close; their frequent letters reveal deep affection and mutual understanding. She alone among the members of his family seems to have shared his Tractarian sympathies. He said the Daily Offices with her when at her home in Taunton and recorded the times when he gave her Holy Communion. He visited her as frequently as his duties allowed and, on 20 March 1858 recorded details of one visit in his diary, 'Talked to me about her Botanical Books – her love for the *Lyra Apostolica*[35] – her belief that she could not go on for many days – her "thankfulness that at such a solemn time as this I am not one of those Low-Church people"'. The next day he gave her communion and said the morning Office, 'and read a part of Dr Pusey's Sermon on the "Rest of Love and Praise". A[unt] L[ouisa] delighted in both the lessons, and made several observations on the sermon.' He saw her for the last time the following day. She died on 30 March 1858, and was buried on 7 April and although he noted in the diary some of the details of the funeral it seems that he did not assist. The account of his aunt's illness and death reveals a good deal about the man and also shows something of his pastoral manner, even when he was not entirely detached. His diary reveals that he found her death difficult to accept. A similar personal attachment lay close to the surface in his devotion to Bishop Hamilton of Salisbury who, after Pusey and Keble, exercised the greatest influence upon him, and as has been noticed, he spent most of 1869 away from Oxford in attendance on the Bishop, first in London and finally in Salisbury.

Other individuals with whom he was not involved emotionally also received his close attention, although he did not have the large numbers of such contacts as did his contemporaries in the parish ministry. In the winter of 1875 he wrote in his diary, 'Called on Mrs Kingslake. She was in bed – had been for four weeks. She thought she should recover. But of late 'God had told her to think much of another world.' She had not thought she was meant to be here for a long time.' He returned after a week had passed, on Christmas Day, and found her 'much altered for the worse since last Saturday', and on New Year's Day 1876, he heard that she had died the day before. He paid a pastoral visit to a relative named Eliza Kingslake on 10 January 1876 after the funeral but did not record any details. Another example of his pastoral activity is to be found in a letter, in the Keble College archive, which is undated except for a pencil note in Liddon's hand 1878. It was from the Reverend and Honourable W. H. Fremantle and asked, 'can you come and read to my dying wife and pray with us? She is fast sinking.' And two diary entries of ten years later provide further examples of his pastoral activity in this difficult sphere of work. On 2 January 1888 he noted that he had received 'a letter from Mrs Barnaby Price telling me that her husband is very ill and asking me to go and see him. Evidently written in great distress of mind.' He called the next day and saw that Barnaby Price was 'evidently dying. I said some prayers with him and talked to him as well as I could on the vital questions.'

Liddon carried this typically Victorian seriousness of purpose into all aspects of his pastoral ministry, and this is particularly noticeable in respect of his work in London which, of all his activities, most closely resembled that of a parish priest. He noted in the diary when he took weddings and he preserved a touching letter from Josephine Hewson requesting that he would conduct her marriage in 1885. The following year he took a wedding at St Peter's, Eaton Square, but a letter filed with the diary suggests that he was not entirely happy to solemnise a marriage during the penitential season of Advent. His book of *Sermons on Some Words of Christ* (1892)[36] contains a strongly worded criticism of some 'society' weddings, but he was very happy to solemnise the wedding of Dean Church's daughter, Mary, to Francis Paget on 28 March 1883.

The Occasional Offices were revived as part of the work of St Paul's Cathedral during Liddon's time as a canon. Colin Beswick, in an unpublished dissertation,[37] noticed that the first baptism to be administered since 1713 took place in 1875 and the first marriage since 1760 was solemnised in 1877, both during Liddon's time as a member of the Chapter. In addition there are references to conducted tours round St Paul's for groups of working men. These were led by Lightfoot and Gregory as well as Liddon, who recorded them with evident enjoyment and who noted that there were often large numbers participating, on one occasion fifty and on another eighty. There are also innumerable entries in the diaries recording visitors who requested advice and spiritual help; the entry for 7 April 1887 sums up this aspect of his pastoral work: 'a very busy day in seeing people'. Among the people who called upon him there were some who were impecunious. Unlike Gore and Holland, Liddon did not seem to possess a particularly active social conscience. Although he often gave beggars the help that they sought, he did not question the fundamental values which produced such inequalities in society. Among his friends it was amusingly alleged that his generosity provided the principal source of income for several match sellers who patrolled the Embankment. His willingness to minister in this very practical way was, however, the result of Christian conviction about his duty as a wealthy man to assist the poor, it was not merely the response of a generous nature. He claimed that the object of the parable of the Unjust Steward was to teach the rich that they have an obligation to the poor. But such obligation arose out of a kind of enlightened self-interest in matters of eternal significance. He illustrated this, in a sermon in 1884, by a reference to Alvarez of Cordova, a fifteenth century Dominican who was tutor to King John II of Spain:

> who wrapped up in his robe the leper who was lying, deserted of all men, by the roadside, and who set him down on his bed, to find that he had already passed away, but also to discover on his brow and hands and feet the marks of the Passion, [the story of Alvarez] embodies the reason why the poor can be said to receive [sic] into everlasting habitations. They are not alone, they are identified with One Who has shared their sufferings without sharing their weakness, and Who knows how to reward what is done to Himself in them.[38]

However, Liddon did exercise a degree of pastoral common-sense and he sometimes turned people away. One individual, at least, over-taxed his generosity but evoked a pastoral response. A man named Richards, who claimed to be ordained, received several sums of money for himself and his family, but 'when he became importunate' Liddon urged him to find parochial employment and even offered to call on the Bishop of London 'and do what I could to smooth matters for him.' The man did not accept Liddon's offer and kept away for a long time. When he reappeared Liddon wrote to a Mr Shaw Stewart who sent him a copy of a confidential report on Richards, produced by the Mendicity Society. This stated that Richards, after serving several curacies in the Diocese of Exeter 'has had only occasional duty and has relied on the proceeds of begging letters'. He was 'much in debt – nearly £100 it was believed – and he was found to be extravagant.' In addition, Liddon made enquiries in East London, but Richards was not known to the Rector of Bow, with whom he claimed to be acquainted, nor even to the vicar of the parish in which he lived. A visitor to Richards' home, the sister either of Liddon or the Rector of Bow, it is not clear from the context, had come away 'strongly of the opinion that it is a case of imposture.'

Another category of visitor who called upon Liddon consisted of those who wished to use him as their confessor. At first these included many of the students at Cuddesdon, as the diaries of the fifties reveal including the remarkable entry for 29 April 1856, 'heard Allsopp's confession. He fainted during it.' In later years large numbers of people went to him both at Oxford and in London. The list of names is incomplete because of the confidential nature of the consultations, and no details are given, except that once he recorded that on 23 January 1858 he deferred absolution until the following day. His penitents included priests such as V. S. S. Coles, who served on the staff of Pusey House from 1884 to 1909, and friends such as Alfred Barff, formerly Chaplain to Cuddesdon Theological College and Rector of St Giles', Cripplegate, and also W. J. Sparrow Simpson as well as numerous laymen and women. Among the laymen were Lord Halifax, as has been noticed, and also G. W. E. Russell, and the latter included a description of Liddon as a confessor in the short biography which he published. His phraseology is a little extravagant, but the picture is clearly conveyed:

To resort to Liddon in Sacramental Confession was to realise, perhaps more vividly than the penitent had ever realised it before, what Sin means to a saint, and, therefore in some faint and broken way, what is means to the All-holy GOD. As the tale of wrong-doing was unfolded, Liddon seemed to shrink, as from the sight of the Evil One who had been at work. He seemed to perceive not merely the power, but the very presence of Satan. On his lips the Word of Absolution sounded like an exorcism. But, with all this horror of the sin, there was conjoined the tenderest kindness to the sinner; the most loving sympathy with human frailty; and the most inspiriting confidence in the Bloodbought Pardon.[39]

Liddon himself described his own convictions regarding the teaching of the Church of England about confession, in a letter quoted by Johnston and written to an unknown clergyman in 1872:

The Prayer-book teaches distinctly
(1) that a priest has the power of pronouncing Absolutions which are ratified in heaven. This can only be evaded by an unhistorical and nonnatural interpretation of the plain words of the Ordinal, and 'Visitation of the Sick' Service. If preaching forgiveness in Christ's 'Name' was all that had been meant, a very different form of words would not merely have answered the purpose, but would have answered it much better.
(2) That Confession to a priest is advisable (a) when persons 'cannot quiet their own consciences', and (b) under any circumstances in illness 'the sick person is to be moved to make a special confession of his sins, if he feel his conscience to be troubled with any weighty matter'.
In insisting upon these words, you keep within the letter of the law. You are strictly in your right in saying that the Church of England leaves the healthy laity at liberty to come to Confession, and that she leaves you free to receive confessions, and to tell people that you are free to do so, by the law of the Church.
(3) When you tell the Bishop that it is *best* for the penitent to come to Confession, you go a step beyond this. I agree with you, of course. It is the common sense of faith; it is a fair *inference* from the premises with which the Church supplies you in her Ordinal and elsewhere. Still, it is an inference.
The actual *letter* of the formularies does not cover it. If men preach (1) the reality of Absolution through the application of the Blood of Jesus Christ to the soul; (2) the liberty of coming to Confession granted by the Church of England; (3) the nature of sin, which can never leave an instructed and sensitive conscience at peace until there is an assurance of forgiveness; – it is all we want. The teaching is within the lines of the Church Formularies; we need say nothing about its being *best* to come. People will ask to come, just as they will for medicine when they are sick and in pain. And this is better than the Roman system, which by enforcing Confession mechanically often makes it sacrilegious.[40]

In the light of Bishop Wilberforce's unease about Liddon's use of confession with the students at Cuddesdon, there is an interesting parallel here with what Bishop Westcott said was Wilberforce's view, that sacramental confession 'is medicine and not food.'

Liddon was one of the signatories of the Declaration drawn up in 1873 in response to a petition of 483 signatures to Convocation urging the bishops to appoint Licensed Confessors. The petition to Convocation was published in full in *The Guardian* in May 1873 and presented High Churchmen with the dilemma that they could not support its plea for the licensing of confessors because they believed that the Church of England ordinal in fact licensed every priest to be a confessor; however, opposition to the petition would easily have been misinterpreted and could have put the growing practice of sacramental confession in jeopardy. The Upper House of Convocation responded to the petition by forming itself into a committee to consider the teaching of the Church of England regarding confession; the committee presented a report on 23 July 1873. This document strengthened the case of those who believed that a reply, in the form of a Declaration, to the original petition was required. It seems that Liddon had doubted the wisdom of the Bishop of Brechin (A. P. Forbes, sometimes known as the 'Scottish Pusey'), who was supported by Pusey, and whose idea the Declaration was. Liddon thought that the production of such a document would prolong the controversy and give the assertions of the Church Association a weight which they did not deserve. However, as was so often the case in his relationship with Pusey, he allowed himself to be persuaded and with Bright and T. T. Carter, he assisted Pusey who 'spent more thought over this Declaration than over any other work of the kind in which he had been engaged.' The Declaration was published in *The Times* on 6 December 1873, but the most accessible version of it is now to be found in the fourth and final volume of Pusey's biography, pp. 266–270. This was put together after Liddon's death by Johnston, W. C. E. Newbolt and R. J. Wilson, and reveals that Liddon also spent much time on the Declaration, which comprises a clear and unequivocal statement of the teaching of the catholic wing of the Church of England with regard to the sacramental nature of confession. It is valuable for this reason and, in fact, largely reflects Liddon's own teaching as described earlier. There were twenty-nine signatories to the Declaration including, in addition to those already mentioned, Edward King, Thomas Keble, R. M. Benson, A. H. Mackonochie and W. J. Butler.

The growth of the practice of confession in the nineteenth-century Church of England was a sacramental expression of the counselling role of the clergy. In addition, Liddon was frequently asked to give specifically spiritual advice in a less formal manner. First, an example of Liddon at his most stern pastorally. A priest named Court had formed a relationship with someone who was only identified by the initials 'E.M'. Liddon wrote to Court on 21 October 1860:

> I write to you in great pain. It is not necessary for me to tell you that all that has passed between us, being based on falsehood, is null and void. Your communions have been sacrilegious. Your confessions – what have they been?
>
>   ... I can only add that it appears to me that resumption of clerical work by you must be <u>indefinitely postponed</u> ... And I beg you on no account approach the Blessed Sacrament, until we have seen each other.
>
>   I entreat you if there be any remaining root of bitterness, to disclose it. No disclosure can add to your deserved humiliation. And only by perfect honesty can you hope at last for penitence and peace.[41]

As a postscript he added a shred of comfort: 'do not despair. All may yet be well. But Oh! pray that you may be perfectly true and honest.'

To Verney Cave, a former Cuddesdon student, he wrote in 1863 to repudiate the assertion that, through giving advice he took responsibility for Cave's thoughts and actions. Cave was troubled by the claims of the Church of Rome, and Liddon advised him to keep away from the capital because

> I think that London has special trials for persons whose faith in the Catholicity of our Church has been weakened. And I advise you to leave London, just as I do not myself, for instance, eat veal. Veal is very good for persons of a strong digestion; it makes *me* ill.

He emphasised, however, that his advice was not a command, and he was careful to claim that it was impartial.

A third interesting example of the exercise of his ministry of pastoral advice is to be found in a letter written in 1876 to a clergyman named Cross. His correspondent was distressed at the state of affairs in the Church of England and was inclined to retire into what he had evidently called 'lay communion.' Liddon's reaction to Cross is the more interesting because of his and Pusey's feelings at the time of the proposal to amend the Athanasian Creed. On this occasion Liddon suggested that if Cross' statements about the Church of England, which have not been retained, were true then the reception of Holy Communion as a layman would be as impossible for him as the priestly obligation to administer it. Indeed, said Liddon, whatever one's beliefs concerning the validity of orders, 'in God's sight no valid orders can be effaced ... But putting this grave point aside – there is a <u>moral</u> difficulty beyond, I mean the difficulty which is presented by voluntary self-consecration to God ...' He apologised for writing 'with such freedom' and although he believed Cross to be wrong in his assessment and intention, Liddon concluded with a statement that effectively describes his attitude to the whole concept and work of priesthood: '... I am sure you will always try to act from some motive that will hold good at the Day of Judgement.'

Chapter Six

'Truth the bond of love,'[1]
Liddon and Church unity

Enough has been written to confirm that Liddon's loyalty to the Church of England was never in doubt. There were times when the strength of his personal certainty was recognised by others as a source of help with their own difficulties. This was particularly apparent on the occasions when he was consulted by Roman Catholics with problems. A letter to an unnamed recipient, dated 19 September 1880, was included by Johnston with the heading, 'To a Roman Catholic proposing to join the Church of England.'[2] It contained theological comments and also advice on practical matters. A more tantalising example of this phenomenon is to be found in the diary entry for 29 January 1883 which reveals on that day a visit from a Roman Catholic deacon who was deeply troubled about the question of Papal infallibility. During the interview he disclosed that, sometime before, the man had also consulted Dr Pusey. Frustratingly no details of either interview were recorded.

Unfortunately Liddon's loyalty was not always apparent to others among his contemporaries. He was pained when people who knew him drew the wrong conclusions. One such instance occurred in 1863 when a friend who had just become a Roman Catholic wrote in a way that brought forth an unequivocal reply from Liddon:

> I fear from your letters that you suppose me likely – one day – to join the Church of Rome. This, believe me is an entire mistake . . . By God's grace I am thankful to live, and earnestly hope to die, where He has placed me, in the belief that it is His Will that I should do so.[3]

This was forcibly expressed, but Liddon's language was no stronger than that of other religious controversialists, and often he tried to be eirenic. Nevertheless, Liddon believed the Roman Catholic position to be false and that it was not the only route to salvation; and he said so. His distress when he heard of secessions of members of the Church of England arose not only from his sure belief that the English Church is truly catholic, but from his equally firm conviction that the Roman communion is not exclusively so.

With regard to his personal loyalty, he was obliged to endure misinterpretation by some of those who did not share his Anglo-Catholic views. Even so, at the height of the controversy surrounding the proposals to revise the Athanasian Creed, as set out in *The Book of Common Prayer*, and its use within the Church of England, when Liddon and Pusey both threatened to retire from public ministry, he was clear that 'we could not go to Rome.' In those heady days, opponents of Tractarianism tended to see the Oxford Movement and its adherents as, at worst, crypto-papists working to destroy the Church of England or, at best, as misguided men who were playing into the hands of others who were trying to destroy it. This was a naïve, and sometimes wilful, reading of the situation. Perhaps it was inevitable at the time because there were a large number of secessions to Roman Catholicism and some of those who remained were unwise, and sometimes foolhardy, in what they said, wrote and did. Liddon's experience in Rome in 1852 meant that he investigated for himself the claims made by Rome and was never seriously attracted to its system. It is interesting to note that Liddon never indulged in the fiercely denunciatory language used, for example, by J. H. Newman and H. E. Manning in their Anglican days. He tried to maintain a relatively tolerant attitude towards the Roman Church. In this respect he was closer to T. T. Carter, and in the later generation to Charles Gore, both of whom recognised Rome's catholicism but did not accept all its claims. Liddon knew that Rome was not for him; in his view it not only permitted but taught grave theological errors. His pastoral dealings with people for whom the allure of Roman Catholicism was all but overwhelming showed him that it did exercise an attraction which could not be denied. For Liddon this attraction was perhaps, as Johnston thought, more to his imagination than to his theological competence.[4] This view is supported by what he wrote in the travel diary for 1852. After the passage which described the interview with Pius IX in the entry for 30 September, he continued:

It is indeed an awful privilege to have visited the City of St Peter and St Paul, St Gregory and St Leo. God grant that, if all which their successors claim be true, it be not a lost one! At least, it is no fruitless knowledge to have learned the aspect and bearing of her who is enthroned not merely above the palace of the Caesars, but on the more precious and undying treasures of the Catacombs. It is something for which, in some way or other one will have to answer – this privilege of having seen that dust which triumphed over the Roman Empire and was the seed of the Church!'

Liddon's reasons for remaining within the Church of England provide significant insights into his understanding of catholicism. Those reasons were couched in strongly anti-Roman Catholic terms which seem, today, to be anachronistic and harsh. Indeed his attitude is well summarised in his sermon on Jonah preached in 1867:

No English Churchman can satisfy himself that it is a duty to become a Roman Catholic until he has at least satisfied himself of two points. First, he must be sure that the Church of England *is not* – I do not say, a perfect representative in all respects of the Primitive Church of Christ . . . but that she is not – a portion of Christ's Body at all; that she is a dead branch of a Divine Tree, or a mere piece of State-contrivance. Secondly, he must satisfy himself that the Roman Catholic Church is – I do not say part of the Church of Christ, with errors and shortcomings, and also blessings all of her own . . . but that she *alone* is – the Holy Body; that she *alone* on earth represents, and that she represents adequately, to this generation, the fair form and pure countenance and unsullied soul of the Church of the Apostles.[5]

As the tone of this quotation makes clear, Liddon did not believe that the Church of Rome did represent the only, or even the most satisfactory expression of the Church of the apostles, although he did not deny the validity of the blessings which Rome enjoys and conveys to her people. Nor did he deny that the Church of Rome has been a great force for good in the world. Much good had been achieved, he was sure, through the work of her great religious orders and also through the endeavours of her missionaries. Liddon was even prepared to recommend some Roman Catholic devotional material, a hazardous course of action in the light of Pusey's unfortunate experiences a generation before, and Liddon's own experience when he fell foul of Monsignor Capel. Pusey was accused of effectively, if unintentionally, encouraging 'Romanizing' tendencies by supporting the translation and use, by members of the Church of England, of continental Roman Catholic spiritual classics. Liddon pointed out that such material was only valuable to Anglicans users so long as they took care to make allowances for what he described as 'Roman peculiarities.'

The various Acts of Parliament which emancipated Roman

Catholics in England from civil and religious disabilities had consequences that perhaps their proponents did not envisage, including the
increased study of Roman Catholic theology by some Anglicans, not
least in order to be more aware of the differences between the two
communions. This phenomenon was also incidentally reinforced by
Tractarianism. Liddon, as a serious theologian, had studied the
Fathers of the primitive Church, and his studies led him to the
conclusion that the claim of the modern Church of Rome to be the
sole representative of God's kingdom on earth was not reconcilable
with the facts of antiquity. This is an interesting contrast with
Newman who arrived at precisely the opposite conclusion. This
reveals that Newman's mind responded to theological ambiguities in a
way that Liddon's did not. In Liddon's case, his position was reinforced by his disciple's attitude to Pusey's vast but unimaginative
learning. But that was not all, there was a straight-forwardness about
Liddon that gave him a degree of certainty at an unconscious level.
Liddon spoke regretfully of an ecclesiastical absolutism which confis-
cated the ancient liberties of the Christian Churches and which
concluded that the believer faced a stark choice between confessing
obedience to Rome or being classified as an infidel. This 'supposed
dilemma between Rome and infidelity [had been] brilliantly manipu-
lated'[6] in the early days of the Oxford Movement to win converts but
such a choice is, wrote Liddon with a trace of irony, 'very far from
being obviously exhaustive'. In a sermon on 'St Edmund of
Canterbury', preached in St Edmund Hall, Oxford, on 17 November
1861, and published in the *Centenary Memoir* of 1929, Liddon
revealed the extent to which he believed that the Roman Catholic
Church had departed from primitive practice and observed that 'we
may humbly and thankfully rejoice that the See of Rome no longer
imposes upon the Church of England a jurisdiction which was
unknown to the First Ages of the Faith.'

Many others, however, who studied Roman Catholicism were
swayed by the arguments and, despite the unswerving loyalty to the
English Church of men like Pusey, Keble and Carter, Liddon
himself, and many who accepted their lead, the secessions of some
important Anglican thinkers and leaders such as Newman and W. G.
Ward, H. E. Manning and R. I. Wilberforce, made the task of
committed Churchmen considerably more complex even in the next
generation, than would otherwise have been the case. As he wrote in
a letter to his Aunt Louisa in 1857: 'the English Church is rendered
more Protestant, and the Roman more violently ultramontane by . . .
secessions.' Although he was a young man without influence when
the most significant secessions took place, the problem of what

Liddon called the 'Romeward movement' always concerned him. He was convinced, however, that the onus of proving the validity of their new religious system lay with the convert in a way that such proof was not demanded of those who remained within the Church of their birth. This is a sentiment that he shared with Keble.

One of his main contentions against the Roman Catholic Church, one which that Church would have immediately rejected, was that it had 'subjected its polity to an unprimitive jurisdiction, and has surrounded its creed with an encrustation of elements which were at least foreign to the belief of the Early Church.'[7] This was a very Tractarian way of describing what Liddon perceived to be a departure from the primitive ideal of the Church as founded by Christ; it had been a gradual process, but to Liddon's mind it was conclusively demonstrated by the necessity for such theories as Newman's doctrine of development which was 'an hypothesis to account for a difficulty.'[8] Newman's theory had been refined during his last months as an Anglican and was an endeavour to show how he had, without inconsistency, come to accept the teaching and practices of contemporary Roman Catholicism. Liddon saw that although it served to satisfy the Cardinal's mind, it could be used to 'serve other causes, ancient and modern, at least as well as that of the Church of Rome.' However, Liddon offered no alternative theory to accommodate intellectual change. It seems that he did not have the flexibility of mind to do so. This was also a cause of his increasing distress in other areas of theological controversy, such as the problems which *Essays and Reviews* and *Lux Mundi* posed for him. What concerned him at this point was his contention that the Church of Rome's most significant departure from the beliefs of the early Church was the developed doctrine of the Papacy. Liddon was able, without doing violence to his own regard for Scripture, to answer the Roman Catholic argument which seeks to establish that not merely the primacy, but also that the supremacy of the Pope, is based upon a legitimate interpretation of our Lord's words to St Peter. Liddon dealt with this with considerable subtlety when it is remembered that the Eastern Churches also reject the doctrine of the primacy of St Peter. He did so in the important Preface to the sermon 'A Father in Christ,' which was published in pamphlet form in 1885. The sermon was preached at the consecration of Edward King and Edward Bickersteth as, respectively, Bishops of Lincoln and of Exeter. It was King who invited Liddon to preach, and the sermon attracted some controversy at the time, although Bickersteth generously said that he was happy with it. The publication added to the dispute and eventually a second edition was issued. This was preceded by a lengthy preface which Liddon wrote in reply to the strictures delivered by Edwin Hatch, a liberal theologian who had delivered the Bampton Lectures in 1880 on *The Organisation of the Early Christian Churches*, and who held very different views to Liddon on authority and ministry. Liddon referred, by way of contrast, to two of Christ's statements:

> If He said to one Apostle, 'Thou art Peter, and upon this Rock I will build My Church', He said to another, 'Behold thy Mother'. The occasion of these last words was more solemn, the words in themselves surely were not less solemn, not less ample and suggestive, than was the great saying to Peter. If our Lord had addressed to St Peter the words which He did address from His Cross to St John, what would not Roman Catholic theologians have made of the unique, unapproachable relation of the Roman Pontiff to the Blessed Virgin Mother, and to the Catholic Church, of which she is unquestionably the foremost type? As it is, do we ever hear, in any quarter, from any divine, that the successors of St John at Ephesus have any relation, whether to our Lord's Virgin Mother or to His Church, which in any way distinguishes them from other Bishops? Plainly here, by universal admission, was a sublime privilege, involving even a higher proof of love and confidence than any vouchsafed to any other apostle, yet strictly limited to the Apostle to whom it was vouchsafed, and in no sense, spiritual or literal, transmitted to his successors. And the Eastern and English Churches do but apply to the words of St Peter the limiting and restricting interpretation which all Catholic Christendom applies to the precept to St John. Undoubtedly a very different interpretation of the words to Peter has for long prevailed in the Churches of the Roman obedience. But the arguments by which this interpretation is shown to be of comparatively late growth, and of less than universal authority, will be as familiar to Dr Hatch as to myself, and, doubtless, not less convincing.

Turning to the related Roman Catholic claim that the 'keys of the kingdom' are held by that Church alone, Liddon continued:

> Our Lord's words, 'I will give thee the Keys of the kingdom of heaven,' and, 'Feed My sheep', addressed to Peter, may be interpreted, as indeed they are commonly interpreted by our divines, not of any unshared prerogatives of Peter, but either of functions belonging to that whole Apostolate which Peter, as *primus inter pares*, unquestionably represented, or else of the ministerial rela-

tion of an Apostle to the Church, which Peter forfeited by his fall, and which he recovered on his repentance. Those who contend that Peter, alone among the apostles, held 'the keys of the kingdom of heaven' ought to go on to maintain that the other Apostles were never made High Stewards of the Household of Christ. Of this Stewardship the key was the badge or symbol; and as soon as its import is thus stated, the question whether the other Apostles had the power of the keys is practically at an end.

Liddon believed the not unquestioned, but common High Anglican view, that the See of Rome properly and undeniably enjoys a primacy of honour, if not order, in the Western Church. The difficulties arose when the Papacy assumed too much to itself. In a letter 'To a Lady', written in 1872 and quoted in this anonymous way by Johnston, Liddon wrote:

> As to the separation of the sixteenth century: it would never have taken place if the Pope had been content with the position of 'Western Patriarch'. It was because he claimed supremacy towards the whole Catholic Church that the Reformation became possible.

This is obviously an over-simplification of a complex series of events, but Liddon felt that it was arguable, and it is a point which he made again on a number of occasions. He further maintained that the divine origin of the episcopate is not ineluctably bound to the modern Roman concept of the Papacy and in fact pre-dates it by some centuries.[9] He cited, in support of his view, the existence of 'ninety millions of Eastern Christians' who, with the best English divines, have always accepted that the first premiss (the divine origin of the episcopate) is correct, while they have rejected the latter regarding the Papal supremacy.

A third ground upon which Liddon rejected the doctrine of Papal supremacy was that it was based, in part at least, upon documentary evidence which is now known to be forged. This objection was not one that occurred to Liddon alone. It was a standard criticism of the whole basis of the doctrine of papal supremacy. As such it was used not only by catholic-minded Anglicans, but also by members of the Roman Catholic Church who were opposed to ultramontanism. Liddon referred to the problem almost in passing in his final Bampton Lecture. It had originated in the year 865 when Pope Nicholas I, generally thought to have been aware that the documents were indeed forgeries, used the False Decretals attributed to St Isidore of Seville, 'to justify and extend the then advancing claims of the Roman Chair.' Liddon's criticism was based on the identification of a dilemma at the heart of the Papal claims; either the Pope knew the documents to be forged, or he did not. In the first place his supremacy was undermined because he was dishonest; in the second it was undermined because his judgement was faulty. In his reference to the pseudo-Isidoran Decretals, Liddon went on to say that although charity demands that we accept that Pope Nicholas I acted in good faith, such a belief 'is of course fatal to any belief in the personal infallibility of Pope Nicholas I.'[10] Indeed, this is not the only example where the behaviour or attitudes of the occupants of the Papal throne was a cause of embarrassment to the ultramontanes. Many years later, he waspishly observed, in a remark which summarised his whole attitude to the doctrine of papal infallibility, 'Rome, by her own act has recently condemned herself to the task of advocating the equal infallibility of a long line of self-contradicting Popes.'[11] Either way the concept of supremacy, particularly as it was being promoted in the nineteenth century was, he contended, very seriously damaged.

When he turned from the question of the supremacy of the Pope to that of Papal infallibility, Liddon realised that the doctrine of the supremacy was, in fact, a necessary pre-condition to the definition made by the Vatican Council of 1870. In this he was following Keble who, Liddon observed, had said 'that when the Immaculate Conception was defined to be a doctrine of the Christian faith by the Pope [in 1854], without a Council, the Pope's infallibility was also implicitly assumed to be an indisputable doctrine of the Roman Catholic Church.' A major protagonist in England on behalf of ultra-montanism was Henry Manning, the former Anglican archdeacon who had converted to Roman Catholicism following the Gorham case, and who rose to eminence as Cardinal Archbishop of Westminster. Liddon referred to an epigram of Dr Pusey's which indicated the immensity of the gulf between the belief of the early Church and the modern concept of Papal infallibility held by Manning and his friends: 'as Dr Pusey used to say, "If St Augustine had believed about the Pope as Cardinal Manning does, his conduct would have been very sinful."'

The gradual process of Papal aggrandizement, as Liddon perceived it, contributed to the view which catholic-minded Anglicans shared with their non-Roman co-religionists that any meaningful *rapprochement* with Rome was impossible until the Vatican abandoned a version of catholicism that is self-defining. He would have approved of T. T. Carter's harsh assessment that the individual Roman Catholic had to endure a 'shifting' faith: . . . most literally a member of the Church of Rome cannot tell today what he may be required to believe tomorrow.' Liddon would have agreed whole-heartedly with a remark that Charles Gore made in 1923 that 'Catholicism is the original Christianity of the New Testament,' and he would have further claimed that attempts to modify that original catholicism, in the way that he believed the Church of Rome to have done, was actually sinful. There was more than a hint of this at the second Bonn Conference, in 1875, when J. J. I. Von Döllinger[12] declared that the blame for the breaks within Western Christendom at the Reformation, especially in Germany and England, properly lay at the feet of the Papacy, and Liddon himself wrote in 1868:

> It is not the fault of England that she is out of the pale of Rome; it is the fault of Rome insisting upon uncatholic terms of communion. The divorce question of [King] Henry [VIII] and the rabid Calvinism of Edward's advisers had been ended by the reconciliation under Mary. With Elizabeth the wound was re-opened; and the excommunication of England by [Pope] Pius V [died 1572] was simply due to the self-asserting spirit of the Supremacy, resolved, at all costs, to maintain an autocratic authority in the West.[13]

The Elizabethan Settlement and its political consequences curtailed the Papal ambitions in England, and had thus been of 'substantial service to the Christian faith' as had the Reformation. Here Liddon was following Pusey who never deprecated the Reformers and their work. Further, he never regarded the Reformation as a mere incident in Church history as did Keble and Newman.

In addition to his rejection of the claims which the Papacy made about itself, Liddon was also unable to accept the teaching of the Roman Catholic Church with regard to the Blessed Virgin. He willingly and naturally accepted her high place in catholic theology as 'our Lord's Blessed Mother,' but believed that the nineteenth century Roman Catholic attitude to her was 'altogether different from her place in the mind of catholic antiquity.' Conversely, he did feel that Protestants ignored the Virgin, but he did not address that problem. As always, it was the practice of catholic antiquity which determined his approach and attitude. He agreed with Bishop Walter Kerr Hamilton's view that it was 'safer' to keep close to the Lord Christ and not to reduce one's devotion to God by an unnecessarily strong attachment to one of his servants, however illustrious in the economy of revelation. In this he was in accord with the feelings of the Oxford Movement generally. A modern writer has observed:

it is clear that a renewal of devotion to Mary, indeed a new development of that devotion, is something which comes from the very heart of the faith and prayer of the Oxford Movement.[14]

Generally, however, he tended to remain silent on the subject of Anglican devotion to the Blessed Virgin, except for his short course of sermons published with the title, *The Magnificat,* (1890) but even these steer a course of blameless discretion.

During Liddon's lifetime, the Roman Catholic Church held as another pious opinion the belief that the Blessed Virgin Mary, at the end of her earthly life, was in body and soul assumed into heavenly glory. Although it was known in the fourth century, it is thought that the belief was unknown to the earliest Church, but by the nineteenth century the Roman Catholic Church had accorded to it a 'devotional expression which rivals Easter Day itself (in the Breviary) in its rank and form.'[15] Liddon himself felt the attraction of the liturgical ceremonies by which the belief was celebrated, describing those ceremonies as, 'supposing it to be justifiable, exceedingly beautiful.' However the aesthetic appeal of the celebration did not overcome his theological judgement and, in a University Sermon preached in 1879, he questioned the origins of the festival in a classically Anglican fashion 'on what does it all rest? . . . Certainly on nothing in Holy Scripture . . . and Antiquity, properly so called, is no less silent . . . It is a pious superstition of a later age, without any proof of a real historic basis.' Privately, Liddon trenchantly recorded his true feeling: 'I confess to you that I never pass the Festival of the Assumption (15 August) without being thankful that I am not a Roman Catholic.'[16]

The dogma of the Immaculate Conception of the Blessed Virgin Mary was proclaimed in the Bull *Ineffabilis Deus* of Pius IX on 8 December 1854, a little more than two years after Liddon's audience. Prior to the Bull, the doctrine had been held by some Roman Catholics as a 'pious opinion.' The effect of the proclamation was to elevate the opinion to the status of a dogma necessary for salvation. However, even when it was no more than a pious opinion the doctrine had not been accepted by all Roman Catholics. Some of its ablest and utterly orthodox theologians had at one time strenuously resisted it, as Liddon had noted in his Bampton Lectures.[17] For Liddon the proclamation had the effect of deepening and dramatising the gulf between catholicism as he understood it, and the Roman Catholic Church. On 25 January 1884, he recorded in his diary an interview with Mr W. Paget, who had recently left the Roman Catholic Church. The entry concluded, 'the Immaculate Conception either was, or was not a fact – either revealed as a fact or not, and not to be settled as might be a question of interpreting language one way or the other.' It is not entirely clear from the context whether Liddon was merely recording the opinion of Paget, although the phraseology used is typical of himself and there is no doubt that he did reject the new dogma on the grounds which the diary describes. At the Conference on reunion which Döllinger called in 1874 at Bonn, Liddon tried, however, to act as a moderating influence when 'Thesis Ten,' which rejected the doctrine of the Immaculate Conception, was debated. He proposed that the Thesis, as the topics for discussion were called, be amended to include the statement that it rejected as 'an article of faith the new Roman doctrine;' this would have softened the content of the thesis in order to make allowance for those who rejected it as a dogma, but who continued to hold it as a pious opinion. He said, 'I myself reject it whether as a dogma or as a pious opinion, but in the interest of liberty I feel bound to make this suggestion.'

Turning from specific dogmas, it is apparent that Liddon's criticism of the Roman Church also sprang from the Tractarian conviction that it was corrupt. However, he knew that 'beyond all doubt' the Church of Rome is a true part of the Catholic Church of Christ. As such it was entirely appropriate that properly catholic-minded English Churchmen should look upon reunion with Rome as a natural and sensible goal. Indeed, Liddon in the University Sermon which has already been quoted, gave expression to the hope that

> though it be against appearances, that a day may come when she, the largest division of the Christian Church ... may virtually abandon untenable positions, without forfeiture of her historic continuity, and that she may ... undertake to reunite the scattered worshippers of the Redeemer in one visible fold.[18]

However, Liddon's ecumenical enthusiasm, like that of other High Churchmen who were not Romanists, was tempered by the fact that he was unable, as a loyal member of the Church of England, to accept Rome's often-repeated belief that it alone on earth is the Church of the Christ. Further, in 1885, he went so far as to maintain, '...in view of Antiquity, the proposition that not to be in communion with the See of Rome is necessarily to be outside the pale of Catholic Communion cannot he maintained except by interpreting Antiquity by the exigencies of a theory of the principle of Unity which is relatively modern.'[19] Thus he believed, as he stated in the memoir of Bishop Hamilton, the catholic unity which the Roman Church claimed exclusively to preserve and demonstrate was, in fact, a spurious unity. It was, he said, achieved only after a redefinition by Rome of the meaning of the term following the schism between East and West and after the Reformation in Europe. Thus it was a sure conviction of Liddon's that the Church of Rome could not legitimately claim the submission of all who sought to be catholic Christians. In this conviction he was holding fast to one of the original Tractarian insights.

In handling the problem of the claims for itself put forward by the Roman Catholic Church, Liddon's personal experience reinforced his intellectual convictions, and he came to believe that there was no real future for the Church of England in relation to eventual reunion with the Roman Catholic Church. Indeed, Bishop John Wordsworth of Salisbury writing an obituary in his Diocesan Gazette, perceptively recognised that Liddon's belief was

> that the Roman claims, especially since the Vatican Council [but by inference before it also], were so obviously at variance with revelation and history that we might hope that people's eyes would gradually be opened as to the necessity of reform.

The situation with regard to reunion with the Church of Rome remained difficult as the nineteenth century wore on, because, convinced that it is the one true Church, the Roman Catholic Church further believed itself empowered, as we have seen, to promulgate additional dogmas as necessary to salvation. To Liddon, as to his Tractarian mentors and to those who followed his own lead, and indeed also to the Eastern Churches as well as the Anglican communion, such a practice was wholly unacceptable. Preaching on 'The Law of Progress,' Liddon emphatically asserted that 'the number of Christian doctrines cannot really be added to'. He readily accepted the need to state doctrines differently in different ages, 'new statements may be necessary to meet new modes of thought, or fresh forms of evasion, or virtual denials of Original Truth', but the gospel as it was 'taught by the Apostles was a final and perfect revelation.' The practical outcome of the Roman Catholic attitude was fatal to the possibility of unity between all Christians in one great Catholic Church. With Rome as it was, unity, ever a remote prospect, was indefinitely postponed; 'The shores of Italy,' as Pusey once said, seemed to be 'perpetually receding.'[20]

Although Roman Catholicism dominated the thinking of Anglo-Catholics in the nineteenth century, not least because they were often accused of imitating it or promoting its theology, it would be inaccurate to assume that theologians such as Liddon gave no thought to other Christian traditions. The decrees of the Vatican Council of 1870 led to a number of excommunications, most notably that of Döllinger, and caused others to leave of their own accord, and these events culminated in the formation of the Old Catholic Churches. Liddon's work with them was his most significant contribution to Christian unity, but it has been largely overlooked when his career has been assessed. He was an important member of an unofficial group of Anglicans who were the first to be involved in serious ecumenical work. The two Conferences at Bonn which he attended, in 1874 and 1875, and which have already been mentioned in passing, brought together 'for the first time, Latin, Anglican, and Orthodox theologians . . . to discuss the differences which separated them,' as C. B. Moss noticed in his significant book, *The Old Catholic Movement, its Origins and History*, published in 1948.

The Old Catholic Church was brought into being as a separate communion by the Union of Utrecht in 1889 but this was merely the culmination of a process that had begun almost twenty years before. The separations from Rome which were largely to form the Old Catholic Church were a reaction to the intractable nature of the Ultramontane movement within the Roman Catholic Church, for although many German Roman Catholics felt able to accept the dogma of Infallibility (particularly with its restrictions to declarations made 'ex cathedra'), there were a number who could not accept the new doctrine at all. In the end the Ultramontanists at the First Vatican Council in 1870 were able to rely on the support of five hundred of the seven hundred members who remained behind for the vote. Among the most distinguished of those who could not support the new doctrine was J. J. I. Von Döllinger, the theologian and historian who was known to a small number of High Anglicans. He had met T. T. Carter in 1873 and Liddon had made his acquaintance at Munich in 1871 while on his annual holiday. Döllinger became a focal figure among the dissentients, although his role in the movement was somewhat ambivalent. Liddon, in a private letter to Charles Lindley Wood, written shortly after he met the German for the first time, described him as very unhappy about an 'addition to and innovation upon the ancient Deposit of the Church', which the decree of the Vatican Council seemed to him to represent. Döllinger did not want to separate from the Church of Rome and was not interested, in his own words to Liddon, in 'setting up another denomination' and he 'had no desire whatever to repeat or extend the work of Luther.' However, his reluctance to move was not recognised by his superiors and, because of his refusal to submit, he was excommunicated by Archbishop Scherr of Munich in 1871. Two years later, in 1873, a meeting was held at Cologne of those who felt compelled to separate themselves from 'the doctrinal aberrations of the Bishop of Rome', but not 'from the communion of catholic Christendom.'[21] Döllinger was not present at that meeting, but interestingly there were some Anglican observers including C. F. Lowder, Vicar of St Peter's, London Docks and a renowned ritualist, and also J. S. Howson who was Dean of Chester from 1867 to 1885. Also present was E. S. Talbot, the Warden of Keble College, and also the Bishop of Winchester, E. H. Browne. As a result of this gathering, committees for reunion were set up. The Germans joined forces with the Dutch Jansenists and the body which was eventually to be the Old Catholic Church was formed. It is conventional to refer to this group as Old Catholics, even prior to the Union of Utrecht. The new communion was not merely a negative body; it did reject the Papal claims but decided to use the vernacular in worship, made sacramental confession voluntary, later permitted clergy to marry, and in 1996 the German branch went ahead with the ordination of women to the priesthood. The early developments should have been of acute interest to catholic Anglicans and Liddon was one of the small number who did respond. Liddon, who later could not remember exactly when it arrived, received a personal invitation to the Conference on Reunion which the Old Catholics called in September 1874. He wrote in his diary 'heard from Dr Döllinger inviting me to the Conference at Bonn. Wish to accept the invitation.' Part of his desire to accept was due to his regard for Döllinger. Years later he said, 'he teaches me more about men and books than anybody else I meet with now.' The Conference, it was hoped, would be an important first step towards eventual catholic unity, but there were great difficulties confronting the participants in such a unique venture. Moss says that modern scholars can see 'that the difficulties were greater than they [the participants] realised, and that the *imponderabilia* were scarcely recognised at all.'[22] But this generalisation cannot be applied to Liddon; his doubts and questions were certainly part of the *imponderabilia*, as an undated note in the St Edmund Hall papers reveals:

Queries on Invitation to Bonn Conference:
(1) What definite propositions would you lay before the Conference if present?
(2) What possible steps do you consider *practical* and feasible towards reaching the desired [illegible]
(3) What conditions would you accept as needful, or very desirable, for 'Restoration of Church Fellowship' between members present at Bonn?[23]

Despite the difficulties, the Conferences were important because, as Moss also observed,

> The Old Catholic leaders had no wish to confine their work to the section of Latin Christendom which rejected the Vatican Council. They perceived that their separation from the Papacy made possible the healing of the wounds in the unity of Christendom which had been open for centuries; and they intended the conferences at Bonn to lead to reunion both with the 'Oriental' and with the Anglican Churches.[24]

The Roman Catholic Church had vigorously criticised the actions of Döllinger and his friends. Liddon sought to protect them, and the concept of a Catholicism which was non-Roman, by refuting the suggestion that the Old Catholic leaders were merely 'religious adventurers who are trying their hands at the creation of "a new Church."'[25] Döllinger, as Liddon had reported to Lord Halifax, was most anxious not to create anything that resembled a new Church, but the meetings that preceded the two Bonn Conferences as well as the Conferences themselves, were in fact the beginning of the process by which the protest against ultramontanism became institutionalised. Whether Liddon and the Old Catholics themselves really recognised this is unlikely, for they argued that nothing new had been created at all. What the Old Catholics sought was a return to the primitive catholicism which was held by all Christians prior to the Great Schism between the Eastern and Western branches of Christendom in 1054, an idea that was close to the heart of Liddon and of the original Tractarians. Thus, as Liddon wrote in the important Preface to the 1874 Conference Report, they were 'strong in their faithfulness to the traditions of a better age', and were simply 'left behind by the fanatical impetuosity of an innovating Church.' Liddon's language was strong, but there could be no doubt of his sincerity, and he was totally convinced that the Old Catholics were doctrinally, and indeed spiritually, correct in their stance. He also recognised the possible consequences for the Church of England although he seems to have been almost alone in this. What the Conference at Bonn offered to the Anglican Communion was an opportunity, unique since the Reformation schisms, of possible intercommunion between the Church of England and a body

> Catholic, yet not papal; episcopal, with no shadow of doubt or prejudice resting on the validity of its orders; friendly with the orthodox East, yet free from the stiffness and one-sidedness of an

isolated tradition; sympathising with all that is thorough and honest in the critical methods of Protestant Germany, yet holding on firmly and strenuously to the faith of antiquity.[26]

This powerfully expressed, and clear-sighted statement was made by Liddon in his lengthy Preface to the Report of the 1874 Conference. Liddon made himself responsible for the English translation of the reports of both Conferences. Although he did not do the actual work himself, he did contribute a valuable Preface to each.

The aim of the Bonn Conference was intercommunion and reunion between branches of the Catholic Church which had previously been separated, but Liddon knew that this was not likely to be possible, although 'if we do not altogether succeed, something may be attempted for the honour of the Lord.' The greatest practical achievement in Liddon's eyes, however, lay in Döllinger's statement about the catastrophic nature of the schism between East and West, and in Döllinger's eventual declaration that he had 'no manner of doubt as to the validity of the Episcopal succession in the English Church.' This statement was supremely important to Liddon, and he recorded it verbatim in the Report.

The ultimate achievement of the two Conferences, however, was reduced by at least two factors. Of these the least significant, comparatively, was that, in an attempt to widen its appeal, the second Conference was convened by general invitation and was consequently much larger and less effective. Indeed, W. E. Gladstone, in a private letter to Döllinger in August 1875, had been 'very anxious about the personell of the English representation; and fearful lest the quantity should exceed the quality.' The chief reason for a low level of achievement was that no participants attended as representatives of their Churches, but were merely there as interested private individuals. Finally, it was planned to hold at least one more gathering, but the 1876 arrangements were abandoned because of the deteriorating political situation in Europe. No subsequent plans were made. Döllinger did hope to start the process again later on, but Liddon was one who advised against it.

The Conferences were a remarkable initiative, and it is unfortunate that they came to nothing and that their Reports, with Liddon's Prefaces, are now forgotten. The potential that Liddon glimpsed was never realised. He continued to be interested in the activities of the Old Catholics, but his opinion of them became less sanguine as the years passed, largely because of the conservative nature of his own temperament. Johnston quoted from a letter which Liddon wrote on 20 February 1888:

During the last ten years there have been considerable changes in the Old Catholic body. In more than one way they have abandoned the position in which they found themselves in 1870, after the Vatican Definition. Their abandonment of clerical celibacy has alienated Dr Döllinger and Professor Reusch; and the lay element in their Synods, in itself anomalous, is, for those who know something of the ingredients which compose it, a matter for anxiety. I should fear that it may mean that they are drifting, or likely to drift. I have never doubted that they were right in making the stand they did in 1870, but I confess that I do not feel as hopeful as I then did about their future.

And there the matter lay for many years after Liddon's death. But the Anglican Communion as a whole did not reject the Old Catholics. Formal contact between the two Churches led to the Old Catholics' acknowledgement of Anglican orders in 1925. Full inter-communion was achieved in 1931, and one of Liddon's ecumenical ambitions was thus fulfilled but not until more than fifty years after his perceptive involvement.

The question of Anglican relations with the Eastern Church was a far less emotive matter for a Churchman in Liddon's position to discuss and write about. An interest in Eastern Orthodoxy was relatively unusual in Liddon's day, and it seems likely that he owed his concern to Bishop Hamilton of Salisbury. Indeed in his memoir of the Bishop, Liddon drew attention to, in Hamilton's words, 'The attempts which Convocation had sanctioned to enter into friendly relations with the Eastern Church.' These contacts, however, had been few and far between, and Eastern Christianity remained outside the purview of most Anglicans. It is noteworthy that Liddon's own attitude to the Eastern Church is one of the relatively few instances where it is possible to record a definite change in his thinking. During his Continental tour in 1852 it seems that he encountered Eastern Orthodoxy for the first time. He wrote in his diary on 19 September, 'Certainly the Greek ritual, beautiful as it is on paper, does not impress me in action. It is very stiff and Jewish. It does look just as though the Church had been paralysed and stereotyped at a particular phase of her existence.' This reaction reveals something of the prejudices of Liddon's early background for as Georges Florovsky observed, 'Protestants tended to be unfavourably impressed by the ritualistic character of the [Eastern] Church, which they would describe as superstitious and even idolatrous.'[27] A little over a month later, however, the diary records the beginning of a change of heart. On 24 October, Liddon amended his criticism of

what he called the 'Jewish' nature of the Greek liturgy by writing
'... more correctly of its oriental nature' and he realised that it
'requires a much more intimate appreciation of Eastern habits and
ceremonies than I possess, to duly appreciate it.' Liddon's ignorance
at this point was no more than typical of members of the Church of
England, even of those who adhered to the principles of the Oxford
Movement but he was not typical in his efforts to dispel his ignorance, nor in his subsequent interest in Eastern Christianity. The
Tractarians were instrumental in bringing about a change, among
them William Palmer of Magdalen College who visited Russia in
1840 and 1842. However, it was John Mason Neale, who was known
to Liddon, who was the first nineteenth-century theologian in
England to develop a true regard for Eastern Orthodoxy. Neale was
an Anglo-Catholic of great learning. He was a priest, an author, a
hymn writer and translator, an expert on ecclesiastical architecture
and the founder of a religious order for women. In 1847 he began to
publish a very large *History of the Holy Eastern Church.*[28] The first
part dealt with the history of the Patriarchate of Antioch, but in 1850
he published the general introduction to the work in a volume of
more than 1,200 pages. Neale's *History* was a large and technical
work, but at a more popular level, particularly through the translation
of hymns, he began to bring the Eastern Churches to the attention of
ordinary Englishmen. On his initiative the Eastern Churches
Association was founded in 1863 and Liddon was a member from its
early days, serving as a member of the founding committee. The
main objectives of the Association were: (i) the education of Anglican
Churchmen on the subject of the Orthodox Churches (ii) the promotion of friendly intercourse between Anglicans and Orthodox (iii) the
financial assistance, where possible, of Orthodox Bishops. Other
members of the committee included the Hon C. L. Wood [later Lord
Halifax], T. T. Carter and John Wordsworth (later Bishop of
Salisbury), thus Liddon once again was numbered among a small
group of far-sighted theologians.

In 1867, when he visited Russia in the company of C. L. Dodgson,
Liddon took full advantage of that unique opportunity to obtain a
fuller knowledge of Eastern Christianity. At this time Liddon's
earlier criticism of the excessively formalist nature of the Eastern
liturgy as a whole was finally reversed, as he told William Bright, 'I
cannot understand anyone coming here and saying that the Eastern
Church is a petrification. Right or wrong, it is a vast, energetic, and
most powerful body... to which I believe there is no moral parallel
in the West.'[29] It has been noted that when Liddon met Bishop
Leonide, the suffragan bishop in Moscow, the two men achieved a

rapport which enabled Liddon to learn a great deal about Eastern Christianity, and to act as a kind of unofficial ambassador for Anglicanism. In an important letter of 14 August 1867 to the Bishop of Salisbury he reported that Leonide had urged him to have the Catechism from the *Book of Common Prayer* translated into Russian 'with notes, in order to point out its fundamental agreement with the Orthodox doctrine. And the English Ordinal in like manner.' For his part, Leonide was willing to circulate such documents among his clergy in order to improve understanding between the two communions. Whether this suggestion was carried out is not recorded, and therefore it seems unlikely that anything happened. However, in addition to Leonide's obvious goodwill with regard to his own personal contact with Liddon, there was the introduction to Philaret the Metropolitan of Moscow, 'probably the greatest theologian of the Russian Church in modern times.'[30] He was an exemplary bishop, a good administrator, a renowned preacher and theologian. Liddon wrote a lengthy account of the interview in a letter to Bishop Hamilton, which Johnston reproduced. It reveals that Liddon was able to make a valid contribution of his own to ecumenical affairs at a time when such work was not only unfashionable but was also unpopular among many Church members.[31]

In later life, Liddon's middle-eastern tour extended his knowledge of the Orthodox churches and increased the numbers of his contacts among them. The tour took place in the winter of 1885–6, and a full account of it was published by Liddon's sister, Annie King, a year after his death. Mrs King had accompanied him on the tour and her account is simply a collection of her letters home, but it is very comprehensive and provides valuable insights into Liddon's thinking. The book bears the title *Dr Liddon's Tour in Egypt and Palestine* and describes how he saw the work of the Church in Palestine in particular and came to the conclusion that the Anglican and Roman communions were each 'an exotic' in Jerusalem, as in St Petersburg.

Despite the relative doctrinal similarities between Anglicanism, Roman Catholicism and Eastern Orthodoxy, Liddon felt that the Eastern Churches had few friends among Western Christians. Protestantism resented Eastern sacramentalism, Rome resented the rejection of the Papal supremacy, and both despised what they believed to be Orthodoxy's excessive rigidity. However, it was the concept of supremacy on which the relationship between the West and the East had foundered. It was alleged in the Bonn Conference Report of 1874 that the Church of Rome, through the ambitions of the papacy, had pushed Orthodoxy into the present state of schism. Döllinger, at the same Conference also took this view and catalogued the historical processes behind the Great Schism, placing most of the blame upon the Roman West, an attitude that was in tune with Liddon's own opinion. Döllinger further claimed that, with the proclamation of Papal infallibility in 1870, Pius IX 'at one blow . . . transformed the eighty million Eastern Christians, who until then had been only schismatics, into formal heretics who denied a fundamental doctrine of Christianity – the doctrine of the absolute sovereignty and infallibility of the Pope.'[32] Despite the exacerbation of the disagreement between East and West which the doctrine of infallibility therefore represented, Liddon perceptively noticed that each side had always had a 'bad conscience' on the subject of Christian disunity. This was not reduced in any way, even by the most strenuous efforts at self-justification, and the failure of efforts to draw the two branches of the Church together, especially the Council of Florence (1438–1445), had added to the sense of the moral necessity of reunion.

The further schisms within Western Christendom at the Reformation had also left what Liddon, in common with many nineteenth century High Anglicans, believed to be an unsatisfactory state of affairs, but it had at the same time enabled a link to develop between Anglicanism and the Eastern communions. This link had not been at all formal, but had existed at least from the time of the Caroline divines and the Non-jurors. It was derived from a shared rejection of papal ambitions. 'Between the English Church and the East there had been an indefinite feeling of sympathy, ever since the Anglican Episcopate had repudiated the usurped supremacy of Rome,' was how Liddon described it in the Preface to the 1874 Bonn Conference Report. It was this feeling of sympathy which Bishop Hamilton had longed to build upon, and Liddon took up the same idea. With the experience gained from continental travel, he was unable to conceal from himself that this sympathy remained rather tentative, and he was acutely aware, as were the Eastern Christians with whom he spoke, that there are distinct differences between the two communions. In the record of his trip to Russia, he noted with obvious regret that the Russian Church 'reinforces Rome in the cultus of the B.V.M.' Most of his observations regarding the differences between the Eastern Churches and Anglicanism, however, are concerned with the former's doubts and problems regarding the Church of England. The reason for this is that the English Church had never doubted the catholicity of Eastern Christianity, but the Orthodox were rather less sure about Anglicanism; indeed Bishop Leonide, Philaret's suffragan in Moscow, 'gently hinted that our loyalty to our rule of primitive antiquity was not as complete either in theory or, still more, in practice, as might be wished.' The most significant area of doubt for the Easterns was the validity of Anglican orders, but interestingly Liddon was able to write that even Bishop Leonide had 'no doubt, I think, about the validity of our Orders.' Professor Rhossis, of the theological Seminary at Rhigarim and Student at the University of Athens, however, was not so sanguine. At the Bonn Conference of 1874, he declared that the question of episcopal succession in the English Church, and therefore the validity of the Church of England's Orders, had not yet been determined by the Greek Church. Liddon regretted that the Russians, at least in the person of Metropolitan Philaret, tended to rest their 'opinion of the consecrations during the reign of Queen Elizabeth simply on the testimony of Roman Catholic writers.' Liddon reported this to the 1874 Bonn Conference, explaining that it came from Philaret himself.

One important theological problem of which Liddon was acutely aware was not, however, confined to the differences between Anglicanism and Orthodoxy, but focused the whole schism between East and West. This was the Western use, in the Nicene Creed, of the Filioque clause. The clause in the Creed refers to the 'procession' of the Holy Spirit 'from the Father,' and in the Western Church, *'and the Son.'* The latter phrase was unacceptable to the Eastern Christians. In the second meeting of the 1874 Bonn Conference, Döllinger summarised the history of the clause and declared that its universal use in the West had 'led to a rupture between East and West, and inflicted a wound on the unity of the Church.' Here Döllinger was merely repeating the conventional view of the Eastern Churches which, since the time of the ninth century Patriarch Photius of Constantinople, had used the clause as a chief ground of the Orthodox attack on Rome. This, however, is an over-simplification. Liddon at the Conference in 1875 refuted the anonymous accusation that the quarrel over the Filioque clause was 'an old fragment of theological metaphysics.' Rather, he said it was a controversy which 'has had consequences which have divided christendom for a thousand years.' To lay all the blame for the Great Schism upon the Western adoption of the Filioque clause in the Nicene Creed would be incorrect. It was, in effect, merely a significant part of a long process. The Church of England was already aware of the reappearance of the problem. Anglican opinion, formulated by such seminal Anglican theologians as Richard Hooker (1554–1600) and Bishop John Pearson, had long accepted the conventional Western use of the clause. However in November 1864 it had been one of a number of matters upon which Philaret had sought information from American Anglicans. The Americans had passed it to the Eastern Churches

Association and John Mason Neale undertook to provide an explanation of the insertion of the clause, but not its doctrine. Similarly, it had figured in the deliberations surrounding the visit to England of Archbishop Lykurgos of the Cyclades in 1869–70. Liddon, as might be expected, was anxious that the clause should be retained, and Pusey was vehement in advising its retention, although the former admitted that it had been 'irregularly' introduced into the Creed. Liddon gave two reasons for its retention. One related directly to the position of the Church of England:

> ... to eject the Filioque from the Western Creed would entail on the English Church certain and serious disaster. It would erect a fresh barrier – and what true Christian would desire this? – between ourselves and the larger portion of Western Christendom. It would introduce, we cannot doubt, confusion of the most painful description into churches of the Anglican Communion ...

His second objection to the excision of the clause was of wider significance. Such an action 'would aggravate in the Western Churches wide-spread uncertainty as to the basis and worth of other creeds.'[33] In his determination to retain the clause he was, as has been noted, at one with Pusey although he thought that the older man was over-reacting to the extent that Liddon dreaded 'lest his arguments should diminish the great authority which was attached to his name.'[34] Liddon's lengthy explanation of his position in the Preface to the Report of the 1875 Bonn Conference is largely a public expression of this. Pusey's own vigorous defence of the Filioque appeared the following year with the title *On the Clause, 'And the Son'*, in the form of a lengthy 'open letter' addressed to Liddon.

In his desire to promote understanding in order to encourage unity between Anglicanism and the Churches of the East, Liddon seems to have restricted himself to modest actions and recommendations. Probably that was all that was possible at the time, but he was, perhaps unwittingly, laying the foundations for the genuine *rapprochement* which has occurred in the twentieth century. The visit to Russia in 1867, as noticed earlier, had coincided with the jubilee of Philaret's consecration to the Episcopate. Liddon and Dodgson had been present at the special celebration of the liturgy which marked the occasion, although they were not able to see as much as they hoped. In his conversation with Philaret, Liddon had taken it upon himself to offer formal congratulations to the Metropolitan. His later action in writing to Bishop Hamilton and to Bishop Mackarness of Oxford, urging them to write short formal letters of congratulation to the Metropolitan, and his request that the latter should ask the Archbishop of Canterbury (Longley) to write similarly, all indicate the importance that he had come to attach to good relations with Eastern Orthodoxy. Another coincidence of his visit to Russia was that it took place in the year of the first Lambeth Conference. Bishop Leonide told Liddon that the Russians were profoundly interested in the proceedings of 'the Synod of Anglican Bishops' which had been summoned by Archbishop Longley.

The third area in which Liddon was active in relation to other Christian Churches was to do with the theological position of non-conformity in England. The first observation to make, and it one which overshadows the whole matter is that Liddon did not much like what he and his contemporaries called 'dissent'. But it was part of English life and the Church of England was obliged to recognise its existence. In fact he went further and was prepared to admit that the behaviour of the Church of England had sometimes been responsible for driving people from its fold, but while deploring this he regretted that such people had allowed subjective feelings to push them into dissenting groups which were outside the embrace of the Church founded by our Lord with his disciples. He readily acknowledged, however, that much non-conformist protest had political roots. As he explained in the Preface to the Report of the Second Bonn Conference (1875):

English dissent has many motives for its existence and activity. Sometimes it is little more than a form of political opposition to the order of social life in England, with which the position of the Established Church is so intimately bound up. Sometimes it is a profoundly religious protest against the strange and deplorable anomaly which still invests secular bodies, whose members may be of any or no religion, with the power of legislating for a purely spiritual society. Sometimes, like the old Montanism,[35] it expresses mistaken yearnings after a higher spirituality; sometimes, like Donatism, it seeks refuge in a private schism from those contrasts of good and evil which ever recur within the fold of the Catholic Church.

Whatever might be the origins of the various forms of non-conformity, Liddon shared the hard-line Anglo-Catholic theological conviction that all dissenting bodies suffered from an inadequate understanding of the nature of the Church. This failure was, in effect, focused in a similarly inadequate concept of the nature of Christian ministry. The episcopate as the basis of ministry is essential to the nature and structure of the Church, as Newman had proclaimed in the first of the *Tracts for the Times*. This standard view of the Tractarians was, of course, held by Liddon and shared with Rome and the Eastern Churches but it was no help to non-conformists and did nothing to improve relations with them.

Liddon emphasised the distinction between election to a Church Office (as he believed to be the non-conformist practice to appoint ministers) and ordination or consecration which is a commission to discharge a ministry bestowed as 'as gift of Jesus Christ . . . through the Bishops who represent him.' Liddon shared the conviction that the only truly valid ministry is that which is based upon the episcopate, and this insight posed insuperable problems with regard to unity between episcopal Churches, such as the Church of England, and the non-conformist bodies. Following the same logic, he believed that the sacraments administered within the dissenting Churches were also invalid with the exception of Baptism. The exception was made in accordance with traditional Catholic order, as Liddon said in a sermon, 'supposing the matter and words of that sacrament to be duly administered; since lay baptism is of undoubted validity.' It is at this point that the uncompromising nature of Liddon's attitude to non-conformity is revealed. His conception of the essential nature of episcopacy would have involved non-conformists in submission to the Church of England, although he did not say so. This was an unlikely prospect and Liddon was held fast in a theological strait-jacket which would have prevented any serious ecumenical achievement, even if the other Christian bodies had been willing to think about it in those days. Liddon's attitude was revealed in an insignificant but amusing letter in which his uncle, John Bilke, teased him about being 'uneasy' when it was declared legally permissible for non-conformist ministers to use the title 'Reverend' in 1876. A more important and practical example of his rigidity is to be found in the fact that he opposed the Burial Laws Amendment Act of 1880. This permitted the burial of non-Anglicans in parochial Churchyards, with or without the reading of the *Book of Common Prayer* burial service, provided that the incumbent of the parish was notified in advance and that any ceremony was Christian. He was on holiday in Vienna at the time the Bill was going through Parliament, and wrote critically about it in a letter to his old friend C. L. Wood. However, the Act did become law and won acceptance with little opposition from Anglo-Catholics or others.

But his belief in the inadequacy of non-conformity did not mean that Liddon was unwilling to admit that real spiritual benefits have been transmitted and received by the ministrations of dissenters. His generosity of nature and his common-sense combined to acknowledge that the non-conformist churches were the recipients of real, but in his view secondary, blessings. He wrote, 'I have no doubt whatever of the excellence of many Dissenting ministers.' This ambivalence about non-conformist ministries was not entirely untypical. A similar position was occupied by Charles Gore a few years later. In his *The Mission of the Church*, published in 1892, he too acknowledged that the fruits of the Holy Spirit are discernible in the ministry of many dissenters, and continued, 'it is impossible for one who thinks seriously to ignore or underrate the vast debt which English Christianity owes to non-conformist bodies, to bodies which have fallen quite outside the action of the apostolic ministry.' He, like Liddon before him, went on to place much of the blame for the present situation on the bad behaviour of the Church.

Liddon readily acknowledged that Presbyterians and Congregationalists who 'stand aloof from the Church or oppose it . . . are often bright examples to many of its professing members.'[36] His personal contacts with Dr R. W. Dale, his contemporary the famous Congregationalist theologian (they usually sent one another complimentary copies of their new publications), reveal Liddon's willingness to accept the friendship of dissenters on a personal level. But personal friendship between individuals was as far as such contacts should go, and he disapproved of a meeting between a group of Anglican clergymen and dissenting ministers at the City Temple which took place in 1875. Informal contacts did not mean that he accepted the theological viewpoint of non-conformist clergy. He believed that '. . . personal character, and the mentally beneficial effect of high personal character upon those who come in contact with it, proves nothing as to the question of Ministerial Commission.'

However, he maintained that friendship could be legitimately employed in helping those of his acquaintances who laboured under difficulties as dissenters but his help was not at all 'ecumenical'. On Palm Sunday 1867 he wrote to Lord Bute, an undergraduate at Christ Church with a Presbyterian background, who was tempted to become a Roman Catholic, encouraging him to be confirmed in the English Church. Bute, who was under twenty-one, would not change until coming of age. Eventually, though, he did convert to Roman Catholicism, but in the meantime Liddon was pleased that he had

resolved to delay a step involving such momentous consequences . . . Of course I do not advise you to remain a Presbyterian. God forbid! But I do think that if you would consider fully and fairly what there is to be said on behalf of the Catholic character of the Church of England...you would see reasons for admitting her claims and so of following the providential leading of your life.[37]

Similarly, his 1874 diary records pastoral and theological support to another young man in a difficult situation. His name was Jenkins and he had been at Christ Church. He dined with Liddon who recorded on 1 December, 'he has a great deal to put up with at home: his parents are rigid dissenters. He hopes to take Holy Orders. On Sundays he is obliged to go to "Chapel" ... morning and evening; and he teaches in the Wesleyan Sunday School ...,' and Liddon concluded mischievously, '... applying High Church doctrines.' At the end of the same month, the diary records that Jenkins received Communion at St Paul's and spent the day with Liddon. It is clear that such an attitude would have been resented by non-conformists, but it remained consistent with Liddon's theological convictions even though these were sometimes at variance with his pastoral experience.

Thus, in his relations to non-conformity, Liddon had a curiously ambivalent attitude. On the one hand he longed for unity between Christians as theologically desirable, but on the other was unable to accept non-episcopal communities as parts of the true Church. This unease, although reflected in his pastoral and personal contacts, is not apparent in his theology of the Church, which remained uncompromising and which ultimately prevented him from taking an imaginative or original line of thought. In his Preface to the Report of the 1874 Bonn Conference, he referred to the 'soreness' of conscience which has existed, not only between East and West since the great schism, but also to that which has been felt by 'all the noblest souls' on each side of the 'chasms' in Western Christianity. Clearly the desire for reunion is in accordance with the will of God, but nothing would be achieved by men who 'have little in common beyond a certain stock of sincere and fervent feeling, and who are content to ignore great and primary questions respecting the Divine Mind and Will.'[38] Liddon believed, of course, that he did not ignore those questions; on the contrary, they were constantly before his mind, but, in effect, they kept him where he was and reduced his work for unity to the status of a feeling of good will which, although sincere and fervent, achieved nothing.

Chapter Seven

Liddon's spirituality

There is an inbuilt ambiguity in examining the spirituality of any priest. On the one hand there is the need to look at those aspects of the spiritual life which informed and produced the person concerned. On the other, there is the task of analysing this within the context of the priest's public ministry. In Liddon's case the two come together, as they should ideally, and the public *persona* reveals much of his inner and personal spirituality. Liddon was utterly convinced that God speaks to the heart and will of every Christian, not just to the intellect. With regard to the clergyman it is necessary that special care is taken to redress any imbalance that has occurred whereby 'his spiritual life at school and college' has failed to keep pace 'with his intellectual life,'[1] an observation that may have been a reflection of his own schooldays at King's College School. This care should ensure that the priest is adequate for his public role. It is an implied criticism of the tradition that a university education on its own was sufficient training for the clergy of the Church of England. Liddon reflected the view that was gaining ground throughout the Church, that the newly-founded theological colleges helped to provide a necessary corrective. At Cuddesdon he had set himself to counter this imbalance between intellectual growth and spirituality by creating circumstances where education and prayer were both seen to be relevant for the future. Another motive was the desire to avoid the situation where theology can be divorced from spirituality, which has sometimes been a tendency in Church in the West. In Liddon himself these two aspects of the Christian life had come together in such a manner that his theology and spirituality were genuinely complementary. He always remembered his mother's warning and was aware of the false nature of such a dichotomy, as is revealed in the observation that even 'bad men . . . have been good theologians' and he cited King Henry VIII as an example. He also referred to some modern journalists who, although hostile to the Christian faith, take a keen and discriminating interest in the affairs of the Christian religion, but who do so from outside the community of faith for reasons that are primarily concerned with the possibility of controversy. Even among believers a frivolous approach is sometimes found. It is possible 'to meet with men who treat their faith as though it were a mental toy; who are never tired of discussing its speculative or controversial bearings.'[2] It was this conviction which made him so critical of the work of both continental and English radical scholars. He tended to interpret their approach to Christianity as being precisely opposite to the attitude which a genuinely devout person should maintain and to be derived from a cynical approach to the inspiration of scripture and the divinity of Christ, combined with a failure to accept the divinely-inspired origin of the Church. This rather simplistic reaction was only partly countered by his willingness to acknowledge the integrity of those whom he opposed. He had a powerful intelligence and was ready to enter upon disputes, and the belligerence with which he often engaged in controversy suggests that sometimes he found it difficult to accept that his opponents were acting from valid motives. The possibility of falling into what he called a 'rationalist' way of thinking was to be vigorously avoided by members of the ordained ministry and by candidates for it, who were urged to set about the cultivation of a properly devout way of life.

This is in accordance with what he saw to be the 'general aim and effect of religion,' which is 'to create in the human soul, first of all, an awe of the Unseen and Almighty God.'[3] Once again the Tractarian understanding of holiness can be seen here, for, he continued, when a man's heart and mind lives in the light of such awe, an irreligious attitude to the Christian faith cannot develop; 'when reverence for God is rooted in the soul, the soul sees God in all that reflects Him on earth, and yields it for His sake appropriate recognition.' Such recognition will issue in a loyalty to God that finds much of its expression in prayer and worship. Prayer was later defined by Liddon, in a Christmas sermon of 1876, as, 'in its broadest sense, an act by which man in seeking God seeks his true Home and Resting-place. And therefore prayer always ennobles a man, not less now than in the early days of history.' Thus it was inevitable that holiness, as understood by Liddon and the Tractarians, would issue in a reverent and devout attitude to life. It was part of the vocation of Liddon and his contemporaries to promote this attitude among Church members. Two sermons preached in St Paul's, with an interval of five years between them, together illustrate Liddon's approach. The first, an Easter sermon dated 27 April 1873, has the simple title 'Reverence' and offered a definition of 'reverence as the sense of truth put in practice,' which is perfectly compatible with love. On the Third Sunday in Advent 1878, Liddon answered the false supposition that reverence is in some way merely 'a kind of professional ornament or accomplishment' for a clergyman. It is a profound virtue in itself which is no mere 'ecclesiastical or religious excellence', but is 'the sincere acknowledgement of a greatness higher than ourselves,'[4] and as such rightly comes to the fore in a man's relationship with God. In the Bampton Lectures, Liddon maintained that the soul can 'hold communion with God in the Life of Light and Righteousness and Love,' but only 'through communion with His Divine Son.'[5] This is because all our prayers, as he lucidly claimed in an Easter sermon many years later, are 'but the language of immortal spirits addressed to One Who has neither beginning nor end.' In practical terms this issued, for Liddon, in endeavours such as that described in his diary on 22 November 1884, when he took his customary walk alone and 'tried to feel thankful to God for all His goodness.' This rather sentimental note found fuller expression in the claim that the sincere Christian is one who consistently works at his spiritual life and is 'found to be making the most of what He has lent, be it much or little.' This is the proper concern of love, and 'it is by such love as this that the Church was built up . . . by thousands of poor men and women, whose hearts were filled with the love of our Lord . . . they lived in the unseen world rather than in this.'[6] For Liddon, the secret prayers of faithful believers were the strength of the Church.

The sermon, 'Our Lord's Example the Strength of His Ministers,' preached in Christ Church Cathedral, Oxford, on 23 December 1860, drew out for the clergy some of the corollaries which relate these generalisations to ministerial work:

> . . . our people have the bible in their hands, and they recognise, even where they cannot describe, the true mien and outline of prophets and apostles. They are not satisfied by a claim to steer the bark of Peter, when the men who handle the Gospel nets are unlike Peter in their whole spirit and bearing. They are keenly alive to the power of holiness . . .[7]

He therefore found himself reiterating the familiar claim that the clergy must be men of prayer if they are to avoid heartless formalism, dryness, and what Liddon, in the sermon quoted above, called 'dearth'. He claimed that there have been many whose lives, however hidden and undramatic, reveal a holiness through which their

intelligence gazes upon Jesus with a faith so clear and strong, whose affection clings to Him with so trustful and so warm an embrace, whose resolution has been so disciplined and braced to serve Him by persevering obedience, that, beyond a doubt, they would joyfully die for Him, if by shedding their blood they could better express their devotion to His person, or lead others to know and to love Him more.

As can be seen from such a passage, there was a clarity and perceptiveness about Liddon's own spirituality which communicated itself to his hearers and readers. It is this quality which made him stand out and which accounted for his popularity as a religious thinker, teacher and, especially, preacher. The passage quoted above comes from the third of Liddon's Bampton Lectures, 'Is The Sermon on The Mount a Dead Letter?' It continued by claiming that the Church of England has been blessed with its share of such pious individuals. He cited as particularly shining examples the non-Juror[8] Bishop Thomas Ken (1637–1711), and also Bishop Wilson who had served in the Isle of Man for fifty-seven years until his death in 1755. Then came a reference to the recently deceased John Keble, who epitomised many others whose names 'have never appeared in the page of history' and who was, in Liddon's far from unique view, a particularly fine example of contemporary clerical holiness.

Central to Liddon's concept of clerical spirituality was the unfailing recitation of Morning and Evening Prayer, 'always and everywhere.' An important part of Liddon's enduring contribution to the life of the Church of England is that he helped to re-establish the clerical practice of daily Matins and Evensong, as required by the *Book of Common Prayer*. This arose from his conviction that the spiritual life of priests must be lived according to rule. Here again is a continuation of the teaching of the Tractarians. Thomas Keble, John Keble's brother, had introduced the 'Daily Service,' as the Tractarians tended to call it, when he became Vicar of Bisley as early as 1827. Newman had followed his example in 1834, when he had been Vicar of St Mary's, Oxford for six years. Owen Chadwick expressed the view that Liddon's conviction about a rule for regular prayer arose because many of the Cuddesdon students cited, as an excuse for doing very little, the dangers of formalised mechanical approaches. They allowed their spiritual life to rest upon sentiment or emotional feelings, he feared. Certainly this is suggested by an ironical sentence in which Liddon referred to people who 'suppose that their prospects of reaching heaven are dependent on the irregularity of the efforts they make while upon earth.' This remark is found in Liddon's long essay, *The Priest in his Inner Life,* written during the period when he worked at the College. It is an unrecognised classic of priestly piety, which is most accessible now as the first item in the still-valuable *Clerical Life and Work*. Taking to himself the conviction expressed by Thomas Keble and Sir George Prevost in *Tracts for the Times, no. 84: Whether a Clergyman be now bound to have Morning ... and Evening Prayer Daily in his Parish Church*, published in 1838, Liddon devoted a significant part of his essay to considering the place which the Daily Offices ought to occupy in the devotional life of the clergy. Liddon's essay is of particular importance because it is a clear statement of Tractarian thinking about the Offices, and it also encapsulates his opinions which remained unchanged; the following draws chiefly upon it. He believed that the consistent use of a set form of prayer was desirable for any one who lives 'perpetually on the vestibule of heaven,' for to approach 'the everlasting God with words of our own, or selections of our own from His Word involves an element of risk.' The nature of the risk is not specified, but he argued that recognition of it would lead to the conviction that the Daily Office is a 'merciful and welcome provision.' This seems to have been Liddon's interpretation of a quotation from Bishop Cosin, a seventeenth century divine who was exiled during the Commonwealth and who later became Bishop of Durham, to which he referred with approval and which led to his next conclusion. Cosin wrote:

> We are to remember that we which are priests are called 'Angeli Domini'; and it is the Angel's office, not only to descend to the people and teach them God's Will, but to ascend to the presence of God to make intercession for the people, and to *carry up the daily prayers of the Church* in their behalf, as here they are bound to do.[9]

Liddon interpreted the phrase 'daily prayers' in the same way that he and the Tractarians used the phrase 'daily service' to refer to the Offices of Morning and Evening Prayer. For Liddon the obligation to offer intercession was a major reason why each priest should persevere with the whole of the Daily Office. It was not significant that he might be alone. Despite his conviction that it really should be said in Church, the possibility that the recitation of the Office could be a more-or-less private thing was in keeping, in Liddon's view, with the English characteristic, shared by the clergy, to be reticent about religious practices. The priest

may be in his chamber, and they [the parishioners] at their several occupations, but, in the Communion of Saints he is acting with them and for them. The Priesthood of the Great Intercessor has descended upon him; and the spirit of that marvellous chapter, St John xvii, is the spirit of the Daily Office.

Miss Muirhouse has left us a description of Liddon reciting the Daily Office alone during the Christmas vacation of 1864 whilst staying in Pembrokeshire:

> His special delight was to say his offices among the rocks. As he stood bareheaded in their depths, the caves would re-echo with the Glorias as he shouted them out, and he would chant Psalm after Psalm of praise, as if nothing could sufficiently satisfy the exuberance of his thankful heart.[10]

The Office is part of the obedience which an ordained man is expected to offer; thus Liddon felt it is inappropriate for him to abbreviate it for the convenience of his family or to encourage lay attendance. The solitary recitation of the Office may also be conscientiously carried out each day without the fact becoming public. An example of the strength of this conviction is to be found in the following passage which is part of a letter which Liddon wrote to a clergyman named Hill:

> I would . . . add an entreaty to you not to give up the daily service because you cannot ring the bell. We – i.e. 'all priests and deacons' – are bound by the Rule of the Prayer Book, to say the daily service, either privately or openly; and it is better for a parish priest to say it in Church than in private; because there his people may join him if they like; or, if they do not, that they may know that he does not forget them in the representative and intercessory service which he offers on their behalf. I have known a case in which the mere knowledge that daily service was regularly offered in Church had an important share in the sanctification of a soul . . .[11]

It is this identification of the praying priest with the work of the Lord that reveals the logic of Liddon's assertion that the offering of the Daily Office is a primary duty for every clergyman. This is so, even for a newly ordained deacon who may find himself in a parish with an 'incompetent Rector' who does not bother with the Offices, and it is also the case for what he charmingly called 'the stalled member of a Cathedral Chapter.' Liddon wrote this essay fourteen years before becoming a Canon at St Paul's, and his diary attests to his commitment to the Daily Office, although in a rather negative way, for he tended to note the occasions when he did not say it. Examples of this kind of entry, however, can only be found infrequently. Other specific references to the Office are most frequently found in the diary during the periods that he was on holiday, presumably because his practice while at home in Oxford or London conformed to a pattern which did not merit recording.

As might be expected from the high value which Liddon placed upon the use of the Daily Office, he had strong views regarding the rubric in the *Book of Common Prayer* which obliges all priests and deacons to recite the Offices 'not being let by sickness, or some other urgent cause'. It was, he said, a clause 'which is not unfrequently understood to amount to a dispensation from observing it altogether.' The reference to it in the letter to Hill in the Lambeth Palace archives, mentioned above, reflects his considered view. In *The Priest in His Inner Life* Liddon also discussed the history of the rubric and claimed that the present wording, introduced in 1662, removes the initiative for failing to recite the Office from the individual priest and 'referred it to the will of God':

> If the history of the rubric be allowed to throw light upon its intention, we cannot doubt that the Church of England, when she last considered the question, deliberately phrased it in a manner which should make the Daily Office a sacred obligation upon all her conscientious ministers when they were not *physically incapacitated* from saying it.[12]

In response to the claim that, despite the unequivocal nature of the rubric, the Daily Office is not merely 'notoriously neglected' but in 'many quarters absolutely ignored,' Liddon maintained that the assertion was exaggerated and that many clergy did quietly persist with its recitation. This was despite the general assertion of Anglo-Catholics that the obligation was often over-looked before the Tractarians reminded the clergy of it. Another objection with which he had to deal in his essay, although he did not say where he encountered it, was the claim that their plural language made the Offices unsuitable for solitary recitation by individual clergymen. He countered this by stressing the fact that the *Sarum Breviary* was congregational in structure and that the Reformers merely passed on a principle that they found. This was entirely valid because it reveals the conviction 'that the fittest devotions for the interceding priest in his closet were precisely those which he would use if he were in choir.' This was further supported by Liddon's belief, in line with catholic spirituality, that a priest is never without a congregation, for all worship is 'in spirit and reality' offered before the 'throne of God.' A third objection to the literal application of the rule that obliges every priest and deacon to say the Daily Office was, according to Liddon, sometimes found in the fact that the obligation was set out in a mere rubric in *The Book of Common Prayer*, and not in the Thirty-nine Articles nor in Canon law. However, and here he was entering controversial ground in view of the battles over ritual that were already on the horizon, he claimed that the priest suffers 'moral injury' if he sets rubrics aside, for they are meant to be authoritative guides; accepting or rejecting the instructions they contain is not a matter of taste.

But the Daily Office was not intended to be just a form of clerical discipline. It has practical applications to the ministry of the individual which Liddon saw to be valuable. The recitation of the Daily Office by the priest 'deepens his familiarity with the words of Scripture, and the formularies of the Church.' This leads to a deepening of his spiritual perception through the provision of material for meditation, and this in turn would make itself felt in his sermons and in his private ministrations. In this way the criticism to which he referred in the opening paragraph of *The Priest in his Inner Life* is answered, in part at least:

> It is a matter for just complaint with candidates for holy orders, that many books which profess to treat of pastoral work address themselves almost exclusively to the external duties of the Christian Priest. They enter at length upon a consideration of such points as the composition of sermons, visiting the sick, schools, ritual; and they continually insist upon the necessity of bringing the inward life to bear upon the discharge of such outward and visible ministries. The existence of an inward life is indeed assumed, but no attempt is made to determine its specific character, or the laws of its formation.

Liddon wrote the essay in 1856. He had been ordained deacon in 1852, so it is likely that he was referring to his own experience. However, he did not enter into any discussion about specific books of the type he criticised. He moved on to the matter of the Daily Office, which he saw as such a valuable tool in equipping the clergy for their pastoral role. In addition he believed that it was of value to the soul of the individual at what might appropriately be called a non-institutional level. He described the structure of the Office in devotional terms, concluding that, by the time the collect of the day is reached, the soul 'is presumably in a condition widely different from that in which it would have been had it not passed through this varied preparation' for such an act of 'formal intercession'. Thus the Office reminds the priest, twice each day, of his relationship to God. In the same way because it is essentially a corporate act, even when recited alone, it also recalls the priest to his relationship with the Church. This was thought by Liddon to be particularly so when travelling because it is on those occasions that a man is 'exposed to the many temptations which occur in the domestic circle or in general society' which may cause him 'to lay aside the keen and collected spirit of an ambassador from heaven.'

At the end of his examination of the place of the Daily Office in the life of the clergy of the Church of England, Liddon revealed his conclusion that the Church requires its clergy to live a disciplined spiritual life that is not unrelated to monastic ideals. He made the important observation that, 'in prescribing for her clergy the daily use of Matins and Evensong,' the Church of England has 'prescribed to them the Religious Life.'[13] This was in accord with the line taken by the authors of *The Tracts for the Times, no. 84*, Thomas Keble and George Prevost, which identified the practice with the ancient traditions of the Catholic Church, seeing that there is nothing 'modern or "new-fangled"' about it. Although for some people such an unvaried routine might seem unreal and formal, the reverse was the case and Liddon felt able to make the highest claims. He claimed about the Daily Office that

> to the living soul of him who bears Christ's commission, it helps to generate that reverent love and piercing knowledge of the Being of Beings which makes men angels, and fits them for eternity.

Liddon also believed that the Daily Offices as prescribed in the *Book of Common Prayer* could be properly supplemented by the minor Offices or 'Hours.' He encouraged his students at Cuddesdon to observe them, and followed the practice himself. In this he had a seminal influence upon High Churchmen, doing more than any other priest to encourage the revival of the minor Offices. This was the verdict of S. C. Carpenter in *Church and People 1789–1889*.[14] In Liddon's diary there is little reference to the minor Offices in later years, and even in the earlier period he did not produce any systematic argument to support their use, as he did with Matins and Evensong. The occasional diary references to the minor Offices reveal that they formed part of his personal underlying pattern of devotion. For example, on 18 March 1862 he spent the evening reading and concluded the entry in his diary that a man named Payne, who is otherwise unidentified, 'has come to me every night for the last ten days to say Compline.' In the 1858 diary he entered three 'Resolutions' on the first blank page. These were drawn up while he was staying at the Hotel de Rhine in Paris on 27 July. The first resolution concerned a commitment to daily spiritual reading 'solely with a view to the salvation of my own soul'; the third was a resolution to visit one poor villager daily, but the second was 'to endeavour faithfully to observe the Lesser Hours'. That this was a resolution that he was already trying to keep is revealed by an entry from earlier in the same holiday period. On 23 July he recorded that he and his unnamed companion had had a full day of sight-seeing and he added, 'today, we have I am glad to say been thoroughly regular about the Hours'.

With regard to his efforts at Cuddesdon, Chadwick recorded:

> He thought that Mattins and Evensong contained so many elements of the medieval offices of Mattins, Lauds and Vespers that to use these might be held to savour of disloyalty to the system of the Church of England. But this hardly applied to Prime and Compline, which only just overlapped with the offices of the Book of Common Prayer; and it did not apply at all to Terce, Sext and None.[15]

That it was his intention to provide more than just the *Book of Common Prayer* Offices in the College was made clear in a letter to Keble, dated 7 November 1854 just a month after taking up his appointment, 'we hope to induce the Bishop to sanction a Midday Service in the chapel; it would be a great help to forming the men on a truly Christian type.' Johnston, after quoting this, continued by remarking that Liddon was successful in his efforts to persuade the Bishop, for by the end of the term a midday Office was permitted and Compline was also allowed three times a week. However, the gradual increase in what Bishop Wilberforce permitted was not destined to continue. On Palm Sunday 1858, the Bishop was in a critical mood when Liddon called in the evening at the Palace. Liddon was first advised to cut off his whiskers and then was told that devotional practices should be changed; most of their conversation was about the college and included 'many particulars' about which the Bishop had received objections but which Liddon did not record. A week later he recorded the Easter Day services and added '*Terce* in chapel at 9. The last we shall ever have!'

Liddon's most systematic and influential efforts with regard to the minor Offices are to be found in the original version of the

Cuddesdon Office Book which provided five such services although this was later reduced to three. He produced the first version in 1856. It was the version that Golightly said was 'concocted' from the canonical services of the Roman Catholic Church. The pamphlet in which Golightly's letter is included also contains the report of the investigatory commission of Wilberforce's Archdeacons, dated February 1858. With regard to the *Office Book,* the commission reported:

> we have to observe, that the Book in use, which is entitled *Hours of Prayer for daily use throughout the year*, consists of selections from the Psalms according to the Prayer Book version, of short Texts from Scripture, called in the book Antiphons, of short Lessons, also from Scripture, and of Prayers and Hymns, all designed to be suitable to different Seasons of the Church's Year, or Times of the day.
>
> The Book is intended for social or domestic purposes, and not as a substitute for the ordinary Church Services, which last the Students are expected to attend twice every day . . .
>
> . . . The Book is certainly not 'concocted from the seven canonical Hours of the Romish Church', nor, in our judgement, does it contain or suggest any Doctrine at variance with that of the Church of England. It has, however, been cast in a form which bears an unfortunate resemblance to the Breviary of the Church of Rome; and we think it would be much improved if the compilers would abandon the title 'Antiphon,' and the obsolete designations of the 'Hours,' re-arrange the Order and Number of the Services, and remodel the whole Book upon a more simple plan.'[16]

In support of what could be seen as a partial vindication of the contents of the book, the pamphlet also contains an Appendix (Number II) which claimed to give

> transcripts of all the Prayers to be found in the Service Books, accused of a Romish tendency by Mr Golightly, except such as are taken directly from Holy Scripture, or from the Prayer Book or from writings of Anglican Bishops.

The Appendix is in two parts, from Latin sources and from modern original sources. The latter is considerably larger than the former. The whole thing was clearly designed to correct the impression that Golightly had formed and publicised. As a result of the Archdeacons' investigations, which Liddon believed at the time 'gave a fictitious importance to the charges against the College which were either groundless or absurd,' a revised version of the Office Book, which contained three minor Offices, was published on 18 June 1858. This was also Liddon's work, but was evidently supervised by Bishop Wilberforce to whom Liddon submitted at least some of the material, for in the diary for 13 May 1858 Liddon noted that 'the Bishop has lost my litany of the Spirit so I must write it again.'

Even though Liddon's experience with the minor Offices and the *Cuddesdon Office Book* was not entirely happy, he did, along with those who shared his approach, have an effect upon the spirituality of the Anglo-Catholic clergy of the Church of England with regard to Morning and Evening Prayer if not the use of the minor Offices. Obedience to the *Book of Common Prayer* rubric came to be seen as a test of churchmanship. The Tractarians, and Liddon himself, did persuade some previously lax clergy conscientiously to recite the Offices, and thus also improved clerical self-discipline. Liddon by his example and the force of his personality, but more especially because of his career at Cuddesdon, Oxford and London, was in a better position than his Tractarian mentors to encourage clergy and others under his influence and direction to embark on lives of deeper spirituality rooted in the revival of systematic liturgical prayer.

In turning from Liddon's convictions regarding the significance of the Daily Office to examine his belief regarding the Eucharist in the life of the priest, it is significant to notice a connection which Alf Härdelin observed in Newman's work during his Anglican days, that 'the Tractarian endeavours to revive the daily service are also related to the revival of the eucharistic life.'[17] Prior to the emergence of the Oxford Movement, the Holy Communion was celebrated at infrequent if not irregular intervals in the Church of England. The earliest Tractarian advocate of a daily celebration seems to have been R. H. Froude who had promoted the idea of the practice in his 'Essay on Rationalism' which was published in the second volume of his *Remains* in 1839. However, the ideal of more frequent communions was shared by Pusey who had advocated it in his famous sermon, *The Eucharist, a Comfort to the Penitent*, which caused Bishop Wilberforce to ban him from preaching for two years. However, Pusey, when sixty years of age, rose at four o'clock each morning and celebrated Holy Communion in his study having sought and received permission to do so from Wilberforce. The desire for frequent communion services had also figured in the Methodist revival, and the same desire among the Tractarians had stemmed from the insight which they also recovered, although in different ways, that the Eucharist is a means of grace and not simply a memorial or formal religious act.[18] This meant that the clergy themselves experienced a greater enthusiasm for a hitherto neglected aspect of their own devotional life and ministry. Liddon himself, in a reference to Acts 2.46, seems to have believed that the practice in the earliest days of the Church was the daily offering of the Eucharist:

> All through those later summer and autumn months of the year of the Crucifixion, the Apostles and their flock [were] praying together and celebrating daily in private the great Sacrament of our Lord's undying love.[19]

By the time that Liddon was ordained priest in 1853 the old situation in the Church of England had begun to change, but it was still held to be an advanced opinion if a man advocated that the Holy Communion should be received more often than once a week. Liddon was an advocate of this advanced school of thought and indeed went further and did encourage daily celebrations. It is interesting to notice that he had a habit of recording in his diary whenever he celebrated. Towards the back of the manuscript book labelled *Meditations at Cuddesdon,* which is part of the Liddon House archive, Liddon set out a 'Daily Rule of Devotion', dated 26 May 1856, which included as Rule Four, 'Communicate daily, if possible, and if not make a solemn act of spiritual communion, in both cases fasting, except by medical or other authority.' The early date of this recommendation suggests that it was part of the teaching that Liddon had received, probably from Pusey. Although the set of rules was compiled for the use of his students, there was no discrepancy between what he recommended to others and his personal practice in other matters, so it may be presumed that this was the ideal he followed himself. However, it was not until many years after Liddon's departure, and indeed after his death, that a daily Eucharist was instituted at the College. The inclusion of the words 'if possible' in the 'Daily Rule of Devotion' indicates that Liddon was not as rigid in this respect as might be expected. Not only did he accept the situation at Cuddesdon, but he also showed a certain amount of flexibility in his pastoral advice. Many years after leaving Cuddesdon he had a correspondence, now preserved in the Keble College archive, with a man named Hamilton who was distressed that his father had commanded him not to communicate more often than once a month. Unfortunately, the exact nature of Liddon's advice is not known, but a later letter from Hamilton, dated 2 June 1882, reveals that Liddon had probably suggested fortnightly communions. This advice seems to have been followed and the compromise had preserved family peace. Liddon certainly believed that the sacrament of Holy Communion should be received regularly, and a reference to this was slipped almost incidentally into a sermon on an Old Testament subject, 'The Disobedient Prophet', along with serious observance of Sunday, 'regular habits of prayer' and the conscientious use of money. He believed that the ideal was to receive communion regularly and frequently, and although he had been anxious that Hamilton should be able to do so, he was sometimes content to advocate merely 'frequent Sacraments', as in a sermon entitled 'Our Lord's Ascension the Church's Gain,' which he published in the first series of *University Sermons*. According to G. L. Prestige in *St Paul's in its Glory* it was during Liddon's time at St Paul's, on 1 January 1877 that a daily celebration of the Eucharist was introduced, and Henry Scott Holland has implied that Liddon was instrumental in this. This innovation took nearly seven years to bring about. Initially it seems that there had been a proposal to introduce an experimental weekday communion service. This had elicited a letter to Liddon from a priest, R. F. Littledale, who said that in his experience a daily celebration was better attended as it relieved people from having to remember specifically on which days they could expect to communicate. This observation would have been entirely congenial to Liddon. Part of the process had been the introduction in 1871 of celebrations on saints' days. The process of reforming the Cathedral, in this as in other matters, was inevitably slow and St Paul's was a gloomy and under-used place before the energy of the Chapter was renewed by the arrival of Gregory, Liddon and then Dean Church. Liddon, in a quotation given by Johnston from an unacknowledged source, was aware of this: 'You must be patient, an elephant may be taught to dance, but the process is not a quick one.'

Liddon's general advice to lay people is summed up in the sermon 'The Lord's Day', preached in St Paul's on the second Sunday after Easter, 1883:

A well-spent Lord's Day should always begin with that supreme act of Christian worship in which we meet Jesus verily and indeed; the only public service known to the early and Apostolic Church; the Most Holy Sacrament of the Body and Blood of our Redeemer.[20]

This short passage not only suggests that Christians should, in the best of circumstances, communicate weekly, it also refers to the ideal time of day. The regulation of service times was seen by Liddon to be entirely in the control of the parish priest and he urged the clergy to use this advantage in order to improve the devotional habits of congregations: 'let it be boldly confessed that the Church should mould the national habits to the true interests of souls . . .' A few lines earlier he had also written, in an outburst of Victorian moralism:

> Now we are disposed to think that the English habit of lying in bed on Sunday morning is an evil with which the clergy ought to wage unceasing war, as being fatal to the growth of spiritual life.[21]

In this, although he did not say so, he was following Newman, who introduced the early celebration at St Mary's, Oxford, as Härdelin said 'because he was sure that early rising involved real inconvenience, and thus served to safeguard against falling into comfortable religion.'[22] Liddon's occasional references to the desirability of early celebrations of communion are, in fact, supported by a rather more positive reason than that which Härdelin reported of Newman. Early communion is particularly desirable because, when nothing has made any claim upon the attention of the recipient, he can offer his 'freshest' and his 'best' to God and thus win for the soul the strength it needs to cope with the labours, troubles and anxieties that life brings. Thus

> an early communion, where ten or twelve assemble in the twilight to receive the Sacrament of the Divine Redeemer, is likely to be much more useful than an exciting evening sermon in a crowded church.[23]

This remark was made in 1874 when Liddon was at the height of his fame as a preacher. The most consistent expression of the advantages of holding communion services at an early hour is found in Liddon's pamphlet *Evening Communions Contrary to the Teaching and Practice of the Church in all Ages*, published in 1876, where he said that 'the experience of the Christian world is in favour of *early* devotion.' Indeed he went so far as to claim that 'if the Church of England is to recover spiritual vigour in a wide sense, Early Communions must be the cause and chief symbol of such recovery.' In support of the appropriateness of the early practice he countered the objection that early services 'huddle away into a corner of the day its most momentous act' by saying that 'this is reasoning which might have objected to the manger at Bethlehem on the score of its obscurity.'[24]

No doubt reasons such as Liddon's did influence the widespread adoption of the practice of early celebrations of Holy Communion in the Church of England, but there was another consideration of a more pragmatic nature. Celebration at an early hour enabled parish clergy to introduce a weekly Sunday Communion without altering the times of other services and thereby risking the possibility of disagreements within the parochial community. Those who shared Liddon's opinion saw their wishes triumph, but not entirely for the reasons he put forward.

As the title of the pamphlet indicates, these observations regarding the desirability of early worship must be seen in relation to Liddon's reaction to the growing practice of evening celebrations. It was a practice that remained repugnant to old fashioned Anglo-Catholics into the 1950s, at least until Pope Pius XII changed the Roman Catholic regulations. Liddon was so alarmed when this practice began to develop in the Church of England that he wrote a long article about it for *The Christian Remembrancer* in 1860. Some additional material was added in 1861 and the whole thing was reprinted as the pamphlet of 1876. That the practice of evening celebrations had increased is borne out by Liddon's claim that 'at least fifty' London churches were offering them. This statistic is supplemented by Owen Chadwick's reference to a publication called *Guide to the Churches of London and its Suburbs 1886–94* compiled by a man named Mackeson, who claimed that in 1869 there were sixty-five churches with evening celebrations; in 1874, 179; in 1879, 262, and in 1882, 285.[25] It would seem from these figures that Liddon's protest, which is another example of his agreement with Dr Pusey, was unsuccessful. But the reasoning behind Liddon's opposition to the practice is worthy of examination because it throws further light upon his conception of the priestly ministry. Initially in the pamphlet, Liddon expressed the view that the period through which he and his readers were living was a time 'pregnant with momentous results', and that Churchmen must do their best to leave 'entire' to the next generation 'the faith of the Catholic Church.' It was his belief that evening communions would undermine this heritage because the thinking that permitted or encouraged such celebrations was based upon what he called 'Zwinglian propaganda.'[26] Thus his opposition was based on the belief that the practice is of Protestant origin and is incompatible with the catholic faith. Clearly the clergy were in a position to prevent such an unsatisfactory development, and the inference is that a priest with a properly sacramental approach to his work would use his best efforts to prevent such a watering-down of catholic principles. It is clear that the major conviction upon which the argument of the pamphlet rests, and which underlay much Tractarian spirituality, was the desire to re-establish the traditional rule of receiving communion only after having fasted from the previous midnight. Liddon

readily acknowledged that he believed the practice to be very important, and although he made only one reference to it in the pamphlet,
his language was strong:

> It may be said that the dislike to [sic] Evening Communions is at
> bottom connected with the desire to restore the ancient practice of
> fasting before Communion. If this were so, we should, after all,
> only be treading in the steps of Bishop Sparrow and many other
> great English names who might be quoted. But here we will only
> ask, is nothing to be conceded to the practice and instinct of the
> ancient and universal Church of God? Are we to fashion our rule
> by exceptions which she barely tolerated or energetically repudi-
> ated? Are we English of the nineteenth century so much wiser and
> more comprehensive, and deeper and holier, and more jealous of
> God's glory and for His truth than they, that we may safely cast to
> the winds what was treasured up and has been handed down by the
> saints and doctors of antiquity – a portion of that body of faith and
> practice which is the heritage of Christendom – as if it were a
> foolish enactment suited to the stinted and cramped intelligence of
> a darkened age?[27]

Pusey, by comparison, seems to have been rather more lenient than
Liddon in this respect; he urged the custom of fasting before communion, as having been 'the practice of the second century', but
Liddon's biographer Johnston, and W. C. E. Newbolt, who
succeeded him in his St Paul's canonry, together edited Pusey's
Spiritual Letters, and said in a footnote that 'from the nature of the
correspondence ... the stress of the argument is against the
'rigourist' interpretation of this custom.' Liddon, however, believed
that attendance at Holy Communion in the evening would occur with
a 'large neglect of any sacramental preparation.' Even a late morning
attendance was better in this respect, although he was not happy
about mid-day celebrations. In serious families the breakfast table, 'if
attended', would be left earlier and conversation would be likely to
be restrained. What Liddon called 'tension' would be more easily
maintained for the duration of a morning than would be possible if
the 'most solemn act were postponed until sunset.' He illustrated his
point by asking his readers to 'imagine a worthy squire rising from
the wine after dinner to attend Holy Communion in his parish church.
We forbear to dwell upon the picture ...' He did, however, dwell
upon a real incident drawn from the experience of the vicar of 'a
large town in the West of England'. He arranged an afternoon celebration on Christmas Day for 'the servant maids.' But very few

attended although 'other persons came who would else have risen in time to come in the morning – they came "reeking from their Christmas dinners." The vicar did not continue the experiment.' It was Liddon's belief that, not only would the standard of preparation for communion be lower, but also that evening communions would 'tend to lower the popular standard of Eucharistic belief' in the Zwinglian direction. The eventual effect of the practice would be grave and 'we unhesitatingly predict that when Churchmen are so unhappy as to yield to the present current of popular pressure, their higher, better, fuller, truer belief in the Blessed Sacrament will be subjected to a rude shock, and probably abandoned.'[28] The pamphlet was meant to rally the clergy to prevent such a disaster. It received quite a wide circulation for at least 3,000 copies were sold. He did, however, acknowledge that the practice held an attraction for the priest in the parish. Liddon knew the Reverend Walter Farquhar Hook, who was Vicar of Leeds between 1837 and 1859 had in fact adopted the practice in about 1851. Hook is usually described as a follower of the Tractarians although he was a man of independent mind, and he may have been the parish priest to whom Liddon referred. His motive was to make the Sacrament available to parishioners who could not attend at other times. However, he did not persevere with the practice for long. Liddon would have been reluctant to criticise Hook's motives, but in his pamphlet he discussed the temptation which a clergyman might face; such a man 'looks out into his parish' and sees that

> there is a small inner circle of a few communicants; there is the larger circle of church-goers, who do not communicate; there is the zone of Dissent, which never enters the walls of the church, or only occasionally; there is the outer circle of all the irreligious, unpraying, unlistening multitude. Towards all of these he has his duties. But his chief duty lies towards Church people – his strength is the number of his communicants. This is true in a supernatural sense, which he may be slow to apprehend. But it is true in a moral and social sense, patent and obvious to friend and foe. To increase his communicants – that is the question.[29]

Liddon's opposition to evening communions was not simply based on spiritual and pastoral reasons which he felt to be appropriate to the nineteenth century. A large part of his pamphlet is given over to arguing his case from the Bible, beginning with the irrefutable fact 'that our Lord and Saviour instituted the Blessed Sacrament of His Body and Blood after supper, and in the evening.' He continued with a brief study of the *'agape,'* or solemn, loving meal of the very early Church, and then extended his survey into the Patristic period. However, that is beyond the purpose of this examination of Liddon's belief and practice, which is to describe the way in which it affected his teaching and influenced the clergy and lay people to whom he gave guidance.

Another factor that has to be considered is the question of non-communicating attendance at the Eucharist. Härdelin observed that although non-communicating attendance was specifically forbidden in the 1552 *Book of Common Prayer*, the prohibition was omitted in the 1662 version which became definitive and the Tractarians interpreted its removal as permitting the reintroduction of the practice. Many clergy, of whom Liddon was one, permitted and almost encouraged it. As early as 1853 he wrote to his Aunt Louisa about the practice of non-communicating attendance at the Eucharist, 'you see, people ought to come to *worship* without actually receiving, as they did in the ancient Church.' Pusey, however, writing a quarter of a century later, held a slightly different view from that of his disciple, and was concerned about

> spiritual laziness in the non-communicating attendance. I hear that the actual Communions are few. There is no preparation for 'hearing the Mass'. Some go, are satisfied with having performed their duty, but return in a lazy state.[30]

But Charles Gore, however in 1901, was closer to Liddon and said, 'There is in our present service book no direction for those to withdraw who are not at the moment intending to communicate; and they have a perfect right to exercise the liberty to remain without communicating.'[31]

Among the early followers of the Oxford Movement, Robert Isaac Wilberforce, who became a Roman Catholic in 1854, seems to have been the first man to consider this issue in his *The Doctrine of the Holy Eucharist* (1853), and Liddon was aware of his work and had looked forward to its publication, although he made no published references to it. Wilberforce, the brother of the bishop, argued for the propriety of habitual, but not actual, communicants being present throughout the whole service. This seems to have been a line of thought with which Liddon would not have disagreed, for he noted in his diary for Sunday 2 January 1876, 'remained throughout the morning service and Communion, without communicating at 11'. His reasons for refraining from receiving are not given, but we know that he did feel that it was inappropriate to receive if one had not made an adequate preparation, or if his fast was not maintained. There are other references in the diaries to Liddon himself attending the Eucharist without receiving communion, but perhaps one of the most significant is the entry of 26 October 1887 because on that occasion he was not alone, 'at 9.45 went to Mr Beresford Hope's funeral . . . At church made to go into a surplice and sit in the choir . . . [Robert] Gregory and I remained without communicating.' The funeral took place at Kilndown in Kent. Beresford Hope had been a benefactor of the Church, and a politician.

The most frequent references to attending the Eucharist without communicating are to be found in the diary entries for his holidays abroad, for it would have been inconceivable for him even to contemplate the possibility of receiving Holy Communion in a Roman Catholic Church, although he frequently attended. He attended such services because he was convinced that 'the essential catholicity of the Church of England' gave every Englishman the right to be present, although he advised those afflicted by 'Roman fever' and those who could not understand the service to stay away.

In the introductory passage at the beginning of *Tracts for the Times, no. 81: Catena Patrum IV . . . the Doctrine of the Eucharistic Sacrifice,* Pusey had however described two beneficial aspects in such non-communicating attendance at the Holy Communion. One was 'the benefit to the individual communicants'; the other was the 'benefit to the whole church.' From these two points it is possible to conclude that non-communicating attendance is not, as the Reformers had tended to suggest, a denial of participation in worship. This reasoning lay behind Gore's contention that 'we may well feel that to "assist in the prayers" is better than to be absent.'[32] This was a clear echo of Liddon's teaching and lay behind the Anglo-Catholic practice of the celebration of a High Mass on Sundays, usually at about 11 a.m., at which only a small proportion of the congregation or even none at all received the sacrament. This developed towards the end of Liddon's life, and persisted until the development of the Parish Communion in the twentieth century. It is this view which Liddon had in mind in the following undated passage to an unknown correspondent which is quoted by Johnston,

Did I ever tell you how the attendance of non-communicants at the midday Eucharist at St Paul's began? When I first came there, the vergers used to go to people who were remaining after the Prayer for the Church Militant, and say, 'Are you intending to receive?' and if the reply was in the negative, 'Then you are requested to leave the Cathedral.' This went on till, after one Trinity Sunday, I received a letter from a Cambridge undergraduate, saying that he and another had come to the Cathedral to see a common friend ordained. They had communicated early, and were most distressed by being interrogated by the verger ... and turned out of the Cathedral. I felt that this was an opportunity; so I wrote to the undergraduate saying that I was very sorry for what had occurred, and that if he would write me a suitable letter (for which I made some suggestions to him) I would bring the matter before the Chapter. The letter was accordingly written, and I read it at the next Chapter meeting. Thereupon the Archdeacon (ie Bishop Claughton) said he had fears of the reintroduction of the Mass, etc. I replied that the Archdeacon often insisted on the importance of obeying the law, and, as far as I knew, the request which the vergers were ordered to make was a strictly illegal request, failing, as it did, to derive any support from the Rubrics. The order to the vergers was in consequence withdrawn.[33]

Finally, with regard to the Eucharist in the life and ministry of the priesthood, it is necessary briefly to notice the way in which Liddon perceived how belief was expressed in the attitudes which celebrants, or communicants, adopted. There are two diary entries which serve to illustrate this, both come from the year 1882. The first, 18 June, was a comment on the way in which the Holy Communion was distributed at St Lawrence's Church, Southwark. Liddon described it as irreverent, and was critical of the fact that 'they administered to two at a time'. The second incident occurred on 24 August, and Liddon recorded, 'celebrated chorally at the 10 o'clock service. An old clergyman who was present received very irreverently', but unfortunately he was not specific about the man's behaviour, although a reasonable guess might be that he took the cup from the hands of the administrator and followed the old-fashioned habit of drinking from it rather than sipping.

This reference to the devotional practice of another priest reveals an aspect of Liddon's spirituality which it is appropriate to examine at this point because it formed part of his approach in the training of ordinands, and was, at the same time, a significant part of his own prayer life. In the long essay *The Priest in His Inner Life* he devoted much space to advocating and describing the practice of systematic meditation. He believed that it was the best way for priests systematically to deepen their spirituality. The Tractarians, especially Pusey, had touched upon it, but Liddon took it much further; so much so that Chadwick described it as, after the Daily Offices, Liddon's 'second hinge of the disciplined spiritual life.'[34] He believed that meditation was an important part of the process of equipping the clergy of the Church of England to present the catholic truth which the Tractarians had restated in the previous generation. Meditation helped to prevent the clergy from drifting into a hollow formalism through which they would eventually come to look down on the Offices as, in Liddon's words, 'a stumbling block to honest men.' The concept behind Liddon's advocacy of meditation was that the Church of England had, in prescribing the Offices to her clergy, 'implicitly demanded other spiritual exercises as a regular part of clerical life.' Indeed, at the end of the passage which dealt with meditation Liddon almost apologised for devoting so much space to it, but excused himself on the grounds that he believed it to be at 'the root of the priestly life' and thus to be 'of primary importance.' One of the truths which he held to be fundamental to the Christian faith was the belief that God desires the human soul to grow in the devotional life. In a reference to the Psalter, Liddon expressed this conviction in beautiful language, referring to the soul 'as it expands with ever-increasing tenderness and awe towards Him who is its Centre and Sun.' He held that meditation is an essential part of this process, as he declared in a sermon preached in 1868:

> Meditation is an intense act of the whole soul moving forth to welcome and to embrace truth; it is intelligence marking out the exact limits and range of truth; it is affection embracing truth for the sake of its fair and matchless beauty; it is will, sternly resolving to express truth in act and life. Meditation to be of real service ought to be just as regular and systematic as prayer; and when this is so, each of the great doctrines of the faith, each of the acts, and sayings, and sufferings of our blessed Lord, each of the means of grace, become to the soul familiar things, and not, most assuredly, despised or thought lightly of, because familiar.[35]

One of the things which he thought tended to undermine the serious practice of meditation was the fact that it was taken for granted in 'a Bible-reading country like ours.' He drew a succinct word-picture to demonstrate his point: 'you see a worthy clergyman in his study – he is resting his elbow on the table, and reflecting on some portions of his Bible – making remarks at intervals to his wife.' He regretted that what he called 'feeble and dreamy' efforts were often regarded as entirely acceptable and feared that his conviction of the need for more rigorous discipline would be regarded as excessive. Indeed, he went so far as to claim that 'a reason [for] our superficial hold on truth is that we Christians do not meditate.' He wondered whether it was thought that the practice of meditation is inappropriate for busy people. However, he believed that meditation was a means by which the soul of the believer met the Lord and could linger in his presence. Inevitably such a meeting would have a significant effect upon the human character because 'man ... was made for God.' But the process was not something that just happened. Liddon thought that it was necessary to be both disciplined and systematic in devotion, and this applied not least in the practice of meditation. Warmth and feeling is not sufficient. An essential part of meditation, therefore, was seen by Liddon to be the need for a system which taught the soul 'to move just as systematically and reverently when in the Divine Presence as the body,' and he continued, 'such a meditation as this bears the same sort of relation to that of the well-instructed Christian, as does the rant of a meeting-house to the ritual of a well-appointed church.'[36]

He then went on to devote several pages of the essay to a description of the process of meditation which he believed should occasionally be based upon a doctrine, but much more frequently should be based upon a Biblical passage. There may be a connection here with Pusey's 'love of scriptural scenes as subjects of meditations, especially the Passion of Christ.'[37] Chadwick very adequately summarised Liddon's approach in *The Founding of Cuddesdon*. He

taught his men to survey their materials for meditation the night before and to come to it in the early morning when their body was refreshed and their mind undistracted. It was not an intellectual study of Scripture nor a mere resolution, but an act of worship issuing in resolution. It must be made not at the desk but on the knees. After preparatory prayers of penitence and faith, the soul should come trustfully to the Bible, to put aside human reason and to listen to the Word that is spoken. He should seek to picture the incident on which he meditates, to clothe and enliven it by reverent imaginations. Then the understanding should work upon the picture, dividing it into its component parts until it can select one element which evokes response from the will. Here the intellect 'retires' its function ended. 'The point upon which it has fixed as cardinal is transferred to the will.' The whole being now seeks to absorb the moral truth which the intellect has selected, and so passes to resolution, always a concrete and practical resolution.[38]

A profound motive for recommending the practice of meditation is revealed in a passage in a Lenten sermon preached in St Mary's, Oxford in 1868. Liddon said:

Ten minutes or a quarter of an hour of meditation each day is not much for a Christian to give to God; but the man who gives even this, knows by experience at the end of a year that he has thus acquired a quite new grasp and sight of revealed truth. He sees how impossible it is to add to it, how yet more impossible to mutilate it. Between it and all other thought there is in his mind the sharpest line of demarcation. Scripture is no longer a dead letter to him, but a 'living creature'; he sees in Scripture, not a mere collection of documents relating to a distant time, to events and to states of mind which have passed away, but the perpetual Voice and Mind of One with Whom his soul holds constant communion, and in Whose light he traces with clear eye the certainty and the symmetry of the faith.[39]

The process which Liddon recommended is reminiscent of the Ignatian system of meditation although he made no acknowledgement of this, perhaps because he feared an adverse reaction from people who felt threatened by what would have been seen as another example of incipient Romanism within the Church of England. In addition, there had been that curious incident back in 1867 when C. Kegan Paul, in 'The Theological Review,' had accused Liddon of plagiarism from Loyola's 'Spiritual Exercises' in one of the sermons published in his volume *Some Words for God* (later, *University Sermons, first series*).[40]

Writing about meditation in general in *The Priest in his Inner Life*, he did say that 'it is not easy to recommend a good book for beginners in meditation,' and he went on to claim that Hook's *Meditations for Every Day in the Year* is no more than 'pious reflections' which lack what he called the 'method, the nerve, the point of meditations'. The *Daily Steps towards Heaven* was another publication which he thought to be not entirely suitable for beginners, but in a footnote he did say that the *Meditationes* of Avancini, from which the *Daily Steps* was adapted, was written specifically for priests; and 'if we allow for Roman peculiarities – is a very valuable work.' Despite his anxiety to avoid Roman Catholic 'peculiarities' he was very keen to promote meditation, even though, to many Anglicans, the whole idea would have seemed both foreign and exotic.

In addition to recommending the practice, Liddon helped to meet the deficiency of suitable material by compiling some meditations for use by the students at Cuddesdon, reference has already been made to some of the contents. The books themselves are extant in manuscript form in the Bodleian Library, there is one additional notebook at Pusey House and another in the Liddon House archive labelled in Liddon's handwriting, *Meditations at Cuddesdon*.

The latter contains six 'Meditations for those preparing for Holy Orders and clergymen in the Church of England'. None of these follow the pattern of reflective thought upon a Biblical passage, but were designed to facilitate the development of what Liddon believed to be the appropriate frame of mind that ordinands should have. The titles of all six meditations reflect this concern. They are themselves noteworthy and reveal some aspects of Liddon's character:

1. On a right aim in entering a Theological Seminary.
2. On the tone and temper which ought to characterise a Theological Seminary.
3. On the obligation, while living in a Theological Seminary, to make great progress in Holiness.
4. On a Rule of Life: the value we ought to set upon it, and the scrupulous fidelity with which, when settled, it would be observed.
5. On Punctuality and the Inward dispositions essential to a due Observance of a Religious Rule of Life.
6. On Daily Actions: the care with which they should be performed, and the necessity of a Pure intention and right motive to their due performance.'

Each meditation, except the last, has three 'points' which are to do with conformity to God's will or invoking his help through prayer.

There is a further fragment of evidence regarding Liddon's approach to meditation among the loose papers in the 1860 diary. It is a pencil note in his hand-writing and clearly formed part of some larger document which appears to have been prepared for use by others. A paragraph is headed 'Habit of Meditation' and it urged that the habit must be sustained; and it suggested that the Lord's Prayer, the Creed or 'some aspect of Christ's Person' should be reflected upon in the ordinary course of daily events. This process would allow 'the mind to be withdrawn from the world . . . and will have its effect on the inward life.' This short note helps to demonstrate Liddon's belief that the priest should always have the responsibility for his vocation in the front of his mind, a fact which he achieved himself as is evidenced by many diary entries, including (for instance) that for 26 January 1861, where he recorded that he had had 'some thoughts early in the day which I desire to cherish, and for which, O my God, make me thankful and humble.' The meditations themselves reflect the attitude revealed in a quotation which Liddon copied on to the first blank page of the same 1861 diary and which summarised his whole approach to the spiritual life:

It is a rule of the Divine Life that sanctity is more surely shown in doing ordinary things with extraordinary devotion than in doing things which are themselves extraordinary.

Liddon recorded that this passage came from T. T. Carter 'on the imitation of our Lord,' but he gave no other details. It is, however, typical of the emergent spirituality of High Churchmen of the generation of Liddon and Carter. Three practical points, Liddon believed, should issue from the process of meditation, and these apply equally to his specifically Scriptural model as well as to the Liddon House archive material described above:

> ... it would be desirable here, – (1) by casting oneself upon God, to nerve the soul for future sufferings; (2) to resolve to sacrifice any cherished inclination or pursuit which is at variance with clerical or Christian perfection; (3) to make a perfect oblation of self to the Blessed Trinity, as the End and Lord of the Soul by Creation, by Baptism, by Confirmation, by Ordination.[41]

In addition to these practical aspects of the process of habitual meditation, Liddon also believed that it would equip a man with the appropriate words on those relatively rare occasions when extempore prayer is a necessity. He said that extempore prayer is mostly unsuitable. Indeed, he wrote that 'extempore prayer is dangerous, if not almost impossible, in the mouths of those who are strangers to systematic meditation upon dogmatic truth.' But 'it is a very efficient aid in the hands of a clergyman whose inner life is fed by meditation.' Here he echoed St Augustine, to whom he referred as saying that meditation is a necessary preparation for all prayer, but he went further and said that it should be used in addition 'to any more formal preparatory office or needful examination of conscience' by any priest about to celebrate the Holy Communion.

Chapter Eight

Liddon as leader

After 1870, Liddon's time was divided between London and Oxford and punctuated by holidays on the continent and visits, mostly, to his family in the west country in England. Into this even pattern of life he packed a remarkable amount of pastoral involvement and intellectual activity. His personality was such that he did not avoid controversy, although he did not seek it out. He enjoyed spiritual and intellectual stability and his self-confidence made him an effective protagonist. Owen Chadwick, comparing three contemporaries, wrote that William Palmer was 'equipped by learning and temperament to hold his own amidst the dialectics of mediaeval schools. Ward believed controversy to be the very life-blood of intellectual advance' and enjoyed the use of his sharp intellect. Whereas 'if Ward had a rapier, Liddon kept a bludgeon, kept it for the most part mercifully behind his back.'[1]

Occasionally, however, the bludgeon was deployed with a considerable degree of effectiveness. One of the most significant instances was the quarrel, which erupted in 1872, over the so-called 'Athanasian Creed', or 'Quicunque Vult' as it is sometimes known from its opening words in Latin. This Creed has been more widely used in the Western Church than in the Eastern. It is to be found in *The Book of Common Prayer* between Evening Prayer and the Litany, and its use is prescribed at Morning Prayer on fourteen specific days in the year. Unfortunately the Prayer Book version is not an accurate rendering of the original. The biographer of Bishop Wilberforce who had been translated from Oxford to Winchester in 1869, described the dispute as 'one of the greatest dangers which have beset her [the Church of England] in modern times.'[2] That may have been an exaggeration, but the controversy exemplified the differences between the Tractarians and the theological liberals. The objections to its use arose, not so much from its inaccuracies, but from its damnatory clauses. These are well summarised by the declaration at the beginning of the Creed, which asserts the necessity to accept the whole 'Faith', and claims that anyone who fails to 'keep [it] whole and undefiled: without doubt he shall perish everlastingly.' Not all conservative theologians objected to the prospect of amendment or alteration as such, but they were utterly opposed in practice. This was on the grounds that any attempt to make the Creed less objectionable, or alternatively to reduce the number of occasions of its use, could be interpreted as a watering-down or abandonment of the traditional faith. Part of a letter from Liddon to Wilberforce depicts accurately the force of the objections of the traditionalists:

> To give way in this matter is to give a fearful impetus to the demoralisation, so to term it, among our best people, arising from an increasing conviction that high authorities are prepared to make an unpopular stand *nowhere*; almost no stand whatever, except against Rome, and what is supposed to lead to her; that we are on an inclined plane, leading swiftly and certainly towards a Socinianism tempered by indifference.
>
> I feel the depressing force of this conviction in my inmost heart at times, more painfully than I can say, and it takes all vigour out of one.[3]

Archbishop Tait can be counted among the liberals with regard to the Athanasian Creed, and at first he failed to see any danger. In September 1870 the Archbishop declared that the use of the Creed should be discontinued. His wish was expressed in an Appendix to the Fourth and final Report of the Royal Commission on Ritual. The response was rapid. In February 1871 a petition was presented to the Archbishop. It contained eleven hundred and fifty signatures, clerical and lay, and deprecated any change being made, either in the Creed or in its use. The petition was met by counter petitions to Convocation and to the Archbishop urging alterations to the Creed. In June of that year, the Upper House of the Convocation of Canterbury decided to consider the matter, because it was feared that a theological rift could split the Church. This action produced a further response, largely in the correspondence columns of newspapers, in which Liddon and Pusey took part. Bishop Wilberforce was recognised by the traditionalists as their best hope of resisting change, and he was certainly alive to the dangers inherent in what was proposed. He wrote to Liddon in October 1871, although his letter seems to have been written at the instigation of Tait. He enclosed a statement of the objections with a request that Liddon should comment on them. Liddon went to see the Bishop before sending a lengthy reply which dealt with the theological matters and also expressed his alarm at the situation. Part of it has already been quoted, and it is drawn upon in what follows. Dealing with the relatively unimportant matter of the inaccuracies of the Prayer Book version of the Creed, he wrote that, 'no mending of the translation will suffice to reconcile the strictly irreconcilable phases of opinion, the "Liberal" and the believing or Catholic, on this vital question. The differences in question reach the very basis of thought and faith.'[4] This was at the heart of the traditionalists' perception of the problem, although Liddon's distinction between 'liberals' and 'believers' was not particularly charitable. A little later he wrote about the prospect of a selective use of the Creed,

> It will convince a large number of minds that, if only a sufficient amount of negative and unbelieving pressure can be brought to bear, there is no Truth, however central and hitherto undisputed, which the Church of England is prepared to proclaim before God and man as strictly necessary to salvation.
>
> The disuse of the Anathemas will be held to imply that the Arian, the Sabellian, the Nestorian, will, however deliberate their heresy, however great their opportunities of escaping from it, do just as well in the world to come as the faithful children of the Church to whom her Creed is a serious reality.[5]

At this point Pusey, also at the suggestion of Archbishop Tait, tried to calm down the situation. He called together the relevant Oxford Professors and proposed that they should draw up 'an explanatory rubric' concerning the damnatory clauses. However, events moved more quickly than Pusey anticipated, and although the rubric was written, this proposal came to nothing. Two days before Christmas 1871, Liddon wrote to the Archbishop. In the letter he revealed that he could indeed use the bludgeon with which nature had equipped his intellect:

> ... it is not, I trust, obtrusive or other than right of me to state formally to your Grace, that if this most precious Creed is either mutilated by the excision of the (so-termed) Damnatory Clauses, or degraded, by an alteration of the rubric which precedes it, from its present position in the *Book of Common Prayer*, I shall feel bound in conscience to resign my preferments, and to retire from the ministry of the Church of England.
>
> If I should unhappily be driven to this, by the action of the English Bishops, it will become a duty, perhaps, to justify my step

at some length and to point out the wound and insult to *fundamental* Truth, which, as I conceive, would be inflicted by either of the courses referred to.

For the present it is enough to say that, having subscribed the statement that this Creed, in its integrity, 'ought thoroughly to be received and believed,' since 'it may be proved by most certain warrant of Holy Scripture,' I cannot possibly acquiesce in any measure the most avowed object of which is to deny the proposition thus affirmed by the Eighth Article of our Church.[6]

Liddon gave no hint that he was doing more than writing on his own behalf, but Tait was clearly disturbed as the prospect of an Anglo-Catholic rebellion opened like a chasm before him. He was right to be concerned, because Liddon was not a solitary voice, as the Archbishop knew. He feared that Liddon was acting in concert with Pusey, although that was not the case. Indeed, much later, in a letter to Newman written in 1878, Liddon recounted that Pusey, 'when the Athanasian Creed was attacked . . ., had made up his mind, if it had been withdrawn from her, to resign his preferments . . .' At the time Liddon had written to his sister and said, with regard to Pusey, 'we had not compared notes.' Tait tried to take the initiative by deprecating the expression of such a threat by Liddon in what should have been a time of quiet discussion. He was only partially successful in his remonstrance as Liddon demonstrated when he replied in a letter of more than a thousand words which began with a sentence of barely concealed sarcasm, 'I must express my regret that, through any want of clearness, I failed to convey my exact meaning to your Grace.' He explained his reasons in detail, pointing out that he took his stand in the belief that it was consistent with the 'explanatory rubric' of the Oxford Professors to which he had already appended his signature. The substance of his letter is contained in the paragraph which follows the sharp opening:

By the 'mutilation' of the Creed, I meant the omission of any one of its existing clauses. By the 'degradation' of the Creed from its present place in the Prayer Book, I meant, (1) the rendering its use only permissive; or (2) a reduction of the number of days on which it is now appointed to be used; or (3) still more, its removal from the Public Service of the Church, and relegation to a place among the Thirty-Nine Articles. And I ventured to intimate to your Grace, that, in the event of any of these changes being adopted, I shall feel bound in conscience to retire from the ministry of the Church of England, and to give my reasons for doing so.[7]

Rather disingenuosly, Liddon also included a statement that he did not expect his conclusions to be interpreted as a threat, nor did he expect his attitude to affect any final decision on the matter. Whether he really believed that to be the case cannot now be ascertained, but Liddon's observation – he did not want it to be called a threat – was certainly serious, particularly when it became clear that Pusey's name and reputation was aligned with his own. Liddon went so far as to warn his widowed sister, Mrs Ambrose who lived with him in Amen Court, that they could be homeless by the autumn of 1872. He wrote to her from the home of another sister at Brislington. He was there for a lengthy period early in 1872 recovering from a bout of ill health. He was ordered to rest and had to miss a term at Oxford. However by the spring he was better. The threat to the Creed had almost subsided and Liddon was able to do his April period of residence at St Paul's Cathedral and then resume his Oxford work.

In his efforts to resolve the problem, Tait had asked Liddon to speak to his fellow Canon at St Paul's, J. B. Lightfoot. Like Liddon, Lightfoot was a University Professor as well as a Residentiary Canon, but he held a Cambridge chair and theologians from that University had not been so outspoken as their Oxford counterparts on this matter. Also the Archbishop had obviously spoken to Lightfoot, who called on Liddon on 2 January 1872, just before the latter went to Brislington. Liddon wrote at once to Tait:

> Professor Lightfoot has been here today, and we have had the conversation which your Grace desired. Nothing, of course, could exceed his kindness and patience, and, if the object of our meeting had only been attained, I, at least, should look back with unmixed and thankful satisfaction. But I fear I must add that it leaves matters where it found them.

In the meantime, Bishop Wilberforce had been using his influence. It was apparent that he and Tait saw very differently the problem of the Athanasian Creed, but eventually Wilberforce persuaded him that men such as Liddon and Pusey were serious and the Archbishop abandoned his ambitions with regard to that Creed. The final act of the drama came in June 1872 and is summarised in a letter from Liddon to Wilberforce dated 1 July:

> ...Your proposal that the Bishops should have a legal power of dispensing in writing, upon application from an incumbent, with the use of the Athanasian Creed as enjoined in the Prayer Book, does not appear to me, upon further consideration, to involve the

abandonment of principle. Such a power is part of the *jus litur-gicum* anciently believed to be inherent in the Episcopate, although suspended by the Papal usurpations abroad, and, by later legislation, among ourselves. This power never extended, as your Lordship knows, to the *matter* and form of the Sacraments, or to the main features of the Eucharistic Office, but it would certainly have enclosed a right to deal with the contents of such a Service as our 'Morning Prayer'!

As far as this goes, the bishops might, in their collective capacity, have advised the omission of the Creed in such a Service; only they could not, as I believe, do so under the existing circumstances of the Church without being guilty of an act of conspicuous *unfaithfulness to Revealed Truth*.

If all that is conceded be that it shall be within the power of a Bishop to give a permission to disuse the Creed in particular parishes, upon application from the incumbent, and not otherwise, the witness of our Church would still be substantially intact; nothing would be done beyond recognising the toleration of partial disuse which prevails already.[8]

At this point, hoping that end of the controversy was in sight, Liddon went on holiday to Ireland. However, he was a little optimistic. In December 1872, a committee of the two Houses of Convocation finally decided that the Athanasian Creed should not be altered, but that a Declaration should be issued offering an explanation of the damnatory clauses. Those who agreed with Liddon's view sought to press home this advantage and a public meeting was held once again in St James' Hall. Liddon attended and estimated that there were three thousand present. When he rose to speak, he was astonished at what Johnston called 'a tumult of applause; the whole vast assemblage of men, which filled the floor and the galleries . . . rose to their feet and repeatedly cheered him.' After such a powerful demonstration of support for the conservative position, it was clear that no further attempt could be made to alter either the text or the customary usage of the Athanasian Creed 'for a generation.' When he wrote to Pusey, on 10 February 1873, Liddon said as much and observed wryly that he had not heard of Tait's view of how the matter had ended. However, it is clear that Tait was not happy, nor was he reluctant to apportion blame. He did not name Pusey or Liddon, but in his Primary Charge to the Diocese of Canterbury, he publicly attributed the failure of his endeavours to 'certain eminent men whom we greatly respect, that, if certain courses were not taken [had declared] they should feel it their duty to retire into lay communion with the Church of England.'

Liddon's determination to 'save' the Athanasian Creed, even at considerable personal cost, was a unique event in his life. As had been the case with the Jerusalem bishopric, which was described in Chapter Three, Liddon had been in frequent contact with Bishop Wilberforce and, to a lesser extent, with Archbishop Tait. With his national reputation as a preacher and in his University role, he was a well-known public figure and his name was often mentioned with regard to ecclesiastical preferment, or promotion. However, Liddon lived through the period when priests of Tractarian sympathies were almost systematically excluded from promotion, but towards the end of his life some of this prejudice abated. His perception of the epis-copate, and occasionally his response to the holders of episcopal office, meant that in personal terms he viewed the office and work of a bishop as a vocation from which a man might reasonably shrink, and he did much to evade episcopal preferment. Reluctance to accept any preferment was, however, part of the Tractarian mind-set, and was part of Liddon's perturbation when he was offered his canonry at St Paul's. When he was considered for bishoprics his personal modesty was such that he believed himself to be unfit for the task. He wrote in his diary on 23 January 1885:

Arguments against a bishopric. (1) My personal unfitness, (2) I have refused two Scotch bishoprics, (3) Dr Pusey's Life. Impossible to finish it, (4) The spirit of the Oxford Movement against preferment (5) Does Mr Gladstone wish me to accept? I think not. He could have surely asked the Queen first if he had.

The occasion which prompted this self-searching was when, early in 1885 when Liddon was nearly fifty-six, three bishoprics became vacant. They were London and Lincoln, followed by Exeter when Frederick Temple was translated from there to London. At the time there was speculation that Liddon should be given the senior See, London. G. W. E. Russell observed:

it seems . . . likely that if the See of London had been definitely offered, Liddon would have felt it impossible to decline. The opportunity . . . of witnessing for the truth in one of the most conspicuous places in the Church was too great to have been declined; and the charge of London, vast as it is, would not have been fatally incompatible with his state of health and habits of life.[9]

Among those who urged this suggestion on the Prime Minister was

Lord Acton, the Roman Catholic lay historian, who asked, 'who is manifestly worthier to occupy the greatest See in Christendom?' However Acton, who appears to have had a deeper and more profound knowledge of Liddon than he had of many prominent Anglican clergymen,[10] could see that Liddon's churchmanship was an obvious problem, but he maintained his opinion nevertheless, arguing:

> Assuredly Liddon is the greatest power in the conflict with sin, and in turning the souls of men to God, that the nation now possesses. He is also, among all the clergy, the man best known to numbers of Londoners.[11]

Nothing came of Acton's speculative suggestion, although Mr Gladstone, who was Prime Minister for the second time between 1880–85 and had known Liddon since 1853, would have been happy to submit his name to the Queen for nomination to one of the vacancies. In his diary for 2 September, 1886, well over a year later, Liddon made a note to the effect that Gladstone 'meant to offer me the choice [of], if I had proved willing, when asked to accept', either the bishopric of Exeter or Lincoln. Corroboration of this statement was discovered by Owen Chadwick who, in his pamphlet *Edward King, Bishop of Lincoln 1885–1910*, described a consultation:

> on 22 January 1885 at a meeting at 10 Downing Street between Gladstone and the Archbishop [Benson] it was agreed to submit three names to the Queen: Temple (liberal) for the see of London, Bickersteth (evangelical) for the see of Exeter, and Liddon (high church) for the see of Lincoln. But first, it was agreed, Dean Church of St Paul's should sound Liddon to see if he were willing. If he refused, then King's name should go forward to the Queen.

This desire of Gladstone's was in keeping with his policy of ensuring that ecclesiastical appointments were representative of the various parties within the Church. We have two accounts of the sounding process from Liddon's pen; one is a letter to C. L. Wood:

> Here, in justice to Mr G[ladstone], I must tell you something, in entire confidence. Some days before Bishop Temple's appointment was announced, he sent me a message through the Dean of St Paul's to inquire whether I would take a Bishopric! He said nothing about any particular See. And while I should have had great and sore misgivings in answering *any* specific proposal, I could not but answer

the general question in the negative. To have done otherwise would have been false to the whole Tractarian (i.e. the Patristic and Catholic) tradition on the subject. What would St Ambrose have said to a willingness to accept a bishopric in the abstract? What would Dr Pusey or Mr Keble have said? My reply was that I earnestly hoped to be spared the great anxiety of answering such a question. This put an end to the matter for good and all . . .

Part of this letter was quoted by Johnston, but the second account, which is more personal, has remained unpublished. It comes from the earlier part of the diary entry for 23 January 1885, to which reference has already been made:

Letter from the Dean of St Paul's. He has been asked whether Dr Liddon would consent to be made a Bishop. I telegraphed that Dr L[iddon] most earnestly desired never to be obliged to consider the subject. On reaching London, I had one and a half hours talk with the Dean of St Paul's. The Dean urged me to reconsider my answer, and to say that my name might be submitted to the Queen. But I could not make up my mind that this would be right. So that nightmare is, I trust, at an end. This most anxious question has given me a great heartache.'

But the following day he wrote, 'could not dismiss the decision of yesterday as entirely from my mind as I could have wished'. Nor could Dean Church, for two days later Liddon wrote in his diary, 'The Dean called and talked over the decision on Thursday. He thought that I should be happier without being a bishop, but regretted it.'

The involvement of Dean Church in negotiations planned to persuade Liddon to accept an episcopal appointment contains its own irony, for the Dean's daughter wrote of Liddon's own involvement in persuading Church to accept the Deanery in 1871:

when years after, he had been engaged in an attempt to induce Dr Liddon to consider the question of a Bishopric, I remember well the amused smile with which he told me how, as he listened to Liddon's fervid arguments against any such offer being made him, he could not help recalling the way in which that very same fervour had disposed of the very same arguments when he himself had used them to Liddon as his own reason for declining the Deanery.[12]

This note of irony is intensified firstly by the fact that Liddon had hoped that Church would be appointed to a vacant canonry at St

Paul's very soon after his own appointment. He was unsuccessful, but rejoiced greatly just months later at Church's appointment as Dean. A second fact, of which Liddon probably never knew, must also be recalled: that Dean Church himself had declined to be considered for the Archbishopric of Canterbury, following the death of Tait in 1882. The three appointments were completed by the end of January 1885, and Liddon was relieved that the prospect of a bishopric was removed. Although some of his acquaintances were surprised at the outcome, Randall Davidson the future Archbishop of Canterbury who was Dean of Windsor between 1883–91, and a man who did not often get such things wrong, wrote:

> I confess to being myself a little surprised that Mr G is recommending a High Chmn. and did not submit the name of Canon Liddon with whom he is on such terms of friendship. Canon King however wd., I think, be a decidedly better Bp than Canon Liddon, and perhaps Mr Gladstone thinks so . . .[13]

However, Liddon's relief was short-lived, for George Moberly, Bishop of Salisbury since Hamilton's death in 1869, was thought to be considering retirement. In his diary, 27 May 1885, Liddon noted a report in *The Guardian* that Moberly had tendered his resignation. In fact the See became vacant when the Bishop died on 6 July. By that time not only was the usual speculation at work, but the official process of selecting the new bishop was well under way, for on 7 April Liddon recorded in his diary that:

> after afternoon service, the Dean said that Salisbury would soon be offered to me. He hoped that I would not put it aside. Said that there never was such a case of clear call. His eyes filled with tears and he begged pardon in his characteristic way for mentioning the subject. I said that I had hoped this ghost had been laid by what passed in January. He said: No, it had been all along intended, and he was surprised that nothing had yet been said.

This is the most significant of many entries in the diary about the Salisbury proposal, and it was also noticed by Johnston. In addition to the reasons already noted for Liddon's reluctance to accept episcopal consecration, there was again a feeling of anxiety regarding his work on the biography of Pusey. He wrote to Church, 'begging him to write to Mr Gladstone to beg him *not* to submit my name to the Queen for the See of Salisbury' and in the letter he said that among his reasons for declining, 'my choice . . . lies between the book and the See.' Just over a month later on 3 June 1885 his diary records that he again, 'wrote to the Dean, telling him that my mind about Salisbury was still what it had been; hope that he will write and beg Mr G[ladstone] not to submit my name to the Queen.'

Moberly's death and the consequent vacancy at Salisbury came after Gladstone's administration had been replaced by one led by Lord Salisbury. The new Prime Minister was a life-long friend of Liddon, so the threat, as he saw it, of a bishopric was not removed. But the offer was not made and once again the question lapsed. On 15 August he recorded that *The Standard* carried a report that John Wordsworth, the first Oriel Professor of the Interpretation of Scripture at Oxford and an enthusiast for Church reunion, had been appointed Bishop of Salisbury. Later in the month Liddon was on his continental holiday and arrived at Neuchatel where he 'found a great many papers and letters. Among others *The Record*, who expresses her profound satisfaction that I am not to be a Bishop. It is a pleasure, for once in a way, to have given pleasure to her managers.' *The Record* was the first weekly newspaper published for members of the Church of England. It was fiercely evangelical and opposed to the Tractarian point of view.

It is interesting to note, however, that despite his apparent firmness at the time, Liddon was able to write to William Bright in March 1886:

> If Lord Salisbury had offered me the See of Salisbury in the autumn, I had, with much misgiving and after long hesitation, made up my mind that it would be a duty to accept it. . .As you know, he did not offer it.

Chadwick has suggested that Liddon underwent this change of heart having been 'moved because his friend King accepted Lincoln.'[14] It could be that his admiration for King and his friendship with him overcame his reluctance, at least in retrospect.

For a time there were persistent rumours that Liddon had offended Queen Victoria, who took a real interest in episcopal appointments, and that she vetoed any suggestion that he should be given a bishopric. The truth is difficult to get at. The rumours dated back to the occasion when Liddon had preached before the Queen at Windsor, on 28 June 1868. He preserved in his papers a newspaper cutting from *The World,* dated 15 August 1888. In the passage he was described as 'the greatest of living English preachers', and it went on to say that the Queen disliked his style:

Canon Liddon framed his style on that of the great French preachers, and as Massillon, when preaching before Louis XIV, addressed the King as 'Sire', so Canon Liddon in his sermon addressed the Queen as 'Madam'. The Queen, either from ignorance or forgetfulness of the authority on which he based his sermon, was very much shocked and annoyed, and expressed herself in no measured terms, and Canon Liddon has never since been commanded to preach before her.

The same supposition recurred almost two years later when *The Guardian,* a high church weekly, for 5 March 1890, carried the following summary of a report:

The London correspondent of *The Manchester Guardian* hears that Lord Salisbury was very anxious that Dr Liddon should succeed Bishop Claughton at St Alban's, in which diocese Hatfield is situate.

The Queen, however, is unalterably determined that Dr Liddon shall not be made a bishop, and Lord Salisbury has given up the attempt in despair.

The speculation culminated about this time in an article in *The Pall Mall Gazette* to which Liddon said he found it exceedingly painful to refer. But the Queen had heard of the rumours, and Johnston recorded an exchange of letters, initiated by the Queen, between Liddon and Dean Randall Davidson, who urbanely wrote:

The Queen has enjoined upon me a somewhat delicate task, which I must perform as best I can.

Her Majesty has been a good deal annoyed during the past few weeks by certain paragraphs which have gone the round of the newspapers . . . to the effect that she had (with reference to present Episcopal vacancies) been acting with personal disfavour to yourself. The story was sufficiently absurd, and might perhaps have been well left to die of itself, but the Queen, knowing the annoyance its circulation has caused to herself, has feared it may perhaps have vexed you also, and therefore bids me send you privately what will be, I think, an unnecessary assurance, that it has not a vestige of foundation.[15]

Liddon at once replied with a grateful letter in which he regretted the pain that the rumours caused, and expressed courteous sympathy to the Queen. This letter was dated 7 March 1890. However, only two years before, in 1888 when Bishop Mackarness resigned the see of

Oxford, Lord Salisbury had enquired whether the Queen would allow Liddon to be nominated for the vacancy. The Queen had written that 'She is greatly opposed to Liddon being made a bishop', and further-more she asserted that, if he became Bishop of Oxford, 'he might ruin and taint all the young men as Pusey and others did before him.'[16] This strong language is hardly reconcilable with the instruc-tions to Davidson, and it is a matter of speculation to wonder how she would have reacted if Liddon's response to Gladstone's discreet and gentle enquires in 1885 had been different. It may be that the Queen, like Liddon himself, was pleased that no specific offer had to be faced!

However, the Queen's opposition to Liddon's promotion cannot have been considered as absolute by her closest advisers, as is made clear by the chronicle of other men's efforts to persuade Liddon to become a bishop. These continued into the last months of his life and culminated in the offer of the See of St Alban's, to which *The Guardian* had referred. On 22 April 1890, Liddon wrote in his diary, 'Letter from Lord Salisbury, offering me the See of St Albans. Felt as though I had been shot.' He replied asking for time to think, but the diary for 25 April, three days after receiving the offer, recorded, 'wrote to Lord Salisbury, declining to be nominated for the See of St Alban's. Fear that it will vex him very much, but do not see how I could do otherwise.' In the back of the 1890 diary, which he did not live to complete, he wrote a sad private memorandum to which he appended his initials:

> Reasons for my declining See of St Alban's:
>   1) My age 60 – added to my broken health of late.
>   2) The proof afforded by *Lux Mundi* that I have lost the confi-
>   dence of the younger High Church clergy.
> The offer comes too late; and it comes at a time when I have discovered that I have nothing to fall back upon in the way of support.

The man who was eventually appointed was J. W. Festing, a devout High Churchman who governed the See until his death in 1902.

Before leaving the discussion of Liddon's reactions to the prospect of himself becoming a bishop, it is necessary to return to the impor-tant diary entry of 23 January 1885, where he said that he had declined 'two Scotch bishoprics'. It has proved possible to trace only one of these, and it seems likely that the other offer was never made formally. Probably it was no more than an informal sounding-out with nothing committed to writing.

Regarding the offer that is documented. This had occurred in 1875 on the death of Bishop Forbes, and Liddon's diary once again provides the record. The entry for 18 October reads, 'Heard from the Dean of Brechin, through [Malcolm] MacColl, [an old friend] pressing me to be put up for the vacant See, and assuring me that I should be carried unanimously.'

A later, incomplete, entry recorded on 26 October:

> In the evening Mr Nicholson, the Dean of Brechin came here. He was most anxious to persuade me to accept the bishopric. He said that I should be elected unanimously by clergy and laity; he had written out several arguments to move me. I said 'no.' (1) on the ground of nationality; (2) on that of it being necessary to abandon my stall at St Paul's and my professorship . . .

There does seem, however, to have been a suggestion that he could have accepted Brechin without resigning from St Paul's. This was contained in a letter from Lord Kinnaird, dated 27 October 1875, preserved in the papers at Keble College. There is also a copy or draft of Liddon's reply in which he expressed his reasons for rejecting Kinnaird's suggestion. He accepted that the possession of a Scottish bishopric and an English canonry in plurality might not be illegal,

> but morally it would be scarcely possible; at least I had thought so. If our cathedrals are to recover anything like their old position, it must be by much more constant residence on the part of the clergy who belong to them. I am necessarily a great deal away from St Paul's . . .

It is surprising that Liddon did not say that a plural appointment would be disadvantageous to the efficient execution of the work of a bishop, as he conceived it.

In 1886, a year after the diary entry which mentioned the two previous offers, came the offer of another Scottish bishopric, and this time it is well documented. Because the electors tried to present him with a *fait accompli*, and because the offer became public knowledge, his predicament was more acute. It happened while Liddon was away on his trip to Egypt and Palestine. In his hotel at Constantinople he found 'a telegram from the Dean of Edinburgh, announcing that I have been elected Bishop of Edinburgh. *Deus misereatur mei.*'[17] Once again, he declined the offer, but his way of reaching the decision was described by his sister in a letter which she published later in the account of the trip to Egypt and Palestine:

I am afraid that H[enry]'s enjoyment here has been much interfered with by receiving on his arrival a letter from the Dean of Edinburgh, announcing that he had been elected bishop of Edinburgh. He walked his room the whole of that night, and through our thin partition I could hear him imploring God for help and guidance in the step he was taking. When we met in the morning he looked as if he had passed through a great sorrow, but he was quite calm, and by a telegram he gave me to send I saw that he had declined the bishopric. I ventured to remonstrate with him, but he said, 'It is settled; it is not the first time I have had to decline Scotch bishoprics, not because I wish to do so, but I have always taught, and believed, it is essential for the full development of the Church in Scotland that her most important posts should be held by Scotchmen: a foreigner at Edinburgh would mean a fatal mistake.' . . . I think his temptation was very great to accept this bishopric, could he have done so without compromising a principle.

Liddon's perceptive appreciation of the needs of the Scottish Episcopal Church overcame the attraction which the post offered and which the letter went on to make clear: it would have given freedom from those restraints of which the establishment was part, and which generated the 'sorrows, disappointments and anxieties that seem an inevitable condition of his work in England.' That Liddon was appreciative of the electors' confidence in him is borne out by an unidentified press cutting which he kept. It recorded that 'in declining the appointment, [he] expressed a very deep sense of the honour which had been conferred on him. He did, not, however, think it enough to confine his expression of gratitude to words, but shortly after wrote to . . . the Dean of Edinburgh, intimating his desire to make a gift of £100, which should be expended in some way that might stand as a record of the event and his sentiments concerning it'. The cathedral authorities felt that it would be most appropriate to endow an annual sermon for a select preacher to preach a 'Liddon sermon'. The report continued with a reference to 'the modesty of the donor (which is, in truth, one of the great charms of his character) was evidently distressed at the idea of a foundation, which seemed to him too personal and too much akin to a feeling of vain glory.' Eventually, a compromise was reached, and an episcopal chair was made by a London firm at Liddon's expense. The new acquisition, located in the sanctuary, was 'more befitting episcopal dignity than the plain one' previously used but the reporter thought that only at confirmations and ordinations would its 'refinements', because of their 'minute character,' be apparent to 'the eye of the ordinary spectator . . .'

It was ironic that the tour of the Holy Land ended with the offer of

Edinburgh, because it had begun with Liddon receiving a telegram in Cairo with the offer of the Deanery of Worcester.

The Scottish offers, as well as the English ones, reveal the ambivalence of Liddon's attitude to the prospect of serving as a bishop. This ambivalence was in accordance with the views of his Tractarian masters who would have eschewed episcopal preferment if it had ever been offered. However, as the ideals of the Tractarians passed into the life of the Church they gained an influence which made it desirable that some High Churchmen should gain high office. Liddon's attitude largely represents the earlier, purist view. He saw the work of a bishop as that of a teacher and guardian of the flock which he is called upon to govern. It is clear, however, that he believed the work of a nineteenth century bishop carried with it a large number of complicating and frustrating secondary factors. Although Liddon never lacked moral courage and was always willing to champion, even to his own disadvantage, a course of action or an opinion which he believed to be right, it may be that he knew himself to be unable to deal sympathetically with the minutiae of episcopal work. If these personal insights were added to the theological reasons for his endeavours to avoid becoming a bishop, an additional reason may be, as Bishop Francis Paget of Oxford hinted in the concluding chapter of the Johnston biography, that Liddon's own ministry benefited from the fact that he was free of great official responsibility. This freedom led, Paget saw, to 'his doing the most he could of that which he could do best.' Despite this rueful sounding remark of Paget's, it cannot be denied that his gifts were widely used through his work both at Oxford and in London, and that, as an anonymous obituary writer pertinently observed, 'a bishopric would have added very little to Liddon, and would have taken away much. He would have lost his pulpit at St Paul's and received no such pulpit in compensation.' This is probably true and it is now clear that, had he become a bishop, his very considerable but unknown and almost concealed influence upon the Church of England as a whole would not have been so great. Perhaps, despite his self-distrust and his apparent reluctance to accept the mantle of a leader, Liddon knew in his heart that he could best serve the 'church principles' of the Tractarian movement in the spheres of work which he had already made his own. Davidson, in the letter to Henry Ponsonby which has already been noticed, had gone on to observe when reflecting on the failure of the Prime Minister to make Liddon a bishop in 1885, that there might be 'dangers and difficulties' if Liddon came to see himself as an 'excluded leader.' But he did not know his man. Whatever it was that kept Liddon out of the episcopate, whether his reasons were merely personal, or whether they could be justified on theological or other grounds, he recognised as a comparatively young man of thirty-five, preaching in St Mary's, Oxford, on 'Humility and Action', that as St Ambrose had seen fifteen centuries earlier, 'for tender consciences, the lining of a mitre was but a crown of thorns.'

If Liddon had become a bishop he would undoubtedly have found himself facing new difficulties which Davidson would not have appreciated, and he may have seen some of them as dangers, but he would have been spared the inevitable tensions between his two areas of work, a Cathedral dignitary and as a senior academic. He was frequently uneasy about the practical difficulties of combining his two posts, although for almost a dozen years he did run the two together.

When Liddon was twenty-five years old there occurred the first of the nineteenth century reforms of Oxford University and, as a consequence, he felt an ambivalence which developed into unhappiness as the years passed and further reforms were made. He loved Oxford and for almost the whole of his adult life was associated with the University. However, his love was tempered by the nature of the process of the reforms. He wrote:

> Whatever else these changes may have done, they have made the Oxford of today much more unlike that of our fathers and grandfathers than was the Oxford which they knew and loved unlike that of the Middle Ages. More than this these changes have profoundly affected the relations of the University with the Church and religion; they have almost, if not altogether, dissolved a union which had lasted already for a thousand years.

Although he rather over-stated his case, particularly with reference to the time-scale, this unease was not simply that of someone who regrets the alterations that inevitably occur to an institution that had shaped and informed his thinking. Rather it was due to the loss of Oxford as 'the handmaid and home of the Church,' which it had been for centuries. This felicitous epigram was coined by Liddon at the beginning of a lengthy article in the April 1881 edition of the *Church Quarterly Review*, from which the longer quotation above is also drawn. The article was published anonymously, but Liddon's friends recognised his authorship because of the style and because there was no reference to Liddon in it. They felt that no other conscientious author could have written about contemporary Oxford without mentioning the name of Liddon. Characteristically, Liddon failed to see that the relationship of the University to the Church of England was, for the nineteenth century reformers, part of the problem, although he would have been happy for the cathedral of the Diocese of Oxford to be moved from Christ Church to the church of St Mary the Virgin. He wrote in a style of suppressed indignation for most of the article, and its title reveals the nature of his primary concern as a teacher and Churchman: *Recent Fortunes of the Church in Oxford.* He referred only to Oxford, because he had no personal knowledge of Cambridge, where the process of reform took a different line. Taken in conjunction with a survey of his spheres of work, it is possible from this to trace something of his influence as well as his concerns. His work as a teacher began outside the University in 1854 when he accepted the post at Cuddesdon and indicates that he had already perceived what, at first, was a largely unacknowledged need for professional clerical training. This need began to be recognised and led to the founding of the theological colleges. Prior to the implementation of the 1854 University reforms, the Church of England had enjoyed the practical identification of both the ancient universities with its aims and function. Liddon quoted Edmund Burke in support of this contention and devoted several pages of his own article to the historical background behind the assertion. It was his appointment as Vice-Principal of St Edmund Hall that saw the beginning of his more specific work with undergraduates. However, he left there after three years and it was as a Student of Christ Church that most of his work was done. It was at Christ Church that he also enjoyed his deepest relationships with colleagues in the senior common room. Even his growing pessimism about Oxford could not overcome his appreciation of his colleagues. He paid tribute in the article to Dr Pusey who, by this time, was virtually confined to two rooms 'by the infirmities of his eighty years.' He similarly acknowledged Edward King, still the Professor of Pastoral Theology, and William Bright, Regius Professor of Ecclesiastical History, both personal friends.[18]

His formal academic work received its highest recognition in 1870 with his election to the Ireland Professorship of Scripture Exegesis, but his pastoral work, lecturing commitments and his London duties unavoidably robbed him of much time which might otherwise have been devoted to the life of the University as an institution. In 1864 he was elected to the Hebdomadal Council, the executive committee of the University, despite the wish of Pusey that he should not be a candidate. He was re-elected twice, but later he ceased to enjoy the work and was relieved when he was not re-elected in 1875, although Pusey was then deeply disappointed. He had been appointed to his Christ Church Studentship before the changes of 1867 restricted their tenure, and was therefore one of a dwindling number of men who had the right to retain the office for life. By 1885 the number holding Studentships under the old constitution had dwindled to five. They were Liddon himself, R. M. Benson founder of the Society of St John the Baptist, C. L. Dodgson (Lewis Carroll), T. J. Prout, T. V. Bayne and T. B. Strong, later Bishop of Oxford.

During Liddon's career, the University underwent considerable changes and the rise of academic life as a separate profession was both a cause and a consequence of those changes. Two Royal Commissions examined the work of the University. The first, in 1850, brought about the reforms of 1854. The second was in 1877, but in between came the University Tests Act of 1871 which abolished the Church of England's exclusive hold on the University. Liddon was bitter about this and wrote that what he called 'liberal and secular' Oxford had 'dethroned and succeeded' the older 'religious and ecclesiastical Oxford.'[19] A modern scholar has confirmed the pessimistic view of Liddon:

> one had only to look back ... to before the first university commission to gauge the losses which had been suffered by the Church and the revolutionary suddenness of the change. In 1850, Oxford was a predominantly clerical society. All the heads of colleges, with the one exception of Merton, were clergymen. The vast majority of fellowships were not tenable beyond a short term of years except by those in holy orders. Virtually all tutors were clergymen. All undergraduates were members of the Church and about 80 per cent of them were destined to be clergymen themselves. The commission of 1877 continued the work of dismantling this ecclesiastical society, leaving to the Church only two headships and perhaps thirty reserved fellowships in the entire university.[20]

The abolition of religious tests, as a result of legislation passed by Gladstone's government in 1871, had opened all degrees and University offices, except those specifically tied to Anglican orders, to men of any religion opinions, or even none. This too was a blow to Liddon, and he reacted in characteristic manner by claiming that it would, in due course, reduce the University to a totally secular institution. He viewed with considerable alarm the possibility that 'a claim will be advanced, at no distant date, for the admittance of other preachers than the clergy of the English Church to the University pulpit, in order to satisfy the tastes of other religious bodies.' To his mind this would have been a 'desecration of the University church.'[21] His distress about these trends within the University was publicly expressed in a sermon preached in 1881, '. . . we may shortly live to see what has been a home of the Church for a thousand years become a place of purely secular instruction which might have been founded last week by a company of shareholders.'[22] He came to the conclusion, in his long article, 'Recent Fortunes of the Church in Oxford,' that the traditional form of University Sermons were themselves of doubtful value under the new regime, and he put forward a suggestion that they should be replaced by carefully arranged courses of sermons, delivered in term time, but in other parish churches in Oxford, and that St Mary's should be merely one venue among others.

A realistic apprehension of future difficulties was his belief that the secularisation of the University would lead to a decline in chapel attendances and to a drop in the number of vocations to holy orders, and it may be that this was so. Clearly the role of the ancient Universities as appropriate training places for the clergy of the Church of England had changed, and his perception of this caused Liddon, in later years, to strengthen and maintain his support for the theological colleges as he began to withdraw from active involvement in Oxford life. Although this view was not uncommon among High Churchmen, it was by no means universally held by those of different ecclesiastical views. The liberal A. C. Tait, even when Archbishop, always 'preferred to look to the universities for the training of ordinands, rather than to the theological colleges . . .'[23]

The reforming legislation had, however, left the possibility in existence for the establishment of specifically denominational colleges, and Liddon and his friends took advantage of this. Keble College was opened in 1870 as part of a deliberate endeavour to stem the effects of secularisation. Johnston claimed that 'as soon as news of [Keble's] death came, [in 1866] Liddon determined to do his utmost to perpetuate his memory worthily in Oxford,' and he willingly served as one of the fund-raisers for the building of the College. He was naturally anxious to keep the College for the Church and wrote in his article of 1881, 'Keble College . . . would seem to be secured to the Church by the constitution of its council.' He was later scathingly critical of the Bishop of Oxford who seemed to imply that this was due more to good fortune than to the deliberate intention of those who set themselves to build the College. He naturally showed a keen interest in the College's fortunes, despite his resolute refusal to be its first Warden. He preached at the laying of the foundation stone of the library and the opening of the College chapel on 25 April 1876, having previously insisted that the chapel should not be consecrated in order to protect it from being compelled to follow what G. W. E.

Russell called 'the legal fortunes of the Church in Oxford.' Today, the main quadrangle is named after Liddon, and the side chapel was dedicated to his memory. Similarly, another aspect of his activity on behalf of Christian education in Oxford was to find its eventual expression in the establishment of Pusey House as a fitting memorial to Dr Pusey. In his *Church Quarterly Review* article Liddon had expressed the desire to see set up

> colleges of priests, living in community, but under no strict rule, and in houses having no connection with the colleges or the University. They might or might not themselves be University men. They would devote themselves to everything that interested undergraduates; to their studies, their occupations, their moral and spiritual needs.[24]

Liddon held this as his vision for Pusey House.

After Liddon himself died, a similar desire to perpetuate his ideals was felt by his friends. First chronologically came Liddon House now in South Audley Street, Mayfair. Francis Underhill, its Warden in 1929, described it: as 'a house to which young [middle-class] laymen are welcome to come, to say what they have to say, and to hear what can be said in reply.' It sought to protect such men from both moral and religious dangers; it endeavoured to continue the pastoral work which Liddon did among all classes of people. It is not an educational establishment but was thought to be 'exactly the kind of work which most appealed to Dr Liddon's heart.'[25] Rather different, but perhaps more in keeping with Liddon's Oxford work was the establishment of 'Liddon Studentships' administered by the Warden and Council of Keble College. They were established with the residue of the money collected for Liddon's memorial in St Paul's Cathedral. Similar work was undertaken rather later with the Exhibition Fund which was set up under the auspices of St Edmund Hall to provide financial help to ordinands. Again, in the *Centenary Memoir*, this was claimed to be a particularly apposite memorial to Liddon.

As a teacher Liddon was both conscientious and successful, although dogmatic and conservative. He influenced many hundreds of lives, as the popularity of his informal Sunday evening lectures demonstrates. Despite his high office in the University, he did not exercise much influence on the institution. This was because of his devotion to Pusey, whose views he generally tried to support, but it was also due to his London commitments which removed him regularly from the Oxford scene for a large part of each year. Although his influence upon individuals has sometimes been favourably compared with Newman's, he remained unaware of the true extent of the influence that he did wield, yet he had a formative effect upon many men who, over a period of three decades, went out from Oxford University to work in many areas of Victorian life. While his influence, although very considerable, cannot be measured, it has to be admitted that his increasing pessimism did detract from his usefulness in later years, as he gradually withdrew from involvement with the University and devoted himself to Dr Pusey and then to writing his *Life*.

Chapter Nine

'An Anglican of Anglicans: a very sample of the class'[1]

Liddon suffered a flattering misfortune in that all three of his earlier biographers succumbed to a note of affectionate fulsomeness. This has to be overcome if his work is to be accurately assessed. All three clearly revered their subject, and it seems that he inspired such a response among those who knew him. However, this has not helped succeeding generations to assess him, and it is partly because of this that his importance has been consistently underestimated.

Liddon was a publicist for the ideals of the Tractarians and helped to bring them out of Oxford into the cities, parishes and homes of the country. At the same time, however, Liddon was more than just a populariser. Of all his generation he was the one closest to Dr Pusey, and he acted as his spokesman on many occasions. But he was not just Pusey's lieutenant, although he served to bring Pusey's opinions and teaching to bear upon subjects that otherwise would not have been commented upon publicly by the older man. Of the three original instigators of the Oxford Movement, Pusey alone was left after Newman's secession in 1845 and Keble's death in 1866.

From almost the beginning, Liddon's attitude to Pusey was that of a disciple to his master; he sometimes referred to him affectionately as '*ho Megos*, the Great One.' His devotion was not entirely uncritical, although the verdict of history has maintained otherwise and Liddon tended to foster that view, perhaps unintentionally, after Pusey's death. None of the biographies reveal how the young Liddon found his way to Professor Pusey in the early months of his time as an undergraduate. In the 1840s, Pusey as the unofficial leader of the Anglo-Catholics, was considered by many in Church circles to be a dangerous man. Bishop Wilberforce had taken the highly unusual step of suspending him from preaching in Oxford for two years, following his 1843 sermon, *The Holy Eucharist, a Comfort to the Penitent*. When that suspension was lifted Pusey rejoined the ecclesiastical fray with another uncompromising sermon, *The Entire Absolution of the*

Penitent, which he preached in 1846. In reality he was totally loyal to the Church of England, but the common misconception persisted that he was not. Such was the man whom Liddon soon got to know, probably by the simple expedient of calling upon him. However, he was not unaware of the possible disapprobation he might suffer as a result of his friendship with the great man. Certainly he had been anxious after being seen at Pusey's door, and had not been surprised to receive that note from Dr Barnes.

By the time that Liddon went to Cuddesdon, Dr Pusey had been his mentor and confidant for approximately eight years, but they saw rather less of each other during the next five years, as Liddon's failure to inform Pusey of his departure from Cuddesdon indicates. This was partly because of the absorbing nature of Liddon's work, but also because of the attitude of Bishop Wilberforce. Liddon's refusal to support Pusey's eirenic proposal regarding the endowment of professorships, is an indication that he had learned some independence in the intervening years. Liddon's name, even so, was linked with that of Pusey in terms of Church principles throughout this period and, when he left the theological college, the threads of their friendship were picked up and never laid down again. As time passed and the Tractarians gradually became respected, his reputation was both enhanced and damaged by the development of his role as Pusey's lieutenant and spokesman. Pusey was reluctant to accept leadership of the Anglo-Catholics, and it fell to Liddon gradually to supply the need which existed within High Church circles for a theologian who was able to carry forward and articulate the work of his mentors as Church life developed in the second half of the nineteenth century. His leadership was never institutionalised or expressed in any formal way, nevertheless it has been the theme of this work that his contribution was important at the time and was of lasting significance.

This aspect of his role was emphasised as Pusey grew older and more reclusive as his health failed. Not only did the Church of England perceive Liddon to be the mouthpiece of Pusey, Liddon also began to fulfil that role more specifically. Indeed after Pusey died, Liddon's friend William Bright commented that his veneration of Pusey's memory was 'rapidly becoming a cult.' It is clear that Liddon was willing to inconvenience himself in order to please Pusey. When he lost his place on the Hebdomadal Council of the University of Oxford in 1875 his relief was tempered by the knowledge that Pusey regretted it. As early as January 1879, three years before Pusey died, Liddon recorded in his diary that he had suggested that he should give up the Ireland Professorship in order to work on the old man's biography. Pusey opposed the idea and Liddon dropped

it. A more significant instance of their disagreeing occurred following the death of Charles Darwin, on 19 April 1882. Pusey refused to
serve on the committee which was set up to propose a suitable memorial. Liddon thought this was a mistake, but he also declined to serve
on the same committee in order not to distress Dr Pusey at his age.
Liddon would have liked to serve, and it is ironic that Pusey was
willing to accept that he did have his own rather different view.
Liddon preached on Darwin in St Paul's on 22 April 1882, and the
sermon was published. It was a sermon that lots of people, including
many who were not among Liddon's usual audience and readers, had
waited for with some interest, and it received warm approbation.
Liddon had been apprehensive as the time drew near to preach the
sermon. He knew that approval would not be unanimous. He was
right; he did receive criticism, including at least one anonymous
letter which accused him of being a 'rationalist' on account of his
refusal to condemn Darwin. Indeed he was by no means as alarmed
at Darwin's theories as his conservative cast of mind would suggest.

Liddon, with his own unwavering loyalty to the Church of
England, naturally admired the same quality in Pusey and Keble and
remembered the part which Pusey in particular had played in the
development of his own opinions. In a letter in November 1864, to
an unknown recipient but quoted by Johnston, he contrasted the
loyalty of Pusey and Keble with Newman's change of views. He did
not question the quality of Newman's mind, but declared that his
Apologia pro Vita Sua proves

> his conversion to have resulted from the idiosyncrasy of his genius,
> rather than from obedience to any law, or laws, which can have
> weight with the many. He himself says enough of the learning and
> sanctity of Mr Keble and Dr Pusey; *and they have no doubts.*[2]

Keble predeceased both Pusey and Newman, and Liddon, as a
younger man, was inevitably involved as the end of their lives drew
nearer. He met Newman for the first time in 1872 and recorded that
the Cardinal's manner was 'quite like' that of Keble. At the end of
1872 and the beginning of 1873 at the time of the Athanasian Creed
controversy, Pusey was unwell and Liddon found this 'a terrible
anxiety.' He made a full recovery but in March 1878 he fell ill again
and Liddon thought that he should inform Newman who responded
on 31 March by thanking him for the letter. He went on to express
the wish

> to say to my dearest Pusey, whom I have loved for above fifty

years, that the Roman Catholic Church solemnly lays claim to him as her child, and to ask him in God's sight whether he does not acknowledge her right to do so.

This request, which Newman explained enigmatically he would not have made if Liddon were 'an ordinary Anglican,' not unnaturally posed a difficulty. Fortunately it was resolved by a chance remark made by Pusey which Liddon recorded in the next letter to Newman, which was written the following day.

I have spent more than an hour with Dr Pusey this afternoon. I found him on the whole much better than I had expected. He looked reduced by illness, but he was very bright and joyous, and even energetic ... I told him you had asked for him, and he desired me to write a loving message. But I did not say more about the contents of your letter. He has not a shadow of doubt as to the entire consistency of his position with the Revealed Will of God. Only two days before he became ill (he told me today) he 'quieted' a person who was unsettled about the Roman question; and on Saturday last, when he was in bed and too ill to see anyone, he sent another for the same purpose to Dr King ...'

Liddon gave a few more examples of Pusey's Anglican consistency and towards the end of the letter made the following comment:

You will, I am sure, forgive the explicitness with which I write this; but you would, I think, say yourself that his clear and strong convictions were inconsistent with his being anything else than an English Churchman. Yet his vivid sense of the fundamental verities which bind the whole Body of Christ into one, always made him speak of Rome in tender and respectful language, and without the conventional asperities of Anglican controversialists.[3]

Although Pusey recovered from that illness, when the end came, Liddon did not expect events to happen as quickly as they did. He had gone to the continent in 1882 when his August period as Canon in Residence at St Paul's had ended. While in Turin on 15 September he received a telegram from Pusey's daughter, Mrs Brine. She wrote, 'My father is sinking fast; could you return to England at once?' Liddon's diary entries are sad and graphic.

Telegraphed to Ackland [Pusey's physician] to know if I could arrive in time, and to Mrs Brine to say that I had telegraphed

Ackland. A very miserable evening; no telegram arrived before bedtime.

The following day he received another telegram, 'begging me to return to England at once.' He decided to set out immediately but all the 'sleeping carriages' were taken that night and he was unable to do anything more than wait. He was 'in a most anxious state about Dr Pusey all day,' especially when he discovered that *The Times* and *The Daily News* of the previous day both referred to the seriousness of Pusey's illness and that Archbishop Tait, himself mortally sick, had sent Pusey a message of sympathy. On 18 September he got as far as Paris, where he telegraphed Edward King but received no reply. He was unable to keep still, and walked for a while before returning to the hotel to rest. In the evening he went out again,

. . . bought today's *Standard* at a kiosk. On opening it, saw the beginning of an obituary notice, headed 'Dr Pusey.' Had not got the heart to look on, but walked rapidly back to the hotel. Then was enabled to read it, and also *The Times*. So he has left us, most dear and revered of friends, of whose friendship I have been all along so unworthy. How little I can realise it! Though I have been looking forward to this day for twenty years at least.

Pusey had died quietly at Ascot Priory on 16 September 1882, just a few weeks after his eighty-second birthday.

Liddon arrived in Calais on 19 September, clearly having decided not to hurry to England. Something of his personal desolation was revealed in the privacy of his diary.

The afternoon entirely wet. I never saw more steady and heavy rain continuously pouring down. In harmony with my feelings. After dinner, went to a cafe in the Place, as last year and saw the same black-and-white cat. How things have changed since then! Now that dearest Dr Pusey is gone, the world is for me no more the same world. The whole past seems torn up by the roots. I feel the danger of disbelief in God the Holy Ghost. He Who created and trained Dr Pusey can train successors if He wills.

Liddon arrived in Oxford for the funeral on 21 September,

Many old friends . . . The coffin lying in the large study . . . The whole place so natural; the books and pictures just in their places. At 12.45 went to the Deanery, where I joined the Dean and the

Bishop of Oxford. We then all walked to the w. door of the Cathedral. I read the sentences and all the Burial Service after the Lesson, which the Dean read. The Cathedral crowded with people of all kinds. Mr Gladstone one of the pall-bearers. . .

Pusey was laid to rest in Christ Church Cathedral with his wife, who had died in 1839, and his daughter Lucy who had not survived beyond teenage.

Liddon was immediately involved in the two chief projects designed to perpetuate Pusey's memory. In the afternoon of the day of the funeral, he attended a meeting at William Bright's which resolved, after some debate, to establish what he called 'a College of Clergy.' To start with, Liddon had wanted to build a great church in London which would have been a centre of Anglo-Catholic excellence, but was fairly easily persuaded to change his mind.[4] The 'College' was to contain the old man's library and Pusey House was evolved from it. Liddon went to considerable trouble to help with fund raising, touring the country to preach about the project. In Liverpool he described his vision. Pusey House was to be 'a home for sacred learning and a rallying point for the Christian faith,' it was to be a 'centre of moral and intellectual and spiritual enthusiasm.'[5] It was opened in October 1884, little more than two years after Pusey had died. Charles Gore was its first Principal, having served as Vice-Principal of Cuddesdon from 1880–83. Many people were involved in the project, but 'the chief guide and directing force . . . was the faithful Liddon.'[6] It was Liddon who invited Gore to be the Principal, but he seemed to ignore a number of warning signs which Gore spelled out, and which were to cause Liddon much distress within a few years.

> Gore wrote . . . with a long list of hesitations: he was happy in the pastoral work at Cuddesdon; if he moved he wanted to go into a parish; he did not wish to return to Oxford as a pure academic; he could not accept Pusey's attitude to biblical criticism; he rejected the ideal of Oxford as a purely Anglican institution.[7]

Liddon also began to assemble material for the biography and to reflect upon the magnitude of the task. He already knew that the scale of the undertaking would not be compatible with his existing commitments. The work associated with his Canonry at St Paul's had grown to the extent that it could not easily be held in addition to the Professorship. For some years he had wanted to resign his Professorship and he did so soon after Pusey died. He had experienced difficulty in keeping abreast of developments in New Testament scholarship, with which he had little sympathy, so it was sensible that that should be the task he relinquished. It was, of course a real break with the past. His decision was greeted with expressions of regret from former colleagues, and he noted one in particular from Benjamin Jowett, the theologically liberal Master of Balliol College. Nevertheless, despite this rearrangement of his life, his depression did not lift. Others tried to encourage him in his work on Pusey, and he noted a conversation with Dean Church who advised him to use Stanley's *Life of Arnold* as a model 'of form.' Church also advised the extensive use of Pusey's letters. Certainly Liddon followed this latter advice. He set about compiling books of Pusey's correspondence, retaining copies when the owners wished to have their material returned. Eventually this source material amounted to a considerable archive in its own right. The four volume biography of his master is the work for which he is most remembered. Liddon used his rooms at Christ Church for much of the work. There he was relatively free from interruptions and he felt close to the source of his inspiration. Russell, echoing Johnston, thought that his commitment to the huge task was Liddon's 'great mistake.'[8] The sheer amount of work meant that Liddon, who threw himself into it, was almost overwhelmed. He declined to undertake other tasks because of it, and it dominated his life. At the time of his death he had completed two volumes, had done a great deal of work on the third and had also done some on the fourth. The task was completed from his material by Johnston, R. J. Wilson and W. C. E. Newbolt in 1897. It is not surprising that the size of the undertaking has led to the false conclusion that there is nothing more to be said concerning either the subject or the author.

Liddon was an able theologian in his own right. Because of his learning and his analytical powers, together with his felicity of expression, it has been claimed that in his generation he 'possessed an abler theological mind than anyone in the [Oxford] Movement except Newman and J. B. Mozley,'[9] and, perhaps, Dean Church. This is at least a tenable assertion, but it is undoubtedly qualified by the fact that his mind was of a conservative cast. It is further qualified by Pusey's influence which pushed him in a yet more conservative direction. Consequently, he never came to terms with the new thinking that emerged during his lifetime. 'In all his natural instincts he was intensely conservative,' said Holland who wrote the original article in *The Dictionary of National Biography*. Elsewhere, Holland said 'intellectually, his lines were singularly formal and motionless.'[10] This quality was revealed in Liddon's Bampton Lectures on *The Divinity of our Lord and Saviour Jesus Christ.* His preparation was thorough and the Lectures remain an important although unadventurous exposition of the traditional doctrine of the person of Christ. Writers as different as Horton Davies and Don Cupitt have paid tribute to their significance, respectively describing them as 'the best Victorian re-statement of the orthodox two-natures Christology' and 'the last really able defence of a fully Orthodox doctrine of Christ in Britain.'[11]

Earlier Liddon's reaction to the publication of *Essays and Reviews* had revealed the inflexibility of his approach to new theological ideas, and the same attitude prevailed when another volume of essays, this time by Anglo-Catholic scholars and called *Lux Mundi,* was published in November 1889. The events surrounding this later collection distressed him exceedingly and were commonly held to have hastened his death. His uncompromising adherence to principle made some people uneasy with Liddon. One such person was the future Archbishop of Canterbury, Cosmo Gordon Lang who, while working as a don at Magdalen College, Oxford, read the biography of Dean Church and in a letter about that book made the following observation concerning Liddon:

> And Dr Liddon – well, you know how one feels about some houses or churches – 'the design admirable, the scheme of architecture perfect, but I could never feel *at home* there'. There is ... [about Liddon] ... a hardness, a rigidity of dogmatic outline which somewhat repels one.'[12]

Liddon, who was by no means a cold character, would have been distressed by such a comment as a reflection upon his personality, and his friends would have denied that it was true. But as a commentary on his theological views and as a reaction to them it cannot be so easily dismissed. In so far as Lang's comment about rigidity is consistent with a view of the man as someone who was a teacher and a propagandist for the unaltered catholic faith, it is accurate and Liddon himself would not have seen it as an adverse criticism. He did not share the depth of perception enjoyed by Newman whose conclusions he rejected, but who was a theologian able to provide a new synthesis of old truths. Nor did he share the poetic insights of Newman and Keble and, although learned, he did not enjoy the same erudition as Pusey. These limitations are relative to the Tractarian pioneers, but when combined with his fixity of view they inevitably mean that his work as a theologian was not creative. This does not detract, however, from his contribution to the Catholic Movement within the Church of England, and thus to the Church's developed understanding of itself. Indeed what was needed was a theologian who understood the motives of the Tractarians and who was able to bring their insights to bear upon the next generation's problems and opportunities. Liddon was very well equipped for such a vocation, and without him High Church principles would have taken longer to bring about many of the far-reaching changes which the Church of England has experienced since the Oxford Movement began.

The settled nature of his theological views, along with his reputation of being merely Pusey's biographer, has been a major factor in the failure of Church historians to recognise his significance. But he, naturally, did not consider this conservative tendency to be a disadvantage. He was merely anxious to teach accurately that which he once called the 'ancient tradition.' The conventional view, which dismisses him as unimportant, is inaccurate. Far from being insignificant, Liddon's careful restatement of catholic truth in sermons, in university teaching, in private counselling, in spiritual direction and in letters, meant that he exercised a considerable influence throughout the Church of England for many years. It was an influence upon individuals in the Church rather than directly upon the institution itself. Recognition of this fact is the key to understanding both his real importance and his relative obscurity. Theologically he ably re-stated, at a crucial time, an orthodox interpretation of the Christian faith that was subsequently used as a foundation and basis for development by succeeding generations. His personal and private influence cannot be measured, but extended well beyond the confines of the places where he ministered, and beyond his own lifetime. In a letter to E. S. Talbot, a fellow contributor to *Lux Mundi*, Holland said early in 1885 that Liddon was 'an Anglican of Anglicans: a very sample of the class.' This significant remark hints at the place which Liddon and his theological work really occupies in modern Anglican history.

Despite all that can be said about his positive influence, there was an additional factor that limited his usefulness as a theologian and which detracted from his posthumous reputation. This was his willingness to engage in controversy. There was something of a gladiatorial spirit in the man, which was there from childhood, as Bishop Francis Paget noticed in his contribution to the Johnston biography. Paget was a friend and follower of both Pusey and Liddon and 'surrendered himself to the pessimistic influence of Liddon.' Although he had the highest opinion of Liddon's character,[13] he trenchantly observed that a life spent in controversy is especially difficult for those of another generation to analyse. Earlier biographers were careful to minimise the significance of this combative trait in Liddon's character and did not draw attention to the contrast with Pusey 'whose intention was always eirenic'.[14] A good example of this is to be found in the treatment of the controversy with Monsignor Capel at the end of 1874 and early the following year, which was noticed in Chapter Four. This was spread over several months, but Johnston dismissed it in less than two pages; Russell gave it half a dozen lines, and Donaldson who mistakenly dated it all in 1875, was similarly brief. Another earlier example of Liddon's willingness to go to extremes in argument was his threat to retire into what he called 'lay communion' if the proposals to delete the obligation to recite the Athanasian Creed, or to amend its text, were carried out. That he could use his willingness to engage in controversy with greater skill is revealed in his endeavours over the Jerusalem bishopric. But even there, he did not achieve all that he fought for. This sortie into the arena between religion and politics points to the conclusion that Liddon was not effective as a politician, and this was reinforced by his experience with the Public Worship Regulation Act and by his incautious use of the anecdote about Disraeli. It may be that he came to see this himself and consequently kept his involvement in secular politics to a minimum, thereby further reducing his posthumous reputation.

There remains, however, one spectacular involvement in secular politics to be chronicled. In the summer of 1876 there was a genuine fear that the British government, under the leadership of Disraeli, would go to war with Russia in support of Turkey. Liddon, always critical of Disraeli, was dismayed that one Christian country should fight another in support of a Muslim nation. The situation was made more grave when reports of Turkish atrocities began to emerge from Serbia. Disraeli added to the outrage of his opponents by dismissing the accounts as 'coffee house babble' and by making 'odious jokes about the oriental way of executing malefactors.'[15] Gladstone wrote a pamphlet about the political situation, and Liddon decided to go to the Balkans to see for himself as soon as his August period as Canon in Residence was ended. In the meantime, he used one of his sermons to declare his opposition to government policy. He set out for Vienna at the end of the month, probably accompanied by Johnston who was sometimes his companion on continental trips, and travelled as widely as he could, getting up at 4.30 a.m. on 18 September to make what turned out to be a significant river journey. He recorded the details in his diary:

> The steamboat for Semlin left . . . at 6. It was at first cold and raw, but the day improved . . . We passed two chief scenes of the insurrection, and by the bank were a series of Turkish military

stations. In front of each of them sat a group of Turks, grave and imperturbable; and close to each of these stations, surrounded by a palisade, was an impaled man, and other poles on which insurgents had been impaled. Mr Odzic [a Roman Catholic priest and fellow passenger] said that some of them lived for four days, some only twelve hours.

On his return to England, Liddon did all he could to publicise what he had seen. It raised a considerable degree of controversy, and he was accused of believing the propaganda of those who opposed the actions of the Turkish government. He stuck to his own convictions, however. It was, wrote Holland,

> ... a moment never to be forgotten, when Liddon challenged the united hostility of England's Officialdom. And how vivid was his insistence in after years, in making you look through the splendid glasses which had shown him the gruesome sight close at hand: and, then, in contrasting their immediate evidence with that of the British Consul, who, at a distance of eight hundred miles, off and on, from the spot, suggested that it might, possibly, have been a bag of beans on a post . . .[16]

British involvement in the war was avoided. Liddon spoke at a public meeting in St James' Hall on 8 December, but he had said his say in the August sermon when he drew the congregation's attention to what he believed to be the moral outrage of a Christian nation supporting a non-christian state which was guilty of barbaric acts against helpless prisoners and civilians.

It was as a preacher that Liddon's reputation has survived, and his last sermon took the unusual form of a response to an theological controversy. When Pusey House was established, Liddon had full confidence in the Principal or Chief Librarian, the young Charles Gore. He did know that there were differences of opinion concerning scriptural criticism and that Gore did not absolutely reflect the views of Dr Pusey. However, Liddon had convinced himself that these were differences over detail and relatively minor aspects of interpretation. He was not aware of any deep divergence of view and such matters were not discussed by them. Gore said later that he thought that there had been no discussion because each was fully aware of the other's position. He seemed to imply that a kind of conspiracy of silence existed between the two. Liddon, however, claimed to be unaware of the existence of any gulf or any conspiracy and, when the problem was suddenly revealed, he was shocked to the core of his being. Gore had made no secret of his opinions and it seems that Liddon was rather naïve. He included the following, rather pained, observation in a letter to Gore on 29 October 1889:

> When you accepted the Principalship of the Pusey Library, I remember your telling me – I thought it had been in conversation – that you could not always agree with Dr Pusey about the Fathers. I believe I replied, that in so wide a field, within the bounds of which so many questions might be raised, anything like absolute agreement was not to be expected, and I instanced Tertullian, whom I knew you to have been reading very carefully, as a writer about whom people might differ widely on a great variety of points without doing any particular mischief. I do not now remember any allusion to the Old Testament. But this may be due to my bad memory; or, if we were talking, to my deafness; or, if you wrote, to a careless way that I have of reading letters imperfectly; or from my turning the subject out of my mind, from thinking at the time that all you meant was that you could not bind yourself to every opinion of Dr Pusey on matters of detail, or to every interpretation of particular passages of Holy Scripture which he has sanctioned . . .[17]

This statement takes us to the core of the problem which was exposed by the pending publication of the volume of essays entitled *Lux Mundi*. In the summer vacation of 1889, before returning to London for his August period of Canonical Residence at St Paul's, Liddon had visited his erstwhile colleague of eight years, Bishop Lightfoot of Durham. Their conversations did not deal with any potential controversy. The days that Liddon spent in Durham were the last occasion on which the two friends met, and was a period of calm before the controversy that clouded Liddon's last months. Back in Oxford for the Michaelmas term, he heard about the *Lux Mundi* essays. The book was edited by Charles Gore and consisted of twelve essays written by priests who 'found themselves at Oxford together between 1875–1885, engaged in the common work of University education.' They were all Anglo-Catholics and worked, 'for their own sake, no less than that of others, to attempt to put the Catholic faith into its right relation to modern intellectual and moral problems,' as Gore explained at the beginning of his preface. Liddon learned, over dinner one night, that the series was soon to be published. His informant, he recorded in his diary, told him that Gore's essay would 'make great concessions to the Germans.' By those words Liddon perceived that the essay would be more sympathetic to contemporary critical scholarship than he considered acceptable. Gore wrote to Liddon on 15 October 1889, fearing that what he called 'evil rumours' had reached Liddon concerning the book, but he was entirely frank:

> I believe you will approve almost all of it. What you will least like are a few pages at the end, I am afraid, of my Essay. I send it herewith, so that if you wish you may know the worst. Only I hope if you read it you will read the whole Essay . . . Whatever I have said there I have said times out of number to people of all classes in difficulties, and have found again and again that it helped them to a firm footing in Catholic Faith. Where you have found a certain method spiritually effective and useful, and you believe it to be quite orthodox, it seems impossible to refrain from saying it. Something had to be said on the subject. I do sincerely hope that if you read it you will not seriously disapprove. I think I should almost die if it did harm. But certainly experience has led me to hope otherwise. If you seriously disapprove, it would be a great misery. But, at least, I had better send it without delay.[18]

Liddon did seriously disapprove. He was alarmed at the doctrinal implications, and also for the Church. His sister, Mrs Ambrose, later told an acquaintance how distressed he was by the essays. She said that, on the night when he first looked at them, he could not sleep. She heard him pacing his bedroom, repeatedly asking himself, 'What will happen to the Church of England?' Characteristically he responded with a detailed critique which served to emphasise the gulf between their ways of thinking. He hoped that Gore would rewrite or, better still, remove the last pages from his essay. Liddon believed that he made unnecessary concessions to 'rationalism.' He thought that the integrity of scripture, and thus the Christian faith itself, was undermined by those concessions. He was not alone in those views. When the book was published a considerable controversy arose and Gore's essay was the chief cause. Liddon did, however, have a second objection, and it was probably unique to him. Liddon believed that the publication of such opinions by the Principal of Pusey House was an act of violence towards the memory of Dr Pusey. Gore was acutely distressed, but he did not abandon his convictions. He declined Liddon's suggestion that he should submit the text of his essay to various bishops suggested by Liddon, but he invited Liddon himself to approach the Bishop of Oxford, a course of action that Liddon did not feel able to take.

Liddon was plunged into despair because of the apparently rationalistic tone of Gore's opinions, but also because of what he perceived to be the betrayal of the principles underlying the establishment of Pusey House. He had recently stayed at the home of Lord Halifax's sister, Mrs Maynell-Ingram, and she had been persuaded to make a donation of £500 to Pusey House. She had done so on his assurance that it represented the Anglo-Catholic orthodoxy of Dr Pusey, and Liddon felt obliged to offer to return the money. He was, he recorded, 'miserable' about the essay. He also perceived that he was out of touch with the views of the younger generation of Oxford theologians. This was a further cause of despondency. As has been noticed, this was a factor in his decision to decline the bishopric of St Alban's, when the offer came from his old friend from undergraduate days, Lord Salisbury, soon afterwards in April 1890.

His life continued to be busy, and was mainly centred on London, but Oxford claimed his attention when *Lux Mundi* was published. Liddon was already sick at heart when, on 21 December 1889, he was further saddened by the death of Lightfoot. His sense of bereavement gave rise to serious thoughts which he linked to the current state of theology in Oxford. He lamented that theological liberalism would ultimately deprive people of that comfort which orthodoxy provided in the face of human mortality. However, he told himself that a reaction might set in, but in the meantime expressed his sad opinion to C. T. Redington on 2 January 1890:

> sooner or later the sadness with which a non-Christian age contemplates pain and death will lead men to turn their eyes to a Faith which makes these inevitable facts of human life, not merely endurable, but welcome.[19]

On 10 June 1890 he went to Cambridge to receive a DCL degree, and a number of people noticed that he looked ill, although he had put on weight in recent years. A few weeks later he attended the funeral of Lord Carnarvon on 3 July. He felt unwell when he set out, and more so when he struggled back to Oxford. There are so many references to ill health in his diary that there is sometimes an air of hypochondria. He suffered from rheumatism, and often said, 'I am a sort of living barometer; I register every change of atmospheric conditions . . .' This time the situation was serious and there seemed to be a sense of foreboding in his private note about the Bishopric of St Alban's where he referred to his health as 'very uncertain, especially this spring' As the summer developed things got worse. He was in great pain; he described it as 'agony' and 'unspeakable distress.' Johnston said that the cause was 'acute neuralgia of the neck,' but gout was also a problem. A letter to Bishop King of Lincoln was written from Liddon's Christ Church rooms, but addressed 'from my sick bed.' He told King, 'God has laid His hand very heavily upon me; and I have been through the fire . . .' He asked for King's prayers, because 'I never before knew what pain might be.' Even in this extreme suffering his wit did not desert him. The gout, he observed, was 'of no more importance than a burning out-house when the citadel was in flames.' His physician was Sir Henry Ackland, and it was decided that he could not remain at Oxford. Before he moved, however, he asked daily after Charles Gore, but rejected the suggestion that he might be visited by him. Eventually he relented, although he maintained he was too ill to talk. The unfortunate Gore was conscientious with daily visits from that date.

On 19 July 1890, Liddon travelled to the home of his sister, Annie Poole King, at Stonehouse in Gloucestershire. Under her care he appeared to recover. He received visits from various siblings and their children. He had good days, but many painful nights. Throughout his illness he persevered with the Daily Offices. *The Times* was read to him and, as always, he kept up his correspondence although it was sometimes necessary to dictate his letters, and he also dictated his diary. His reading material included Newman's sermons, with which he did not persevere, and Walter Scott's novels, which he found more congenial. Gradually he became able to cope with serious reading and eventually he corrected the proof of the preface to the fourteenth edition of his Bampton Lectures adding, for the new edition, an assessment of the issues raised by the recently published *The Seat of Authority in Religion,* by James Martineau, the Unitarian.

At the end of July 1890, he felt sufficiently well to write an optimistic letter to R. W. Dale, the Congregationalist minister and theologian. This was the last episode of a correspondence which stretched over many years. Liddon wrote frankly about the pain of his illness, using language which was similar to that in his letter to Edward King. He wrote in much the same vein to Lord Halifax in early August when he had suffered a relapse. On 12 August Liddon dictated a record of the death of Cardinal Newman in his diary. He also dictated a letter which he wrote to Father William Neville who had been Newman's closest friend in the final years of his life. In it he regretted that his illness prevented him from attending the Cardinal's funeral. He would willingly have attended in his own right, having met and corresponded with Newman over the years, and also as a mark of respect for the friendship which had existed between Pusey and Newman in the early days. Indeed, he told Neville that both Pusey and Keble would have wished him to be there.

At Stonehouse he was under the medical supervision of his brother, Doctor Edward Liddon, who came to the opinion that a change of air would be beneficial to the patient. Liddon himself did not want to move again, but eventually was persuaded and went to Weston Super Mare on 5 September 1890. Before he left Gloucestershire, his old friend Alfred Barff came to stay for a few days. He arrived on 1 September and gave Liddon what was to be his last Communion two days later. Afterwards he seemed rather better and Barff remarked on the improvement, to which Liddon replied, 'Yes, I have often noticed that the Blessed Sacrament helps the body as well as the soul.'

Edward Liddon travelled with his brother, as did two nieces. It was arranged that Mrs Poole King would join them later. The journey was a success and although he found the last part rather painful, Liddon seemed to be stronger immediately. But within a short time he had received another emotional blow. His godson, Lord Halifax's son Charles, was also unwell. On Monday 8 September, Liddon learned that he had died. He was twenty years of age. One of Liddon's nieces saw how terribly distressed he was on receiving the news, and she noticed how he had difficulty in signing the letter which he dictated to Halifax. This latest death was an event from which Liddon did not recover his emotional equilibrium, and his own health began rapidly to deteriorate once again. The biography by George Russell quoted a description of the closing events which was compiled by one of Liddon's nieces. On Tuesday, 9 September, Liddon's servant found him helpless. He had suffered a similar attack on the previous evening. The eye-witness account continues:

I went in, and found him sitting up, not faint or unconscious, but apparently unable to move. I begged him to let us help him back into bed, but he shook his head and seemed unable to speak. I called my sister to stay with him, and ran off for the doctor, who only lived about five minutes off. Somehow, I was not frightened, for I had often seen him very like this, and he had generally come round suddenly. I noticed though, this time, that his eyes were unusually large and bright and expressive: they had struck me so too on Monday. I found the doctor in, and he came at once . . . He went straight into my uncle's room, and, as he went in, my sister came out. I asked her how Uncle Harry was. She said that he had gradually become easier, and she had sent the servant away; and that he soon fell asleep. At first his breathing had been very laboured, but now he was sleeping so quietly that she could hardly hear him. She went on to say that his sleep was like death, but she remembered to have seen him look like it in the night, and was not really alarmed.

In a few minutes the doctor came to us, and told us that it was all over before he arrived. The face had not a trace of suffering on it. I never saw anything more beautiful than his expression – a certain sweet but rather severe look which he had sometimes, reminding me somewhat of what he had been like as a young man.[20]

Liddon's body was brought to London on the Thursday and lay in his study at Amen Court and moved to St Paul's on the Monday where it remained overnight. On Tuesday 16 September 1890, Gregory celebrated the Holy Communion at 7 a.m. and Holland at 8 a.m. The funeral took place at noon in the presence of a large congregation, Although there were ten bishops present, neither the Archbishop nor the Bishop of London attended. Liddon had made his will in 1885, before setting out on his tour of the Middle East. He had asked to be buried in the crypt of St Paul's, 'if it may conveniently be arranged,' and the will was itself a statement of Christian orthodoxy, and a declaration of loyalty to the Church of England:

... I commit my soul into the Hands of Almighty God, trusting to obtain his mercy only through the Merits of Jesus Christ, and firmly believing the Christian Faith as held by the whole Catholic Church before the Division of East and West, and by the Church of England ...

Dean Church officiated in the crowded church, and it was to be his own last appearance there, for he too died shortly afterwards:

no one who was present ... on the occasion of Dr. Liddon's funeral, could have seen unmoved the wasted fragile figure of the Dean, or have listened without a sense of its pathos and significance, to his broken and scarcely audible voice as it was heard for the last time in the cathedral ...[21]

The two men had been colleagues for nineteen years, but friends since Liddon was an undergraduate. There were many tributes to Liddon, and many people were genuinely saddened by his death and by its suddenness.

Liddon died shortly after his sixty-first birthday and the Church of England was robbed of a doughty champion who, many thought, still had much to give.

His final years were over-shadowed by work on the biography of Pusey whom he survived by only eight years. This, combined with his self-effacing style meant that he was soon largely forgotten, particularly as fresh controversies and challenges erupted to confront the successors and spiritual heirs of the Oxford Movement. It might be that, had he lived for another decade or more, Liddon would have completed his work on Pusey and also have begun to come to terms with the emerging theology which *Lux Mundi* exemplified within Anglo-Catholicism. It may be that, then, his contribution to the Church would be easier to measure. However, his earnest endeavours to promote catholic principles tended to lead him towards an exclusive view of the Church in relation to other Christian bodies, despite his authentic desire for reunion and the genuine efforts he made at the two Bonn Conferences. It is difficult to avoid the conclusion that his most cherished convictions about the Church of England had the unsought consequence of encouraging a tendency to make it theologically narrower. But this danger was recognised by him and he sought to avoid it by his constant references back to Scripture and to the writings of the Fathers of the early Church with their emphasis on the central significance of the incarnation, not only for the salvation of each individual, but also for a proper understanding of the nature of the Church. This true catholicity of view was taken up by the next generation of High Anglican scholars. Ironically, it can be traced in the title of the essays that so distressed Liddon in the last months of his life. *Lux Mundi* was described, in its subtitle, as 'a series of studies in the religion of the Incarnation', and Gore also wrote in the preface to the first edition:

The real development of theology is . . . the process in which the Church, standing firm in her old truths, enters into the apprehension of the new social and intellectual movements of each age: and because 'the truth makes her free' is able to assimilate all new material, to welcome and give its place to all new knowledge.

Despite an apparent divergence, this is not exclusive of Liddon's motive expressed, more than twenty years before, in the preface to the first edition of his Bampton Lectures. He saw himself as dealing with '. . . some of those assaults upon the doctrine of our Lord's Divinity which have become prominent or popular of late years.' Gore, it may be claimed, was taking the battle forward whereas Liddon was defending the citadel. But it was the same war. In lecturing on the Divinity of Christ, Liddon was most certainly standing firm to old truths, but in doing so was unwittingly paving the way for the apprehension of that which was new. He prepared the way for that emphasis on the doctrine of the incarnation that has been such a notable element of twentieth century Anglican theology. He would have rejected any suggestion that his presentation of the 'ancient tradition' was other than properly conservative, but he helped to make it possible for the insights of the Tractarians to be re-worked and to be presented to the generations that were to follow. This is part of his greatness, but it is an aspect of his teaching and ministry that could not be recognised at the time and is only apparent to later generations.

Liddon's thoughts were clothed in a Victorian vocabulary and seem to express theological insights that are dated, but they nevertheless point uncompromisingly to 'the divinity of our Lord and Saviour Jesus Christ.' They were addressed to those who take seriously that divinity, in its bearing upon a developed doctrine of the Catholic Church, and its consequences for each individual soul. The Bampton Lectures constitute his longest and most systematic piece of theological writing. In the third lecture in the series, Liddon declared that Christ was the 'Founder' of the Church because

> He did not propose to act powerfully upon the convictions and the characters of individual men, and then to leave them, when they believed and felt alike, the liberty of voluntarily forming themselves into an association, with a view to reciprocal sympathy and united action. From the first the formation of a society was not less an essential feature of Christ's plan, than was His redemptive action upon single souls.[22]

Liddon rejoiced to be part of that society, and gave all his abilities to strengthening that which he believed to be its authentic English branch. If his books are no longer read, this is not entirely due to the movement of theological fashion, it is partly an indication of the thoroughness with which he did his work. His 'cutting edge' remains sharp in its challenge to those who would deny the centrality of catholicism in the Church of England's self-understanding. It is appropriate that the last words should be his, taken from his last public utterance, the sermon *The Inspiration of Selection* which was published shortly before he died. He rejoiced to have lived as a member of the Church of England and thus to have shared in that catholicity, and to be part of that 'little community' which at Pentecost received the Holy Spirit and was

> hallowed and invigorated from on high, [and] entered on the career which has already lasted for nearly nineteen centuries, and which will end only with the close of time.[23]

Select Bibliography

Part One, Published Works by H. P. Liddon
(the place of publication is London unless otherwise stated)

University Sermons (First Series) (1865), (originally published with the title:
    Some Words for God)
The Divinity of our Lord and Saviour Jesus Christ (1867) (The Bampton
    Lectures of 1866)
Walter Kerr Hamilton, Bishop of Salisbury, a sketch (1869)
    (Reprinted with additions from *The Guardian*)
'The State in its Relation to the Church,' a paper reprinted from 'The
    British Critic' of October 1839, by the late John Keble, MA with a
    Preface by the Rev. H. P. Liddon, (1869)
*A Letter to the Rt. Hon. and Rt. Rev. The Lord Bishop of London by the Two
    Senior Canons of St Paul's Cathedral* (1871), written in conjunction with
    Robert Gregory
Some Elements of Religion (1872)
*Report of the Proceedings at the Reunion Conference Held at Bonn on
    September 14, 15, 16, 1874,* with a Preface by H. P. Liddon (1874)
'*Report of the Proceedings at the Reunion Conference Held at Bonn between
    the 10 and 16 August, 1875,* with A Preface by H. P. Liddon (1875)
Evening Communions Contrary to the Teaching and Practice of the Church
    in All Ages' (1876)
(An Article re-printed from *The Christian Remembrancer*)
Thoughts on Present Church Troubles (1881)
'The Recent Fortunes of the Church in Oxford', article in *The Church
    Quarterly Review,* April 1881, 201–242
Of the Five Wounds of the Holy Church by Antonio Rosmini, edited with an
    Introduction by H. P. Liddon (1883)
University Sermons (Second Series) (1883)
(The Liddon House copy contains, pasted in the back, pages from The
    Oxford and Cambridge Undergraduates' Journal of 13.11.1884 containing
    a report of a Sermon by Liddon on Psalm 143.v8, the sermon is not
    published elsewhere and has no title)

A Father in Christ, a Sermon preached at the consecration of Bishops King and Bickersteth (St Paul's, 25.4.1885); the second edition has a long and valuable Preface by Liddon which is not included in the version of the sermon published in *Clerical Life and Work*.

Easter in St Paul's
   (originally published in two volumes in 1885, a collected version in one volume appeared in 1889)

Advent in St Paul's (originally published in two volumes in 1888, a single volume version was produced in 1889)

The Name of Names a sermon preached in St Paul's 1.1.1889, (published 1889)

Christmastide in St Paul's (1989)

The Vision at Corinth, a sermon preached in Christ Church Cathedral, Oxford. 12.5.1889 (published 1889)

The Worth of the Old Testament, a sermon preached in St Paul's 8.12.1889 (published 1890)

Selections from the Writings of H. P. Liddon (1890) produced by an unnamed editor, but with Liddon's permission

The Magnificat, Sermons in St Paul's (1890)

The Inspiration of Selection, a sermon preached in St Mary's, Oxford, 25.5.1890 (published 1890)

Passiontide Sermons (1891)

Sermons on Old Testament Subjects (1891)

Essays and Addresses (1892)

Sermons on some Words of Christ (1892)

Explanatory Analysis of St Paul's Epistle to the Romans (1893)

Life of Edward Bouverie Pusey (edited and prepared for publication by J. O. Johnston and R. J. Wilson).
   Volume I   1893
   Volume II   1893
   Volume III   1894
   Volume IV   1897 (Johnston and W. C. E. Newbolt)

Clerical Life and Work (1894)

Sermons Preached on Special Occasions (1897)

Explanatory Analysis of St Paul's First Epistle to Timothy, (1897)

Sermons on Some Words of St Paul (1898)

Additional Note

A number of unauthorised volumes of Liddon's sermons were also published. Reference has only been made in the text to publications authorised and prepared by Liddon or his executors; therefore, the unofficial publications are not included in this Bibliography.

Part Two, Other Published Sources
The place of publication is London unless otherwise stated. A number of additional items are listed in the footnotes.

Allchin, A. M. *The Joy of all Creation* (1984)
Battiscombe, G. *John Keble, A Study in Limitations* (1963)
Battiscombe, G. *Shaftesbury, A Biography of the Seventh Earl* (1974)
Bell, G. K. A. *Randall Davidson* (2 vols.) (1935)
Bentley, J. *Ritualism and Politics in Victorian Britain* (Oxford, 1978)
Benson, A. C. *The Life of Edward White Benson* (2 vols.) (1899)
Briscoe, J. F. (ed.) *V. S. S. Coles, Letters, Papers and Addresses with a Memoir* (1930)
Butler, P. *Gladstone: Church, State and Tractarianism* (Oxford, 1982), (ed) *Pusey Rediscovered* (1983)
Carey, K. M. (ed.) *The Historic Episcopate* (1954)
Carpenter, E. *Cantuar: The Archbishops in their Office* (1971)
Carpenter, S. C. *Church and People* (1933)
Chadwick, Owen *The Founding of Cuddesdon* (Oxford, 1954)
The Mind of the Oxford Movement (1960)
The Spirit of the Oxford Movement (Cambridge, 1992)
The Victorian Church, Part I (1966)
Part II (1970)
Edward King, Bishop of Lincoln (Lincoln 1968)
Church, M.C. (ed) *The Life and Letters of Dean Church* (1895)
Church, R.W. *The Oxford Movement* (1891)

Church Quarterly Review, Vol. 60, July 1905 (anonymous review of J. O. Johnston's biography of Liddon)
Clifford, J. *Typical Christian Leaders* (1898)
Cohen, M. N. *Lewis Carroll, a biography* (London, 1995)
Coleridge, J. T. *A Memoir of the Rev John Keble* (1870; republished 1969)
Coombs, J. *Judgement on Hatcham* (1969)
Cowling, M. *Religion and Public Doctrine in England, Vol II* (Cambridge, 1985)

Correspondence Relating to Cuddesdon Theological College (Oxford, 1858)
Cross, F. L. *The Tractarians and Roman Catholicism* (1933)
Davies, H. *Worship and Theology in England*
Volume 3 From Watts and Wesley to Maurice 1690-1850 (Oxford, 1961)
Volume 4 From Newman to Martineau 1850-1900 (Oxford 1982)
de Waal, E. 'New Style Parson, the Professionalization of the Nineteenth Century Country Clergy', *Theology*, Vol 82, No. 687, (May 1979), 169-175
Donaldson, A. B. *Henry Parry Liddon* (1905)
Ellis, I. *Seven Against Christ* (Leiden, 1980)
Engel, A. J. *From Clergyman to Don* (Oxford, 1983)

Fairweather, E. R. *The Oxford Movement* (New York, 1964)
Gore, C. (ed.) *Lux Mundi* (1889)
    The Mission of the Church (1892)
    Dissertations on Subjects Connected with the Incarnation (1895)
    St Paul's Epistle to the Romans, a Practical Exposition (2 vols, 1900)
    The Body of Christ (1901)
Griffiss, J. E. *Church, Ministry and Unity* (Oxford, 1983)
Haig, A. *The Victorian Clergy* (1984)
Hall, A. C. A. *Henry Parry Liddon, A Memorial Sermon* (New York, 1890)
Härdelin, A. *The Tractarian Understanding of the Eucharist* (Uppsala, 1965)
Hatch, E. *The Organisation of the Early Christian Churches* (1881)
    'Canon Liddon's Theory of the Episcopate', *Contemporary Review,* (June, 1885), 860–865
Hempton, D. N. 'Evangelicalism and Eschatology' *Journal of Ecclesiastical History,* Vol 31, No. 2 April 1980, 179–194.
Hinchliff, P. *Frederick Temple, Archbishop of Canterbury, a Life* (Oxford,1998)
Holland, H. S. *Personal Studies* (1905).
    A Bundle of Memories (1915).
    Article on Liddon in Dictionary of National Biography
Hort, F. J. A. *The Christian Ecclesia* (1898)
Hutton, W. H. (ed.) *The Autobiography of Robert Gregory* (1912)
Johnston, J. O. & *The Spiritual Letters of Edward Bouverie Pusey* (1898)
Newbolt, W. C. E.
Johnston, J. O. *The Life and Letters of Henry Parry Liddon* (1904)
Jones, O. W. *Isaac Williams and his Circle* (1971)
Keble, J. *The Christian Year* (1827, reprinted 1977)
National Apostacy (Oxford 1833, reprinted Abingdon, 1983)
King, A. P. *Dr Liddon's Tour in Egypt and Palestine* (1891)
Lockhart, J. *Viscount Halifax* (2 vols.) (1935)
    Cosmo Gordon Lang (1949)
Machin, G. I. T. *Politics and the Churches in Great Britain, 1832–1868* (Oxford, 1977).
Matheson, P. E. *Life of Hastings Rashdall* (Oxford, 1928)
Matthews, W. R. *Memories and Meanings* (1969)
Moss, C. B. *The Old Catholic Movement, Its Origins and History* (1948)
Newman, J. H. *Apologia Pro Vita Sua* (1864)
Newsome, D. *The Parting of Friends* (1966)
Nockles, P. B. *The Oxford Movement in Context* (Cambridge, 1994)
Norman, E. R. *Church and Society in England, 1770–1970* (Oxford, 1976)
Paget, S. & Crum, J. M. C. *Francis Paget, Bishop of Oxford* (1913)
Paget, S. (ed.) *Henry Scott Holland, Memoir and Letters* (1921)
Pawley, B. & M. *Rome and Canterbury Through Four Centuries* (1974)
Pollard, A. *Writers and their Works: English Sermons* (1963)
Prestige, G. L. *Pusey* (1933, re-issued 1983 with an introduction by C. Jones).

The Life of Charles Gore (1935)
St. Paul's In Its Glory (1955)
Ramsey, A. M. *From Gore to Temple* (1960)
Reardon, B. M. G. *Religious Thought in the Victorian Age* (1980) formerly published with the title *From Coleridge to Gore* (1971)
Rouse, R. & Neill, S. C. (ed.) *A History of the Ecumenical Movement, 1517–1948* (1967)
Rowell, G. *Hell and the Victorians* (Oxford, 1974)
The Vision Glorious (Oxford, 1983)
(ed) *Tradition Renewed* (1986)
Royal Commission on Ecclesiastical Courts, 1882, Minutes of Evidence
Russell, A. *The Clerical Profession* (1980)
Russell, E. F. (ed.) *Alexander Heriot Mackonochie, A Memoir by 'E.A.T.'* (1898)
Russell, G. W. E. *Leaders of the Church, 1800–1900, Dr Liddon* (1905)
Edward King, Sixtieth Bishop of Lincoln (1912)
Sandford, E. G. (ed.) *Memoir of Archbishop [Frederick] Temple (2 vols)*
Sinclair, W. *Memorials of St Paul's Cathedral* (1909)
The Times, December 1874; January 1875 on the Capel controversy
Tracts for the Times. A total of ninety *Tracts for the Times* were issued between 1833 and 1841. An appendix to volume III of Liddon's biography of Pusey contains the most conveniently accessible list of titles and authors. They were eventually published in bound volumes from 1834. Those *Tracts* to which there are specific references in the text are identified in the footnotes.
Vidler, A. R. *The Orb and the Cross* (1945)
Weil, L. *Sacraments and Liturgy: The Outward Signs* (Oxford, 1983)
Welsby, P. A. (ed.) *Sermons and Society* (1970)
Westcott, A. *Life and Letters of Brooke Foss Westcott* (2 vols.), (1903)
Wilberforce, R. G. *Life of the Right Reverend Samuel Wilberforce* (3 vols: 1880; 1881; 1882)
Wilson, R. F. (ed.) *Letters of Spiritual Counsel and Guidance, by the late Rev. J. Keble* (1870)

Part Three, Primary Sources
Keble College, Oxford
This is an extensive archive, mostly of correspondence to Liddon beginning in 1856, but it does also contain drafts or copies of important replies, private notes and memoranda which Liddon compiled for his own use, plus press-cuttings and some pamphlets.

Bodleian Library, Oxford
The St Edmund Hall archive of letters by Liddon to relatives and friends, sermons, notes, press-cuttings, notebooks, dating from 1859.
Ripon College, Cuddesdon (formerly Cuddesdon Theological College), uncatalogued material in boxes dating from 1852. Letters of Liddon and Edward King; letters and papers of Liddon, Newman and Wilberforce;

manuscript meditations by Liddon.

Borthwick Institute, York

Papers of the Hon. C. L. Wood, later Second Viscount Halifax, 490 letters by Liddon to Wood, written between 1864 and 1890.

Liddon House, 24 South Audley Street, London W1

Liddon's diaries from 1852 to 1890. It was his habit to retain letters and other papers between the leaves of his diaries. This archive also contains a small collection of printed sermons, some of which were not published in any of the collected volumes, and two 'scrap books' of press-cuttings.

Lambeth Palace Library

Letters of Liddon to Rev C. P. Golightly, undated correspondence with (Rev) Mr Hill.

Pusey House, St. Giles, Oxford

Liddon's pocket diaries, 1847, 1848, 1849. Eleven boxes of correspondence mainly to Liddon with some draft and copies of replies. Several books of press cuttings, some compiled by Liddon and others by J. O. Johnston, also manuscript sermons and a further manuscript book of 'Meditations at Cuddesdon.'

Part Four, Dissertations

Beswick, C. E. 'Liddon of St Paul's 1870–1890' (University of Exeter, MA, 1974)

Willshaw, T. M. 'Two Apologists for Catholic Christology, Henry Parry Liddon and Charles Gore' (University of Kent, PhD, 1984)

Part Five, Additional published material
Essays and Reviews (1860)
Henry Parry Liddon, a Centenary Memoir (1929)

Notes

Notes to Chapter One: 'A man of modesty and sense'

1. Liddon, on 'The secret of clerical power,' see below page 11.
2. J. O. Johnston, *Life and Letters of Henry Parry Liddon* (London, 1904) p.3, n.2.
3. John Henry Newman (1801–90), Edward Bouverie Pusey (1800–82) and John Keble (1792–1866), with others, initiated a revival of interest in the catholic nature of the theological heritage of the Church of England. They worked through pamphlets, *The Tracts for the Times*, from 1833, and their work became increasingly contentious. The bitterness erupted afresh when Newman became a Roman Catholic in September 1845. From that date Pusey was the reluctant leader of the Oxford Movement, and its followers became known as Puseyites and, later, Tractarians.
4. G. W. E. Russell, *Leaders of the Church 1800–1900, Dr Liddon* (London, 1905) p.8.
5. A. B. Donaldson, *Henry Parry Liddon* (London, 1905) p.9.
6. O. Chadwick, *The Founding of Cuddesdon* (Oxford, 1954) p.56
7. Bishop Joseph Butler (1692–1752, Bishop of Durham from 1750) His *Analogy of Religion* was a standard text for those studying theology in Liddon's day, as was John Pearson's *Exposition of the Creed* of 1659. Pearson (1612–86) was Bishop of Chester from 1673.
8. Chadwick, *op.cit.*, p.43
9. F. H. Borsch, 'Ye shall be holy, reflections upon the spirituality of the Oxford Movement' in G. Rowell (ed.), *Tradition Renewed* (London, 1986) p.64.
10. Liddon, *Clerical Life and Work* (1894), Sermon VII, preached 22 December 1867. Liddon lived over a century before the Church of England began to ordain women to the ministry.
11. Liddon, *op.cit.*, p.169, Sermon V, preached 24 September 1865.
12. Liddon, *op.cit.*, p.221, Sermon VII, preached 22 December 1867.
13. Liddon, *loc. cit.*
14. Liddon, *op.cit.*, Sermon VIII, preached 26 May 1872.

15. Liddon, *University Sermons, First Series* (1865/6), sermon X, preached 30 April 1865.
16. O.Chadwick, *op.cit.*, p.80.
17. R. G. Wilberforce, *The Life of the Rt. Rev. Samuel Wilberforce, D.D.*, vol.2 (London, 1881) p.361.
18. O. Chadwick, *The Spirit of the Oxford Movement* (Cambridge, 1992) p.238.
19. R. G. Wilberforce, *op.cit.*, vol.2, p.361.
20. R. G. Wilberforce, *op.cit.*, vol.2, p.365.
21. O. Chadwick, *Founding*, quoted on p.73.
22. O. Chadwick, *op.cit.*, quoted on p.74.
23. O. Chadwick, *op.cit.*, p.73.
24. Additional material in the 1858 diary, including unidentified press cuttings.
25. G.W.E. Russell, *Edward King, Bishop of Lincoln* (London, 1912) p.127.
26. Liddon's diary, 25.10.1862.

Notes to Chapter Two: To 'The Centre of the world's concourse'

1. J.B. Lightfoot (Bishop of Durham from 1879), Liddon's colleague at St Paul's (1871–9), dedicated his *St Ignatius* to Liddon as one 'assigned to preach' at St Paul's Cathedral, set at 'the centre of the world's concourse.
2. See p.Hinchliff, *Frederick Temple, Archbishop of Canterbury, a Life* (Oxford) 1998, p.63. In the opinion of theologians who criticised *Essays and Reviews*, Temple was the author of the least offensive of the contributions.
3. Morton H. Cohen, *Lewis Carroll, a Biography* (London 1995) p.251.
4. S. Paget and J. M. C. Crum, *Francis Paget, Bishop of Oxford* (London, 1913) p.20–1.
5. For his sadness, see Liddon, 'The Recent Fortunes of the Church in Oxford', a lengthy article in *The Church Quarterly Review*, April 1881.
6. J.O. Johnston, *Life and Letters of Henry Parry Liddon* (London, 1904) p.58.
7. Thomas Thellusson Carter (1808–1901), the Anglo-Catholic vicar of Clewer, founder of the Community of St John the Baptist in 1849 and a spiritual writer.
8. William Bright (1824–1901), Regius Professor of Ecclesiastical History at Oxford, from 1868.
9. Bright to Liddon, 16 October 1867, quoted Johnston, *op.cit.*, p.81.
10. Liddon, 'Recent Fortunes,' p.209.
11. Johnston, *op.cit.*, p.82.
12. p.Hinchliff, *ibid.*
13. Quoted by Johnston, *op.cit.*, p.84.
14. Quoted by Johnston, *op.cit.*, p.111.
15. Liddon's diary 6 April 1866, quoted by Johnston, *op.cit.*, p.111.

16. Liddon, 'Recent Fortunes', p.239. Edward Stuart Talbot (1844–1934) was a moderate High Churchman, a contributor to the *Lux Mundi* series of essays (1889), became Bishop of Rochester in 1895, and the first Bishop of Southwark in 1905. He was Bishop of Winchester 1911–24.
17. Liddon to Pusey, 16 April 1869, quoted by Johnston, *op.cit.*, p.115.
18. Quoted by Cohen, *op.cit.*, p.264.
19. Liddon's diary, quoted by Johnston, *op.cit.*, p.100.
20. John William Colenso, (1814–83), first Bishop of Natal. An accusation of heresy led to a protracted legal dispute in England, and much publicity. The affair was a major factor in Archbishop Longley's decision to call the first Lambeth Conference in 1867.
21. Vasilii Drosdov Philaret, (1782–1867), theologian, Metropolitan of Moscow.
22. Johnston *op.cit.*, p.104.
23. Cohen, *op.cit.*, pp.270–1.
24. Cohen, *op.cit.*, p.131.
25. G. W. E. Russell, *Leaders of the Church, 1800-1900, Dr. Liddon* (London, 1905) pp.24–6.
26. The sermon at Hamilton's funeral was on St Luke 24.4–5, and was published shortly after it was delivered, with the title, *Life in Death*.
27. Johnston *op.cit.*, p.120.
28. Robert Phillimore (1810–85), from 1867 the Dean of Arches, the judge in the Court of Arches, the Consistory Court of the Province of Canterbury.
29. Johnston, *op.cit.*, p.120.
30. Johnston, *op.cit.*, p.122.
31. See Russell, *op.cit.*, pp.33–4.
32 Russell, *op.cit.*, p.33.

Notes to Chapter Three: Devotion to the Church of Christ

1. Liddon, *Sermons Preached on Special Occasions* (London, 1897) Sermon XIII, preached 9 November 1873, pp.294–5.
2. For an assessment of Pusey see K. Denison 'Dr. Pusey as Confessor and Spiritual Director' in p.Butler (ed.) *Pusey Rediscovered* (London, 1983), pp.210–30.
3. 'Ritualism' is the term which describes the revival of ceremonial which characterised the later phases of the Oxford Movement.
4. See D. Newsome, *The Parting of Friends* (London, 1966), p.138.
5. Liddon, *Clerical Life and Work* (London, 1894) Sermon XIV, preached 20 January 1884, p.365.
6. Liddon, *Clerical Life and Work, loc. cit.*
7. M. Cowling, *Religion and Public Doctrine* (Cambridge, 1985) p.53.
8. J. O. Johnston, *Life and Letters of Henry Parry Liddon* (London, 1904) p.66.
9. E. R. Fairweather, *The Oxford Movement* (New York, 1964) p.9.
10. Liddon, *Clerical Life and Work*, Sermon XIII, preached 25 April 1876, p.342.

11. Johnston, *op.cit.*, quoted on p.94. Newman's *Apologia pro Vita Sua*, published in 1864, was an account of his spiritual journey which, despite a certain note of self-absorption, received wide acclaim.

12. The two examples quoted are from the Keble College Archive. The Pusey House records also contain at least one other violently phrased example.

13. Liddon, *Life of Pusey*, vol.III p.26.

14. Liddon was involved in two conferences held at Bonn in 1874 and 1875. They were unofficial attempts to work towards Christian unity and were composed of Anglican theologians and some from the evolving Old Catholic Church and a few Eastern Orthodox scholars. Liddon's involvement in the Conferences will be examined in Chapter Six, as will his relationships with the Old Catholics.

15. Peter B. Nockles in *The Oxford Movement in Context* (Cambridge, 1994), argues cogently that the eighteenth century Church of England was not as ineffectual and moribund as has generally been asserted.

16. J. E. Griffiss, *Church, Ministry and Unity* (Oxford, 1983) p.29.

17. O. Chadwick, *The Mind of the Oxford Movement* (London 1960) p.27. See also *The Spirit of the Oxford Movement* by the same author (Cambridge, 1990) p.18.

18. John Keble had preached the Oxford Assize sermon on 14 July 1833. Newman was not present but declared that the sermon had, effectively, been the starting point of the Oxford Movement. The sermon was published with the title *National Apostasy*.

19. This was the Public Worship Regulation Bill, which will be examined in the next chapter.

20. The text of this speech seems to have survived only in a galley proof from an unidentified publication retained in the archive material for 1874 at Keble College. However, the occasion on which Liddon spoke is revealed in G. W. E. Russell, *Leaders of the Church, 1800–1900, Dr. Liddon* (London, 1905), pp.57–8.

21. Liddon included the quotation from Sir John Taylor Coleridge in his *University Sermons, second series* (London 1880), Sermon XVI, preached 28 February 1869, p.317.

22. Liddon, *loc. cit.*, pp.318–19.

23. O. Chadwick, *The Victorian Church, part 2* (London, 1970), p.430. Liddon did not ignore the controversy, as is evidenced by his republication of Keble's 1838 review of Gladstone's book.

24. G. W. E. Russell, *op.cit.*, p.30.

25. Peter B. Nockles, *The Oxford Movement in Context* (Cambridge, 1994).

26. Charles Gore (1853–1932) was Liddon's protégé as the first Principal of Pusey House, but disappointed him deeply by editing the *Lux Mundi* volume of essays. Gore ended a distinguished career as Bishop of Oxford.

27. Henry Scott Holland (1847–1918) also a contributor to *Lux Mundi*. From 1884–1910 he was a Canon of St Paul's, and from 1910 Regius Professor of Divinity at Oxford.

28. Liddon, *Clerical Life and Work*, Sermon VII, preached 22.12.1867, p.220.
29. Liddon, galley proof of report of speech in St. James' Hall, Keble College archive. He was referring to Richard Hooker (1554–1600) classical Anglican divine, author of the seminal *Laws of Ecclesiastical Polity*.
30. P. Butler, *Gladstone: Church, State and Tractarianism* (Oxford, 1982) p.85.
31. A. R. Vidler, *The Orb and the Cross*. (London, 1945), p.155.
32. E. R. Norman, *Church and Society in England* (Oxford, 1976) p.194.
33. Liddon, *Sermons on Some Words of Christ* (London, 1892) Sermon V, preached 3 August, 1873, p.69.
34. Liddon, *Walter Kerr Hamilton, Bishop of Salisbury*, p.110.
35. Quoted by Vidler, *op.cit.*, p.96.
36. Charles Lindley Wood (1839–1934, Second Viscount Halifax from 1885) was a leading lay devotee to the principles of the Oxford Movement, having come under the influence of Pusey whilst an undergraduate. A deeply devout man, he longed for the reunion of the Church of England with Roman Catholicism but remained an Anglican. For many years Liddon was his spiritual director, and their correspondence in the Borthwick Institute of the University of York is a small but important Tractarian archive, reference A4.210/Liddon.
37. A. B. Webster 'Church Order and Reunion in the Nineteenth Century' in K. M. Carey (ed.) *The Historic Episcopate* (London, 1954) p.95.
38. G. Battiscombe, *Shaftesbury, a Biography of the Seventh Earl* (London, 1974) p.137.
39. Battiscombe, *op.cit.*, p.140.
40. A. C. Benson, *Life of Edward White Benson* (London, 1899) vol.2, p.165. E. W. Benson (1829–96), was a Cambridge don, the first Headmaster of Wellington, the first Bishop of Truro from 1877 and Archbishop of Canterbury from 1883.
41. G. K. A. Bell, *Randall Davidson, Archbishop of Canterbury* (London, 1935), vol.1, p.116.
42. A. B. Smith *Dean Church, the Anglican Response to Newman* (Oxford, 1958) p.206.
43. A.p.King was Liddon's sister, who wrote a series of long letters home and then published them after Liddon's death with the title, *Dr Liddon's Tour in Egypt and Palestine* (London 1891, third edition) p.162.
44. Bell, *op.cit.*, p.117.
45 Liddon, *Life of Pusey*, vol.2, p.250.

Notes Chapter Four: 'Prejudice and experience' Ritualism

1. J. O. Johnston, *Life and Letters of Henry Parry Liddon* (London, 1904) p.269.
2. A. B. Donaldson, *Henry Parry Liddon* (London, 1905) pp.87–8.
3. Liddon, *University Sermons, first Series* (London 1865) Sermon XII, preached 9 June 1867, p.322.

4. Thomas Pelham Dale was imprisoned between 30 October and 24 December 1880, and Richard William Enraght between 27 November 1880 and 17 January 1881. The other clergy who were imprisoned were Arthur Tooth, 22 January to 17 February 1877; Sidney F. Green 19 March 1881 to 4 November 1882 and J. Bell Cox, 5–21 May 1887.

5. Johnston, *op.cit.*, p.216.

6. Johnston, *op.cit.*, p.97.

7. Johnston, *op.cit.*, p.180.

8. C. E. Beswick, 'Liddon at St Paul's 1870–1890,' University of Exeter, 1974, unpublished dissertation, p.72.

9. Alexander Penrose Forbes (1817–75), Bishop of Brechin from 1847 where he worked to promote Tractarian principles in the Scottish Episcopal Church. It is not clear why he persuaded Liddon to work on Rosmini's *Five Wounds*, for he shared Liddon's dislike of ultramontanism.

10. Quoted by O. Chadwick, *The Victorian Church*, part 2 (London, 1970) p.324.

11. The Church Association was formed in 1865 specifically to resist the growth of ritualism, which it sought to do through exerting legal pressure on bishops, through the courts and also through public protests.

12. The full text of this exchange, and the suggestion that Pusey and Liddon's letter was written by the latter, can be found in *Alexander Heriot Mackonochie, a Memoir*, by 'E.A.T' edited by E. F. Russell (London 1908), pp.221–6.

13. Keble College Archive, Liddon papers 1874, galley proof of speech. The (First) Vatican Council of 1869–70 is chiefly remembered for its increased emphasis on the primacy and infallibility of the Pope (ultramontanism). It was this that led to the breaking away of some Roman Catholics and the excommunication of others, mostly in Germany and Austria, and the eventual formation of the Old Catholic Churches. The Council's deliberations on other dogma also included an enhancement of the Roman Catholic devotion to the Blessed Virgin Mary.

14. J. G. Lockhart, *Charles Lindley Wood, Viscount Halifax, part I, 1839–1885* (London, 1935). Also E. Carpenter, *Cantuar, The Archbishops in their Office* (London, first edition 1971) p.347, says that the Queen 'must accept a large measure of responsibility for the legislation which was subsequently passed, though she tried later to exercise a moderating influence.'

15. Carpenter, *op.cit.*, p.348

16. The Purchas Judgement was made by the Judicial Committee of the Privy Council in 1871 and condemned the Vicar of St James' Brighton, the Reverend John Purchas, for ritualistic offences. The case made High Churchmen more vulnerable to censure for matters of ritual.

17. Johnston, *op.cit.*, p.180.

18. Minutes of Evidence to The Royal Commission on Ecclesiastical Courts, 7287.

19. J. Bentley, *Ritualism and Politics in Victorian Britain* (Oxford 1978), p.117.

20. G. W. E. Russell, *Edward King, Sixtieth Bishop of Lincoln* (London, 1912) p.155.
21. G. W. E. Russell, *Leaders of the Church 1800–1900, Dr Liddon* (London 1905) pp.98–9.
22. M. C. Church, *Life and Letters of Dean Church* (London, 1895) p.349.
23. A. C. Benson, *Life of Edward White Benson*, vol.2 (London, 1899) p.336.
24. J. Bentley, *op.cit.*, p.114.
25. Minutes of Evidence, 7371.
26. Minutes of Evidence, 7272–7. Liddon referred to Keble's opinion in the republication of Keble's review of Gladstone's book on Church and State. He quoted Keble, 'We never ought to rest until that unhappy court is either reconstituted or abolished.'
27. Minutes of Evidence, 7379, 7383 and 7321.
28. Minutes of Evidence, 7300.
29. Minutes of Evidence, 7388. Grindal was exiled under Mary I, but appointed Bishop of London in 1559, was Archbishop of York 1570–75, and of Canterbury from 1575. He was suspended by Elizabeth I in 1577, until 1582, with regard to his legal, but not spiritual functions, for refusing to suppress Puritan 'prophesyings.'
30. Minutes of Evidence, 7348.
31. Minutes of Evidence, 7354.
32. Bentley, *op.cit.*, p.114.
33. Minutes of Evidence, 7399; see also 7400–7401.
34. Minutes of Evidence, 7309.
35. Quoted by Liddon, *Life of Pusey*, vol.IV (London, 1897) p.272.
36. G. W. E. Russell, *Leaders of the Church, Liddon*, p.146.
37. P. G. Cobb, 'Leader of the Anglo Catholics' in P. Butler (ed.) *Pusey Rediscovered* (London, 1983) p.358.
38. Johnston, *op.cit*,. p.288.
39. Liddon, *Thoughts on Present Church Troubles* (1881) p.59.
40. Johnston, *op.cit.*, p.149.
41. W. H. Hutton (ed.), *The Autobiography of Robert Gregory* (London, 1912) p.115.
42. Johnston, *op.cit.*, pp.150–1, quoting Liddon to Miss Muirehouse, 3 July 1871.
43. Johnston, *op.cit.*, p.137; also Hutton, *op.cit.*, p.157.
44. The re-ordering at Christ Church had been on a larger scale and included the re-location of the organ to a position suggested by Liddon and C. L. Dodgson. The reredos was donated by Liddon and Bright.
45. G. L. Prestige, *St. Paul's in Its Glory* (London, 1955) p.212.
46. W. R. Matthews, *Memories and Meanings* (London, 1969) p.261.
47. Johnston, *op.cit.*, p.329.
48. Liddon, *Walter Kerr Hamilton, Bishop of Salisbury, a Sketch* (London, 1869) p.25.

234 The Life and Work of Henry Parry Liddon

Notes to Chapter Five: Liddon's preaching and pastoral ministry

1. J. O. Johnston, *Life and Letters of Henry Parry Liddon* (London 1904) p.192.
2. Horton Davies, *Worship and Theology in England*, Volume 4, *From Newman to Martineau, 1850–1900*, (Oxford, 1962) p.283.
3. P. A. Welsby, *Sermons and Society* (London, 1970), p.281.
4. A. Russell, *The Clerical Profession* (London, 1980), p.89.
5. Liddon, *Advent in St. Paul's* (originally published in two volumes in 1888, a single volume version was produced in 1889, all references are to the latter), Sermon XLII, preached 7 December 1884, p.253.
6. Liddon, *Easter in St Paul's* (originally published in two volumes in 1885, a single volume version came out in 1889, from which references are taken) Sermon XXIV, preached 8 April 1883, p.287. See also W. Sinclair, *Memorials of St Paul's Cathedral* (London, 1909) p.473.
7. Johnston, *op.cit.*, p.175.
8. O. Chadwick, *The Victorian Church*, part 2 (London, 1970) p.381.
9. G. W. E. Russell, *Leaders of the Church, 1800–1900, Dr Liddon* (London, 1905), p.33.
10. Isaac Williams (1802–65), priest, contributor to the *Tracts for the Times*, and a spiritual writer.
11. Keble College Archive, 1870, packet 1, item 29.
12. A. Pollard, *English Sermons* (London, 1963), p.52.
13. Brooke Foss Westcott (1825–1901) Bishop of Durham from 1890 in succession to his friend (and Liddon's) J.B. Lightfoot. Westcott was a scholar; at the time to which Liddon referred, he was Regius Professor of Divinity at Cambridge.
14. S. Paget, *Henry Scott Holland* (London, 1921) p.154.
15. Johnston, *op.cit.*, p.53.
16. Johnston, *op.cit.*, p.302.
17. A. B. Donaldson, *Henry Parry Liddon* (London, 1905) p.49.
18. A. C. Benson, *The Life of Edward White Benson, Archbishop of Canterbury* (London, 1899), vol I, p.403.
19. Horton Davies, *op.cit.*, p.288.
20. P. A. Welsby, *op.cit.*, p.13.
21. Peter Nockles, *The Oxford Movement in Context* (Cambridge, 1994) p.6.
22. Johnston, *op.cit.*, pp.396–7.
23. Liddon, *Advent* ..., Sermon XXXII, preached 11 December 1881.
24. Russell, *op.cit.*, p.125.
25. Liddon, *Clerical Life and Work* (London, 1894), Sermon VII, preached 22 December 1867, pp.216–17.
26. Liddon, *Clerical Life and Work*, Sermon I, preached 10 June 1968, p.48.
27. Liddon *Clerical Life and Work*, Sermon V, preached 24 September 1865, p.163.
28. Keble College Archive, 1882, packet 2, item 6.

29. This interesting exchange is stored in the Keble College Archive for 1873, packet 2, item 1.
30. F. W. Filson (ed.), *The Letters of Spiritual Counsel and Guidance by the late John Keble* (London, 1870) p.100.
31. Halifax Papers, Borthwick Institute, University of York, A.4/210 Liddon.
32. G. Rowell, *Hell and the Victorians* (Oxford, 1974) p.111.
33. Liddon, *Advent*, Sermon VII, preached 22 December 1872, p.89.
34. Liddon, *Advent*, Sermon IX, preached 14 December 1873, p.113. Robert Banks Jenkinson, 2nd Lord Liverpool (1770–1828): Foreign Secretary 1801–3; Home Secretary 1807–9; Secretary of State for War and the Colonies (1809–12); Prime Minister 1812–27. Charles Lloyd (1784–1829): Bishop of Oxford (1827–29), formerly Canon of Christ Church, and Regius Professor of Divinity, which he held in plurality with his Bishopric.
35. *Lyra Apostolica* is the title given to a collection of religious poems which were published in 1836 and ran through many editions. Composed by Keble, Newman and others, they appeared originally in *The British Magazine*.
36. Liddon, *Sermons on Some Words of Christ* (London 1892) Sermon XI preached 29 December 1889, p.174.
37. C. E. Beswick, 'Liddon of St Paul's 1870–90', University of Exeter unpublished dissertation, 1974.
38. Liddon, *Sermons on Some Words of Christ*, Sermon XIII preached 10 August 1884, p.204.
39. G. W. E. Russell, *Leaders of the Church, 1800–1900, Dr. Liddon* (London, 1905), pp.140–1.
40. Johnston, *op.cit.*, p.191.
41. Keble College Archive, 1860, item 9.

Notes to Chapter Six: 'Truth the bond of Love,' Liddon and Church unity

1. Sermon title, 1871.
2. J. O. Johnston, *Life and Letters of Henry Parry Liddon* (London, 1904) p.290.
3. Johnston, *op.cit.*, pp.89–90.
4. J. O. Johnston, *op.cit.*, p.93.
5. Liddon, *Sermons Preached on Special Occasions*, (London, 1897), Sermon VIII, 3 March 1869, pp.183–4.
6. Liddon, *Clerical Life and Work* (1894) Sermon XIII, 25 April 1876, p.351.
7. Liddon, *op cit*, Sermon X, 30 November 1863, p.276.
8. Quoted by G. Rowell, *The Vision Glorious* (Oxford, 1983) p.69.
9. Liddon, Preface to sermon 'A Father in Christ,' p.xxxiv.
10. Liddon, Bampton Lectures, *The Divinity of Christ* (1866), p.478ff.
11. Liddon, *Clerical Life and Work* (1894), sermon VIII, 26 May 1872, p.245.

12. John Joseph Ignatius Von Döllinger (1799–1890) was the principal German Roman Catholic theologian of the nineteenth century, but he was excommunicated by the Archbishop of Munich because of his refusal to accept the doctrines promoted by the Vatican Council of 1870. His name was linked with the Old Catholics, although he never became formally one of their number. Liddon met him in Munich in 1871 and they became friends. It was through this link that Liddon was able to attend the Bonn conferences on reunion in 1874 and 1875.

13. Johnston, *op.cit.*, p.128.

14. A. M. Allchin, *The Joy of All Creation* (London 1984) p.114.

15. Johnston, *op.cit.*, p.93. In 1950 this opinion was also elevated to the status of a dogma necessary to salvation.

16. Johnston, *op.cit.*, p.93.

17. Liddon, Bampton Lectures, *The Divinity of Christ* (1866), p.441.

18. Liddon, *University Sermons, Second Series*, Sermon VI, 15 June 1879, p.115.

19. J. O. Johnston, *op.cit.*, p.338.

20. A. B. Donaldson, *Henry Parry Liddon*, p.71, unacknowledged quotation.

21. B & M. Pawley, *Rome and Canterbury through Four Centuries* (London, 1974) p.235.

22. C.B. Moss, *The Old Catholic Movement, its Origins and History* (London, 1948), p.260.

23. St Edmund Hall archive, Bodleian Library MS 69/9.

24. Moss, *op.cit.*, p.260.

25. Bonn Conference Report (1874) English translation, p.xxii.

26. Bonn Conference Report (1874), *ibid.*, p.xxv.

27. G. Florovsky, 'The Orthodox Churches and the Ecumenical Movement prior to 1910' in *A History of the Ecumenical Movement 1517–1948*, ed. R. Rouse and S. C. Neill (Geneva, third edition, 1986) p.177.

28. See L. Litvak, *John Mason Neale and the Quest for Sobornost* (Oxford, 1994) and M.J. Chandler *The Life and Work of John Mason Neale* (Leominster, 1995).

29. Johnston, *op.cit.*, p.102.

30. G. Florovsky, *ibid.*, p.195. See above p.32.

31. Johnston, *op.cit.*, p.103–6.

32. Liddon, Bonn Conference Report (1874) p.27.

33. Liddon, Bonn Conference Report (1875) English translation, p.xliii.

34. Johnston, *op.cit.*, p.189.

35. Montanism was a second century apocalyptic movement started by a heretic named Montanus in Phrygia. Donatism is the name given to a fourth century group of heretical rigorists founded by Donatus in north Africa. It was vigorously attacked theologically by St Augustine of Hippo.

36. Liddon, preface to the pamphlet edition (1892) of his sermon, *A Father in Christ*, pp.xl–xli.

37. Keble College Archive, 1867, 2/26.

38. Liddon, Bonn Conference Report (1874), pp.ix–x.

Notes to Chapter 7: Liddon's spirituality

1. Liddon, *Clerical Life and Work* (London, 1894) Sermon I, preached 10 June 1868, p.63.
2. Liddon, *Advent in St Paul's* (London, 1889) Sermon XLVII, preached 4 December 1887, p.583.
3. Liddon, *Easter in St Paul's* (London, 1889), Sermon XXVIII, preached 17 April 1873, p.329.
4. Liddon, *Advent*, Sermon XXVIII, preached 15 December 1878, pp.333-4.
5. Liddon, *The Divinity of Christ*, Bampton Lectures (London, 1867) pp.240-1.
6. Liddon, *Advent*, Sermon XL, preached 16 December 1883, p.455.
7. Liddon, *Clerical Life and Work*, Sermon III, preached 23 December 1860, pp.115-16.
8. Non-Juror was the title given to eight bishops and several hundred priests who refused to take the Oath of Allegiance to William and Mary in 1688 on the grounds that they were bound by their earlier Oath of Allegiance to James II. The bishops included Archbishop Sancroft of Canterbury, but Thomas Ken of Bath and Wells is remembered as a particularly devout example of the type.
9. Liddon, *Clerical Life and Work*, p.15. The quotation is from Bishop John Cosin's (1594-1672) 'Works' vol.2.
10. J. O. Johnston, *Life and Letters of Henry Parry Liddon* (London, 1904), p.70.
11. Lambeth Palace Archive, Ms 2547 f68. The context suggests that Hill's problem regarding the bell was to do with physical incapacity. Liddon's advice is reminiscent of Isaak Walton's *Life of Mr George Herbert* where men in the fields 'would let their ploughs rest when Mr Herbert's Saints-Bell rung to prayers that they might also offer their devotions to God with him.'
12. Liddon, *Clerical Life and Work*, p.11.
13. Liddon, *Clerical Life and Work,* p.21.
14. S. C. Carpenter, *Church and People 1789-1889* (London, 1933) p.407. See also O. Chadwick, *The Founding of Cuddesdon* (Oxford, 1954) p.38.
15. Chadwick, *op.cit.*, p.37.
16. Quoted from the pamphlet, *Correspondence Relating to Cuddesdon Theological College in Answer to the Charges of the Rev C. P. Golightly*, p.8.
17. A. Härdelin, *The Tractarian Understanding of the Eucharist* (Uppsala, 1965), p.322, see also p.76.
18. Härdelin, *op.cit.*, p.272.
19. Liddon, *Christmastide in St Paul's* (London, 1889) Sermon XI, preached 26 December 1886, p.178.
20. Liddon, *Easter*, sermon XXIV, preached 8 April 1883, p.285.
21. Liddon, *Evening Communions Contrary to the Teaching and Practice of the Church in All Ages* (London, 1876), p.24.
22. Härdelin, *op.cit.*, p.325.

23. Liddon, *Sermons on Old Testament Subjects* (London, 1891) sermon XXVIII preached 30 August 1874, p.264.
24. Liddon, *Evening Communions,* p.25.
25. O. Chadwick, *The Victorian Church*, part 2 (London, 1970) p.308. Liddon's figure is given in *Evening Communions*, p.5.
26. By the phrase 'Zwinglian propaganda' Liddon was implying that the practice of evening celebrations of Holy Communion was based on the belief that the sacrament was no more than simply a memorial of Christ's actions at the Last Supper.
27. Liddon, *Evening Communions,* p.20.
28. Liddon, *Evening Communions,* p.27.
29. Liddon, *Evening Communions*, p.21.
30. J. O. Johnston and W. C. E. Newbolt (ed, *The Spiritual Letters of E. B. Pusey* (London 1898) pp.276-7. The letter is dated 'Advent eve 1879.'
31. C. Gore, *The Body of Christ* (London, 1901) p.277.
32. Gore, *loc. cit.*
33. Johnston, *Liddon,* p.219.
34. Chadwick, *Founding,* p.39.
35. Liddon, *Sermons Preached on Special Occasions* (London, 1897) sermon VII, preached 28 February 1868, pp.159–60.
36. Liddon, *Clerical Life and Work,* p.23.
37. G. O'Donnell, 'The Spirituality of E.B. Pusey,' in P. Butler (ed.) *Pusey Rediscovered* (London, 1983), p.241.
38. Chadwick, *Founding,* pp.39–40.
39 Liddon, *Sermons Preached on Special Occasions, loc. cit.*
40 see above, page 27.
41 Liddon, *Clerical Life and Work,* p.33.

Notes to Chapter 8: Liddon as leader

1. O. Chadwick, *The Mind of the Oxford Movement* (London, 1960) p.62. W. G. Ward (1812–82) was a fellow of Balliol College, Oxford, until his conversion to Roman Catholicism in 1845.
2. R. G. Wilberforce, *Life of the Right Reverend Samuel Wilberforce, D.D.* vol.III (London 1882) p.392.
3. J. O. Johnston, *Life and Letters of Henry Parry Liddon* (London, 1904), p.157. Socinianism is the rejection of the doctrine of the Trinity and is one of the origins of Unitarianism. The term is derived from the name of Faustus Socinus (died 1604).
4. Johnston, *op.cit.*, p.160.
5. Johnston, *op.cit.*, p.160. The three heresies listed all derived from the early Church and were variations of the debate about the true nature of the person of Christ, which orthodox doctrine asserts is that of a single Person, at once both human and divine.
6. Johnston, *op.cit.*, p.161.
7. Johnston, *op.cit.*, p.162.

8. Johnston, *op.cit.*, p.169.
9. G. W. E. Russell, *Leaders of the Church 1800–1900, Dr Liddon* (London, 1905), p.81.
10. C. E. Beswick, 'Liddon of St. Paul's, 1870–1890' (University of Exeter, unpublished dissertation, 1974) p.102.
11. H. Paul (ed.), *Letters of Lord Acton to Mary Gladstone* (London, 1904) p.201–4.
12. M. C. Church, *The Life and Letters of Dean Church* (London, 1895), pp.207.
13. Davidson papers, Lambeth Palace Library. Davidson to Henry Ponsonby, 25 January 1885.
14. O. Chadwick, *The Victorian Church,* part 2, (London, 1970) p.339.
15. Johnston, *op.cit.*, p.373.
16. G. E. Buckle (ed.) *The Letters of Queen Victoria, 3rd Series, 1886–1901* (London, 1932) p.427.
17. Johnston, *op.cit.*, p.327.
18. Liddon, 'Recent Fortunes of the Church in Oxford,' in *The Church Quarterly Review*, April 1881, pp.239.
19. Liddon, *op.cit.*, p.206.
20. A.J. Engel, *From Clergyman to Don* (Oxford, 1983) *op.cit.*, p.177.
21. Liddon, *op.cit.*, p.233.
22. Liddon, *Sermons on some Words of Christ* (London, 1892) Sermon XVII, preached 21 August 1881, p.264–5.
23. E. Carpenter, *Cantuar: The Archbishops in their Office* (London, first edition 1971) p.355.
24. Liddon, 'Recent Fortunes of the Church in Oxford,' in *The Church Quarterly Review*, April 1881, p.240.
25. F. Underhill, 'A Centenary Fund for Liddon House,' in *A Centenary Memoir* (1929) pp.49–51.

Notes to Chapter 9: 'An Anglican of Anglicans: a very sample of the class'

1. Henry Scott Holland to E. S. Talbot in 1885, see below p.208.
2. J. O. Johnston, *Life and Letters of Henry Parry Liddon* (London, 1904), p.95, italics used by Johnston.
3. Johnston, *op.cit.*, pp.245–6.
4. G. W. E. Russell, *Leaders of the Church, 1800–1900, Dr. Liddon* (London, 1905) p.105.
5. Liddon, *Clerical Life and Work*, London, 1894) Sermon XIV, preached 20 January 1884, pp.372, 375.
6. G. L. Prestige, *Life of Charles Gore* (London, 1935), p.49.
7. A. Wilkinson, *The Community of the Resurrection, a Centenary History* (London, 1992), p.11.
8. Russell, *op.cit.*, p.73 and Johnston, *op.cit.*, p.300.
9. O. Chadwick, *The Mind of the Oxford Movement* (London, 1960) p.60. J. B. Mozley (1813–78) was a moderate Tractarian theologian who, from 1871 was Regius Professor of Divinity at Oxford.

10. Holland, *Personal Studies* (London, 1905) pp.139–52. This article is a reprint of an obituary for Liddon.
11. H. Davies, *Worship and Theology in England (Volume 4) from Newman to Martineau*, 1850–1900 (Oxford, 1962), p.196, and D. Cupitt (ed.) *The Myth of God Incarnate* (London, 1977), p.134.
12. J. G. Lockhart, *Cosmo Gordon Lang* (London, 1949) pp.112–13.
13. H. S. Holland, *A Bundle of Memories* (London, 1915) p.65.
14. P. Butler (ed.) *Pusey Rediscovered* (London 1933), p.350, in an essay by p.Cobb, 'Leader of the Anglo-Catholics?'
15. Russell, *op.cit.*, p.61.
16. Quoted by Russell, *op.cit.*, p.63, source unacknowledged.
17. Johnston, *op.cit.*, pp.364–5.
18. Johnston, *op.cit.*, pp.362–3.
19. Johnston, *op.cit.*, pp.369.
20. Russell, *op.cit.,* pp.136–7.
21. M.C. Church, (ed.) *The Life and Letters of Dean Church* (London, 1895) p.348.
22. Liddon, *The Divinity of Christ* (Bampton Lectures, 1866) p.101.
23. Liddon, *The Inspiration of Selection*, p.4. The copy of this sermon in the Liddon House archive bears the following hand written note: 'These were the last words which were spoken in public by Dr Liddon – in St Mary's Church, Oxford, on Whit Sunday 25 May 1890.

Index

NOTE: For the purposes of this index all ecclesiastical titles below the rank of Archdeacon have been omitted. Those above that rank have been described using the highest rank they attained in the Church, whether or not they held this position prior to Liddon's death.